Praise for *I Know Nothing!*

"This is an engaging and often touching account of someone who has gone through life hell-bent on squeezing as much
"

"There is a lot more to the memoir than Manuel ... as well as telling a jolly showbiz tale, he can also strike a more serious and insightful tone when the subject matter requires it."
– *The Times*

"The harrowing, inspiring life of Andrew Sachs."
– *The Spectator*

"A feast of stories, funny and sad, name-droppings par excellence, thoughtful opinions and a 54-year-old love story."
– *Yours*

"A much-cherished read."
– *Camden New Journal*

ANDREW SACHS
I Know Nothing!
THE AUTOBIOGRAPHY

The Robson Press

This edition published in Great Britain in 2015 by
The Robson Press (an imprint of Biteback Publishing)
Westminster Tower
3 Albert Embankment
London SE1 7SP

ISBN 978-1-84954-900-4

10 9 8 7 6 5 4 3 2 1

A CIP catalogue record for this book is available from the British Library.

Set in Caslon

Printed and bound in Great Britain by
CPI Group (UK) Ltd, Croydon CR0 4YY

For Melody – this book would never have been written without her.

Acknowledgements

In writing this very personal book, I have been mindful of the many people who have played an important part in my life, from my 'mongrel' childhood on – my brave and dear parents in particular, and my wife Melody, who really has brought music into my life. Without her enthusiasm, together with the encouragement of my agent, Lynda Ronan, I might well have given up writing the book halfway through.

I was lucky to have in David Cohen a skilled and sensitive editor who was always understanding when the day job got in the way. My publisher, Jeremy Robson, has been caring and supportive throughout.

Additional important parts have been played by Brian Rix, impresario of impresarios; Roy Hudd, for kindly donating his timely birthday poem; and Nick Horridge, whose splendid drawing of Manuel I am delighted to include – which brings me to that supreme hotelier, John Cleese. Always a loyal and inspiring friend, it was John who brought Manuel into my life, and nothing has been quite the same since. So, thank you John! *Gracias* Manuel.

Contents

Foreword by John Cleese

I am delighted that Andy Sachs asked me to pen this brief foreword to his memoirs, because it gives me a chance to express my appreciation of him, both as a great farceur and as a friend of forty years.

The first time I set eyes on him was at the Lyric Theatre, Shaftesbury Avenue, in the autumn of 1973. Andy was appearing with Sir Alec Guinness in Alan Bennett's *Habeas Corpus*, an exquisitely crafted sex-farce about the impact of the permissive society on a respectable family in Brighton in the 1960s. Andy was playing the role of a piano tuner, but the magnificent Margaret Courtenay mistook him for the man who was coming to measure her for a custom-made bra. When Andy started on the standard pianist's hand-and-finger stretching routine, she began to register anticipation of nameless carnal delights, producing one of the funniest farcical moments I have ever seen. Weak with laughter, I managed to open my programme and underline his name.

Only a few weeks later, I was casting a short film called

Romance with a Double Base, and I asked Andy to join us for a few days' shooting. It turned out to be a very happy collaboration, and I observed what a wonderfully inventive comic actor I was working with. Luckily, Connie Booth and I were already writing the pilot episode of *Fawlty Towers*, and so I had the inspired idea of casting Andy as Manuel.

Inspired? Let me explain something. If you met Andy socially it would never occur to you for one moment that he was an actor. You would guess he was a senior civil servant, or a physician, or an academic, or perhaps a research scientist. He is quiet, thoughtful, beautifully mannered, well informed, observant and extremely kind. But once you put that moustache on him... *¡Ole!* Manuel appears, as if from nowhere.

I salute you, Andy. You created one of the great comic characters.

John Cleese

Prelude

I write in peaceful Kilburn today, the north London suburb where my wife and I live. I have spent much of my career trying to make audiences laugh and being very happy when I have managed to do so. Since I turned fifty, I've been rather identified with a much abused Spanish waiter called Manuel, who was born in Barcelona and, somehow, landed a job at Fawlty Towers, a surreal seaside hotel which glories in the worst of British cooking and the best of British chaos. People sometimes, in fact, think I am Manuel.

But my beginnings were far away from the safety of leafy Kilburn. They were in the increasingly dark world of 1930s Berlin, where I was born to a Jewish father and a Catholic mother, and that is where I spent the first eight years of my life, quite unaware of what was to come.

CHAPTER 1

The Mongrel Boy

On 30 January 1933, Adolf Hitler became Chancellor and Germany became the world's most wonderful country in which to live – if you happened to be a Nazi, or a Nazi sympathiser, that is. Many Germans hoped nervously that a strong leadership might restore the prosperity and self-confidence that had been lost as a result of their defeat in the First World War. The country was desperate for an end to mass unemployment and hunger.

But not all Germans were optimistic, given Hitler's policies; many were afraid and some were in total despair, and others could not face the reality of the Nazis taking power. The result was a discordant hubbub with a headlong dive into apathy.

My aunt Barbara echoed a popular opinion when she declared that Hitler and his cronies were a bizarre affliction that would surely self-destruct within a few months. The man himself, after all, was a clown.

Then a wise old rabbi spoke. 'My good people, tell me please – if this devil man is a clown, where are his jokes? I'll tell you: in a

1

circus of horrors, that's where. And you *meshuggeners*, you crazy people, want to buy tickets to see the show. Do me a favour!'

The Jews slapped their foreheads. '*Gevalt!*' they called out in unison. 'You're right, Rabbi. What is a Jew if he can't have a laugh? Let's get out fast!'

Getting out fast is a fine Jewish skill honed over centuries of practice as the strategy of Last Resort.

Over the following months and years, some – but tragically all too few – packed their bags and saved their lives as, indeed, Albert Einstein did. He renounced his German citizenship, dare I say, at the speed of light and infuriated the Nazis. They were angry they had not managed to revoke his passport before he told Hitler what black hole in the universe he should disappear down.

As for me, I was neither flushed with optimism nor in despair. I was having fun just being alive. That fateful January day was two months short of my third birthday. I was learning how to laugh and gurgle and get attention. I was learning how to scream louder than the day before and how to turn a full potty upside down to get attention.

'Don't be alarmed, Katarina,' said my Jewish father to his wife, 'but there's something going on with our youngest.'

'I'm trying to make dinner,' she said.

'He's worried about Hitler. I can tell.'

My mother sighed. 'Oh, for heaven's sake,' she might have said, putting her arms about him. 'Everyone's worried nowadays. Well, a lot of people are. We'll get through this.' I write *she might have said* because I don't have a photographic memory and I could be criticised because this book reports many conversations dating back to the 1930s. Let me plead guilty – and not. These remembered conversations may not be word perfect, but they are accurate as to their general sense and the feelings evoked. I once wrote a play called *Dramatic Licence*, so I'm taking some. Let me carry on with my memory of what my father said:

'How? Let me in on the secret. What does our future hold, dear mother of three?'

'It holds dinner so get your hands washed. And theirs. And don't try so hard to be miserable.'

Only when I was much older did I begin to appreciate the difficulties my parents had to cope with during the 1930s. And they turned out to be among the lucky ones: the survivors.

My parents were, and still are, my heroes. My father, Hans Sachs, was born in 1885 and married when he was quite young. He had a son but the marriage didn't last. He and his first wife divorced so he was free again. He met my mother, who had never been married, at a dance and it was love at first waltz. She fell for him. (I presume he danced well, a trait I did not inherit.) They got married in early 1925, not long before my older sister Barbara was born.

My father's family were bankers and business people. They had a huge house but, after the First World War, they lost everything as a result of hyperinflation. Maybe not quite everything. A family story says that their circumstances were so reduced they were down to a mere four servants.

I don't know how they could have coped.

Mother was born in Eutin, a little town in the very north of Germany, but her heart lay in the Austrian birthplace of her father, the mountains of the Austrian Tyrol. He was a writer, so it is not strange she became a librarian.

When my mother got engaged, she and my father were living together which was, of course, extremely unusual for the time. One day she got a phone call. She was a lapsed Catholic, which made it very surprising that the man on the other end of the telephone was one of the Pope's advisers, apparently calling from Venice.

'I believe you are engaged to a Jew,' he said.

'Yes,' she said.

'Well, are you sure you are right to be so? You are a Catholic girl and it is not wise,' the Pope's man replied.

Marrying a Jew might lead to excommunication and she would certainly not be asked to arrange the flowers in church. Mum was horrified. She replied, 'But I love him.' In the next minutes, the Pope's man tried but could not sway her.

When he finally hung up, my mum was in a terrible state. She called for my father and hurried into the next room, only to find that her beloved was putting the extension phone down. He had made the call, pretending to be the Pope's man, disguising his voice with an Italian accent. I may not dance as well as my father but, like him, I am not a bad mimic.

My mother was born in 1898 and was thirteen years younger than my father. With a Catholic father and a Protestant mother, she was a double-whammy Aryan, who ought to have produced blond, blue-eyed, tall members of the Master Race, all so ready to deserve a mention in the Third Reich roll of honour.

Instead, her three bonny toddlers – Barbara, my brother Tom

4

and I – turned out dark-haired, brown-eyed and smallish. The full catastrophe was that our mother had married a Jew.

Oy vey!

Her husband had won the Iron Cross in the 1914 war. He had a solid-gold Prussian ancestry. He even had blue eyes and almost blond hair.

None of that mattered.

A Jew could have all the military decorations the German Army could award but it would not count. Hitler ignored the brave fighting record of many Jews who served in the German Army in the First World War. Their sacrifices for the Fatherland were not going to stop the Nazis sacrificing them.

This may be a fantasy – because children do have fantasies about their parents – or it may be based on a story my parents told me: my mother once told Nazi officials that she loved my father.

The officials hesitated for a moment. Could it be their hearts were touched? They nodded benignly. 'We are human.'

Her spirits perked up. 'Of course you are! Haven't I always said so? Tell me what I can do.'

Their superior features cracked into a smile … or perhaps they were just baring their teeth.

'Get a divorce,' they said.

By the age of seven, when my parents were going through this turmoil, if I had had an understanding beyond my years, my own identity would have confused me too. I might well have toyed with being Aryan at breakfast; superior subhuman at tea time; *nebbish* in the bath; and degenerate member of the master race while feeding the ducks. But if I had a split personality, I didn't realise it.

My caring father would have understood perfectly and brushed aside my curls, saying, 'It's a tough life, my son, but a good one if you keep your wits about you. Relax, and I'll give you a bit of bedtime philosophy.'

Being a good linguist, he would sometimes recite Rudyard Kipling's famous poem about possibilities to me: if you could talk with crowds and talk with kings, and many other ifs, then such and such would happen. I stayed awake, though nearly all of it passed over my head. The poem had too many 'ifs', but I do remember him ending with the words: '… and which is more, you'll be a *mensch*, my son' – *mensch* being Yiddish for a proper man with integrity and courage.

That phrase, 'you'll be a *mensch*, my son', took root in some mysterious way and guided me to maturity by the time I was seven and a half. My identity became clear: I was neither one thing nor another. My subconscious reasoning was as follows:

(a) I would never qualify as a proper Jew because, for one thing, my private anatomy had not been interfered with.

(b) Nor would I pass easily as a non-Jew since, even then, I never had any difficulty in seeing the funny side of almost every aspect of life. This would make me stand out – just like a Jew – and cause suspicion in a Germany where gravitas counted for far more than mirth.

One of my earliest memories is of being rebuked by an Erich von Stroheim-type bullet-headed neighbour for trying to make him laugh. He remained stony-faced and felt it his duty to inform me that, 'We Germans may have our faults, my boy, but I am happy to say that a sense of humour is not among them.'

(c) Although I certainly had fifty good Aryan credentials, my shape, size and colour was –

(d) – plain wrong.

I was one of a kind, I decided, and revelled in my uniqueness – until I learned there were thousands of others in Germany just like me.

Inevitably we attracted the attention of our busy rulers. Their dedication to bureaucracy drove them to examine our validity as acceptable human beings and to give our breed the title of *mischling*. 'What does that mean?' I asked my mother. Apparently it meant 'half-breed', something like a mongrel, according to her.

Did it? I thought to myself. Being designated a mongrel made me glad because it gave me an affinity with dogs, the most excellent creatures in the world. It was the next best thing to having one of my own. I glowed with pride.

Both my parents were highly literate and had a comprehensive knowledge of German literature. Mum, the daughter of a novelist, was well versed in the works of Goethe, Schiller, Lessing, Mann and the rest. Dad was fluent in French, had studied ancient Greek, spoke good English and some Italian, found his way around Hebrew, and even knew how to write it back to front. The overwhelming majority of the books in our library were in German – including many of the English ones. We had the complete works of Shakespeare, for instance, in German; *The Canterbury Tales*, in German; a selection of Dickens, Thomas

Hardy, Oscar Wilde, Conan Doyle ditto. Our library had, in fact, probably every book ever written since Gutenberg invented printing and published the Bible.

My siblings and I were allowed access to this treasure house of culture. When my brother Tom and I were eleven and eight years old respectively, we devised a brilliant method to help us make good choices.

The most reliable clue to a book's readability, we decided, lay in the distance between the front and the back covers. This measurement was the basis for other subtle judgements. For example:

(a) Books measuring up to 2.5 cm between covers were classed as volumes of the highest quality.

(b) Those that were 3.5 cm thick without pictures, or 4.8 cm with, could also be regarded as praiseworthy.

(c) Because of our age-related low boredom threshold, anything thicker than 5.5 cm was graded as inferior and not worthy of attention.

(d) Books in a foreign language and, therefore, meaningless to us were despised, disallowed and preferably destroyed. It took some time to perfect our theory. We named it *Die Relative Arithmetik der Literatur*; a phrase not as snappy as $E = mc^2$ but more subtle.

Our parents were impressed by our ground-breaking achievement, but alerted us to the Nazi bonfire of 1933 where they burned so-called undesirable books written by undesirable authors like Jews, Communists and other degenerates. I learned later they had burned books by Freud, Malinowski, Einstein and Stefan Zweig. Three of these geniuses I would become connected with. Given Hitler's decision to burn the books the Nazis did not like, Dad suggested one or two of the more fascist-type clauses in our work needed revising.

Ever obedient to long words we didn't understand, we agreed to make adjustments, such as rescuing the works of 'Karl Dickins' from oblivion, despite the disgraceful thickness of his books. His bad habit of writing sentences measuring up to 30 cm before reaching a full stop proved to us he should never have been allowed near a typewriter ... or whatever he used to write those huge works.

We gave the accolade of Best Book Ever Written to the foreign, but extremely thin (at 1.5 cm), *Of Mice and Men*, even though we never read it.

Tom and I had to cope with our age difference. As the officially older and supposedly wiser brother, Tom claimed the right to choose thicker books. This caused friction between us, and culminated one day when he picked out a really fat book of an unbelievable 700 pages. 'It's for my research,' he squawked indignantly. In fact, he was just showing off and trying to make me feel even smaller than I was. He was also cheating. I managed a quick glance into the massive volume before he snatched it back. But I had seen enough to expose his deceit. The book simply did not qualify as a single work in accordance with our rules as it contained a collection of forty separate and stupid stories about some man who played the violin at a place in London called Bäckerstrasse 221b.

Our agreement fell apart.

Once, our parents, in a rare moment of carefree abandon, took their three children to a cinema to see *The Gold Rush*. It was a revelation. I realised the mighty Führer was nothing but a vulgar plagiarist, an *ersatz* Charlie Chaplin without any of that comic genius's talent; a common fraud with a pathetic excuse for a moustache.

At this time that other dictator, Joseph Stalin, was always in the papers, but he looked like everybody's favourite uncle one could really trust. Furthermore, he and I shared similar political views regarding the other Great Dictator. Uncle Joe won the hair stakes as he had a real man's moustache, almost big enough for a young lad like me to swing on. There was really no contest. I knew I would embrace Communism until death – even if I didn't completely understand what it all meant.

My devotion to the hammer and sickle made itself felt almost immediately. One day, a military parade swaggered past our home in full fascist brio with a brass band, swastika flags, shiny leather boots, glittering insignia and crisp uniforms with black or brown shirts specially designed never to show the dirt – or even blood. Starry-eyed bystanders cheered while the goose-stepping Hitler Youth belted out songs of glory from lusty lungs unsullied by the filth of tobacco.

While all this was going on, I was leaning out of our front window and, impulsively, shouted at the top of my own little unsullied lungs: 'Hitler isn't funny!' and, even more recklessly,

'Workers of the world unite!' It earned me a pat on the back from my elder mongrel brother and a clip round the ear from my even more senior mongrel sister, Barbara, who knew the likes of us had to keep a low profile. Fortunately, none of my political declarations was heard above the general din.

As soon as the area was calm again, I rushed down the road to see my very best friend, who lived just a few doors away. Buschi had been ill for some time but I wanted to boast of my bravery. I hoped that perhaps he had been allowed out of bed to witness the rumpus.

But Buschi hadn't witnessed anything; he was in his bedroom as usual, looking tired and pale. His devoted parents had piled colourful packages of toys onto a table by his bed in readiness for his coming birthday. The presents were stacked well ahead of time to encourage him to get better.

His problem, they had told me, was poison in his blood. This wasn't reassuring. Poison conjured up something out of a Grimm's fairy tale. Did some wicked witch come down the chimney every night and drain the blood out of him with foul apples and ghastly spells?

Buschi died before his big day. For the first time in my life, I experienced a sad, empty space in my world, though it didn't stop me wondering what would happen to all those presents. The sadness stayed with me for months; the presents were soon forgotten.

I had another very best friend to whom I could boast. Ralph and I sat next to each other in our class, which was ruled over by Herr Plischert, an avuncular authority figure who, remarkably, did not have a moustache. He taught us all about patriotism and the need to help the Führer with his war effort... I mean, of course, his peace effort.

Sorry – slip of the tongue.

Herr Plischert often made slips of his tongue, too, but he meant well. His grasp of facts was often shaky, though – not a good trait in a teacher. According to him, Japan was the capital of Tokyo; and a mathematical problem involving dividing oranges between a number of boys could mysteriously turn into a question involving girls and bananas. But he was extremely focused on the future of Germany and the need for his pupils to do their bit.

Schools at the time were assigned patriotic duties. Ralph and I were once given the task of going to each home in our Berlin suburb to persuade the householders to contribute metal items for the peace effort. We collected milk-bottle tops, silver foil, crumpled toothpaste tubes, empty food tins, unwanted saucepans and plumbing paraphernalia. Money was considered especially acceptable, in the form of coins or, even better, bank notes, despite their lack of metal content. We were armed with official swastika-stamped notebooks in which to record the names and addresses of all donors, together with a short description of their contributions. A second list was to be made of those who contributed nothing and thus failed to honour their National Socialist obligations.

Ralph and I handed in boxes and boxes of goodies to our loopy teacher, plus our notebooks recording the loyal and the traitors. Our efforts got us a glossy certificate, decorated with colourful party-approved artwork, and signed by our headmaster, Herr Plischert and Adolf Hitler himself, as a special mark of his gratitude. We were very impressed that the Führer could devote so many hours of his precious time to signing personal autographs for thousands of high-achieving schoolboys and girls.

It had been a good week's work. But a little confusion tugged at my conscience. What about my Communist loyalties? Was I faltering? If so, exposure as a defector would surely invite severe punishment.

It struck swiftly, but in an unexpected way. Ralph spoke to me one morning in the playground. He mumbled awkwardly and eventually blurted out that his parents had ordered him not to play with me again.

I asked him why. He shrugged his shoulders, but I already knew the answer. Ralph and I had no secrets from each other.

'You promised not to tell anyone I'm a Communist,' I said.

'I didn't.'

'I'm going to hit you.'

'It's nothing to do with Stalin. It's your father.'

I was puzzled. 'What about him?'

'Well, you know, he's a Jew.'

This was hardly news. I waited for enlightenment. 'Go on.'

'That's why I can't play with you any more.'

I couldn't follow his logic. If Ralph had been forbidden to play with my father, that would have made sense, but why me?

'Tell me the truth or I will hit you.'

'I am telling you. It's because – well, I think it's because

13

the Jews don't like Hitler very much and that's not very nice of them.'

'Who says?'

'Everyone does.'

That rang true all right. It was time for a lie. 'I like Hitler,' I said.

'No, you don't.'

'Well, neither do you.' I was struggling a bit. 'Only we do really, because we collected all that stuff for him and he gave us his autograph, so the three of us are mates now.'

In the end I managed to convince Ralph, but he didn't convince his parents. They were – I realise now – normal. Everyone in Germany was scared and everyone felt they were being watched. So we stopped playing together.

It caused another sad, empty space in my world. And one in his too, I think.

But I was not short of other friends. A favourite was a neighbour in one of the flats in our modest apartment block: Frau Fellenberg. She was a warm, elegant lady and must have been about my mother's age.

We usually exchanged a few words when we passed each other on the stairs. Often she invited me into her home, where a mouth-watering treat always awaited me. My favourite was a spoonful of cocoa straight from the packet, mixed with sugar. Nothing tasted better. We had our ritual. She settled herself at the kitchen table with a cup of black coffee; I squatted on my usual wooden stool and munched away. Our intimate *kaffeeklatsch*, a chat over coffee, covered at different times art, astronomy, animals, politics, embroidery, ice skating, the price of food. I was even willing to talk to her about school.

I grabbed every chance to do small chores for her, carrying shopping bags up the stairs, posting her letters, watering plant pots or running messages. When I knew she was at home, I would go up to her floor, peer through her letter box and ask, 'Is there anything I can do for you today?' which was my unsubtle code for 'Can I have a treat?' It nearly always worked.

As far as I was concerned, she and I were in a relationship for life. But, of course, we weren't. In late 1937, we moved to the city centre and I had to leave Frau Fellenberg behind. I did not imagine we would ever meet again. But I turned out to be wrong about that – thanks to the BBC.

During the school holidays in the summer of 1938, my brother and I were sent to a youth camp on the Baltic coast. He was given this treat because he had missed out the year before; I was given it as a reward for ingratiating myself with Herr Plischert until he put 'top of the class for everything' on my report. He said I had a great brain, clever hands and my mechanical aptitude was second to none. It was news to me, but it wasn't my place to disagree with a teacher. I persuaded myself that perhaps for once he wasn't confused. My brother Tom was highly suspicious, until proof of my talents soon made him think again.

The proof was dramatic. When I was only eight-and-a-quarter years old, I built a U-boat made out of sand, the only material available on our Baltic beach. To be fair, it was not a solo achievement. I was assigned a crack team of fellow campers who had been conditioned to obey orders without question from their superior – namely me. As a result, the second prize was ours. Unfortunately, the top prize went to a luckier – but in our opinion far less skilful – team that came up with a Messerschmitt 109E. Our failure was a shock. However, the military discipline that had been drummed into us as good Germans (thank you, Herr Plischert) allowed a fast recovery from humiliation. We soon stood tall again and gloated over the inferiority of a group that included my pitiful brother, who had scraped into the third prize category with their *Panzerkraftwagen*. The complexities of the word alone should have put them off. To try and fashion caterpillar tracks, a turret and an enormously long gun barrel just from sand showed they had the brains of, well, caterpillars.

My team's success gave us licence to throw sand into the eyes of the *Panzerkraft* despicables while the Messerschmitt supermen did the same to us. Even I, the good Communist mongrel Jew boy, looked forward to the day when, as a member of the Hitler Youth, I would earn the right to perform yet greater acts of heroism and put my inferiors even more firmly in their place.

One disturbing incident spoiled our fun-packed fortnight, however. In the pitch dark one night, I was woken by a car screeching to a halt in the street outside. A door slammed, people ran and shouted, and I heard one piercing cry. Even to my innocent ears that cry combined panic and despair. Then, it stopped suddenly. Doors opened and slammed shut again, then the car drove off fast, tyres squealing, leaving behind only the sound of waves lapping against the beach. I stayed awake for a long time after that.

Had anyone else in our dormitory heard the noise? I can't

remember. My brother? I don't know. Was it mentioned the next day? I have no idea. I only knew the event was as real as could be and the memory of it is still vivid. Imagined or not, it was certainly an ill omen of things to come.

Tom and I had been sent away to the seaside for a more serious reason, too. Our parents wanted to keep us out of the way while plans for the family's future were being arranged. Our superior sister Barbara had stayed behind to help.

Father had studied law and obtained a doctorate, but now was an insurance broker in what was virtually a one-man business. New laws, however, targeted the earning potential of Jews, and the big companies he dealt with were strenuously discouraged from dealing with the Jewish community. Long-standing clients found it necessary, often reluctantly, to take their business elsewhere. 'Nothing personal you understand, Herr Doktor Sachs … but our position … family … children, you understand…' Ordinary people were scared and did not, could not, behave decently, though they knew they were making life even harder for individual Jews they often liked and had been on good terms with.

Our best hope was in getting to England. Former business colleagues of my father had emigrated to London and offered him a job with a guaranteed income, albeit a small one. This was vital. There were many other requirements before a UK entry visa would be granted for a family. Crucially, one had to be sponsored so that Jewish refugees would not cost the British economy one penny.

My parents negotiated a debilitating obstacle course around

countless government departments for exit visas, property and wealth assessments, hefty tax demands, interrogations, certificates and other documents. Jews who wanted to leave also had to obtain an expensive permit to allow desertion from the Fatherland.

Insurance brokers, being experts in assessing risk and human folly, do sometimes develop a black sense of humour. My father had a well-developed one (or he would hardly have pretended to be the Pope's right-hand man). In the interest of autobiographical truth, I must admit I'm not sure if I got the story that follows from him, but I like to think so. It also throws some light on Germany after 1933.

A comedian called Valentin would go once a week to a smart café in Munich. He was in his fifties and had starred in many silent films. Some called him the Charlie Chaplin of Germany. Audiences loved him. He often improvised in this café and was perhaps an early version of a stand-up comic. But when Hitler came to power, he perhaps thought improvisation was a Jewish conspiracy. The manager warned Valentin he had to be more formal, given the new regime. He would have to bow to the audience, click his heels respectfully, raise his right arm and say, '*Heil* Hitler.'

'Of course, I understand perfectly,' Valentin said.

'Because my licence may be in trouble if you don't,' the manager replied.

'Of course, I understand perfectly. I will click my heels and say "*Heil* Hitler",' Valentin reassured him.

A few minutes later Valentin went on stage and clicked his

heels. Perfectly. He glanced at the nervous manager, who was a little less nervous now.

Valentin then looked at the owner, paused and said, '*Heil.*' Paused some more. '*Heil* … What was his name again?' The audience apparently laughed – nervously.

Valentin survived the war despite making fun of Hitler and working with the Communist playwright, Bertolt Brecht, who wrote a wonderful satire which likened Hitler to a Chicago gangster: *The Resistible Rise of Arturo Ui*. In 1959, admirers opened a museum in Munich which celebrates Valentin's life and work. I visited it years later.

Those who wanted to leave Germany did have other options than Britain. In 1937, Austria still had undeniable advantages. It was close by, so there would be no problem keeping in touch with family left behind, who would welcome refugees back as soon as the domestic situation recovered. It was also believed there was less official anti-Semitism in Austria than in Germany. A Jewish community had existed there for centuries – over 100,000 lived in Vienna alone. Austria was also a German-speaking country, so one still had opportunities to work. Many jittery hopefuls endured the bureaucratic rigmarole and breathed a sigh of relief when they were allowed to emigrate there.

These optimistic Jews had hardly unpacked their bags when, in March 1938, the German Army marched across the Austrian border and declared the *Anschluss*. Austria had joined the Third Reich. Hitler, who had been born in Austria, went to Vienna, where he was hailed as a hero. There may have been less official anti-Semitism in Austria, but unofficial anti-Semitism was virulent. The Nazis were welcomed by locals eager to celebrate their good fortune as the latest privileged partners of the Thousand-Year Reich. The SS newspaper – they had one – was astonished that the storm troopers did not have to encourage the locals to persecute Jews; it came naturally to them.

Once again the cry of 'Let's get out fast!' was heard, this time even more urgently.

There was still a choice of other countries nearby, more or less sympathetic to the plight of the Jews: France, Belgium, Denmark, Holland and Czechoslovakia among them. All of them safe havens, surely?

Shortly after my brother and I came home from our summer break, the family's emigration date was finally set for December. It was time for a cautious celebration. We went to the magnificent *Zirkus Krone*, where the clowns were famous. As a further treat – and to use up money that would only have to be surrendered at the German border when we left – we stopped off for supper on the way home.

It was by now quite usual to see notices that forbade entry to Jews to various places, including restaurants. Our favourite neighbourhood restaurant had put up a sparkling new sign – though it was put in a more customer-friendly way than was usual. Jewish patronage, it stated, was no longer *willkommen*, or welcome.

We stood at the entrance deciding what to do. My father sighed and lost his appetite. My mother didn't. She said, 'What nonsense! I'm supposed to eat in there while you have to wait outside? Ridiculous! And the children – what about the children?'

'One foot out, one foot in, I suppose,' Father said, trying to keep his spirits up.

My mother didn't see that as funny. 'It makes one ashamed to be German. I'm not going to stand for it. Wait here.'

'Can't we just—'

'No, we can't. We are old customers. I know Gustav will look after us.'

She marched in and, a few moments later, returned with the apologetic restaurant owner, Gustav, who mumbled about the new and regrettable legal requirements. Then he whispered, 'It's a disgrace! Especially where innocent children are involved. Exceptions will of course be made.'

My father said, 'Please, we don't want to cause—'

'No, no, I insist. You are old friends. Please follow me.' He led us to a discreet corner table and we were soon tucking into good food. Even my father regained his appetite.

As bad luck would have it, soon after we had sat down two officers in black and shiny leather arrived to inspect the papers of all diners. It was routine in those days, and always a bonus for officials when a capital 'J' for *Jude* stamped in bright red on someone's papers could be found, as it allowed them to indulge in their favourite pastime of bullying and terrifying Jews. As an adult, I know that many non-Jews opposed the Nazis and some even saved Jews. However, it did not feel like that at the time.

My father lost his appetite a second time as he was made to empty his pockets. The other diners 'politely' turned away and got on with their chatter, no doubt to spare us any embarrassment. The contents of Father's wallet revealed a newspaper cutting of a satirical version of Little Red Riding Hood in which the innocent heroine represented the German people and the Big Bad Wolf the Nazi Party. Oh dear.

Four law-enforcing eyebrows shot up at the likelihood of a promising evening. A leather-gloved finger tapped the offending article.

'This is a serious violation against the authority of the state.'

The blood drained from my father's face but not, luckily, from his nimble brain.

'No question about it, Officer,' he said, with a confidence that surprised his wife – and even himself. 'It is a scandal that this seditious nonsense was, as you see, actually published in one of our most popular national newspapers. Furthermore, it reveals gross negligence on the part of the as yet unidentified government censor appointed specifically to prevent the dissemination of subversive material of this nature.'

He had their attention now, and continued while the going seemed good.

'You will see from my papers that I am a doctor of law. Yes?'

No reaction.

He pressed his advantage with surprising authority. 'Yes?'

Another moment. Then a wary 'So?' from one of them.

'With doctorates from both Heidelberg and Freiburg universities.'

Another moment's silence.

Father pointed to the cutting. 'This article is the one vital piece of *evidence* needed for our proposed legal proceedings that will swiftly bring the offenders to justice. It must not be mislaid.'

The officers became confused and one said, 'But you are a Jew.'

'Yes, er, Herr Sachs,' said the other one.

Father was not slow to sense they had made a mistake of etiquette.

'Herr *Doktor*, *Doktor* Sachs, if you please,' he said, as impressively as he could. 'I believe it would be in your interest, gentlemen, to prioritise my academic distinctions – both of them – as the relevant ones in this matter.'

In those days it was quite acceptable to flaunt multiple academic credits on formal occasions. Father started pocketing the cutting and his other possessions with a chutzpah only another Jew would have appreciated.

The officers decided, however, to do their Nazi duty. 'Halt! This is not satisfactory. You will come to headquarters for further questioning.'

They allowed no excuses and hauled him to his feet. Then, turning to my mother as they left the restaurant, one of them said, 'You will not see your husband again.'

There was a bewildered silence. The good Gustav had witnessed the incident from a distance and become increasingly agitated. There was now a real danger he might lose his catering licence but, ever the professional, he put the thought behind him and hurried over.

'Dear lady, what can I say?' he murmured reverentially. 'That this should happen in my establishment! It is unforgivable! But I think,' he continued, even more reverentially, 'I think the wisest course now would be to leave my restaurant and take your dear children home as quickly as possible – you never know what these dreadful people will get up to. I will arrange for Carlo, my very best waiter, to see you safely home. No, no, I insist.' He managed to place a comforting hand on her shoulder and the bill discreetly on our table, while calling for Carlo to carry out the proposed errand of mercy.

A few minutes later in the street, Mother collapsed with an awful cry that echoed the one I had heard only a few weeks before at the seaside. Carlo took her gently by the arm and escorted us to our front door as she was recovering, her spirit by no means broken. She immediately got in touch with family members and friends, who hurried over to work out a plan of action. They hit on a potentially helpful contact: a high-ranking officer in the Berlin civil police. He had been a long-term client of my father's but, like so many others, he had had to stop his dealings with Jews. Our family nevertheless approached him in the faint hope of gaining his support. They struck lucky. Ignoring the risk to his own career, he gave the necessary orders. It was a brave act and resulted in my father, grateful but distraught, coming back home just a few days later.

But the danger had hardly gone away. Our top priority now was to ensure Father's safety. What was he, the one Jew in our family, to do? Our parents faced each other and nodded. 'Get out fast,' they said as one.

Mother took charge. Father stayed out of the public eye as much as possible, while she marched along endless corridors of power to battle with an army of stony-faced officials. Nothing could daunt her. By turns bullying, cajoling, shouting, crying, bargaining or charming her way through, the bureaucrats

24

finally agreed. 'Get your damned Jew out of the country! *Schnell! Schnell!'*

'*Heil* Hitler,' she said. It choked her, but she said it with a happy smile, and left.

Father bought a one-way ticket to freedom. Actually, to Southampton. Armed with his UK entry visa and the address of his prospective employers in London, he packed his bags and saved his life. We still have his old passport stamped with 'J' for *Jude*, imprints of the German eagle and a spread of five swastikas.

Just five days after Father reached London, Mother was out and about in Berlin a few hundred metres from our home and came across a building in flames. It was one of many that burned that night, a night that became known as *Kristallnacht*.

Our local synagogue was already past saving, with no fire engines in sight. Many onlookers were enjoying the spectacle. Mother instinctively expressed her dismay. It was not in her nature to keep quiet. An argument began. She was accused of being a Jew-lover – a charge she was quite willing to admit. The argument got more heated. A bystander grabbed her and dragged her away so she would not get into further trouble. For a second time in a matter of days, she was escorted home. The man tipped his hat and was gone.

Kristallnacht means literally 'night of crystal'. It took place on 9 November 1938 and got its name because the windows of Jewish shops, offices and synagogues were shattered in an organised spate of attacks. German officials later said it was a spontaneous outburst of public sentiment, of fury, because a Jew had gone into the German embassy in Paris and shot dead Ernst vom Rath, a German embassy official. It was a pretext, of course. The 'killer' was Herschel Grynszpan, who was just seventeen years old. A few days earlier the Nazis had expelled thousands of Jews who had Polish citizenship. Herschel's parents had been living in Germany since 1911, but they too were booted out and sent to live in a refugee camp. Their son had gone to the German embassy and asked to see someone who could help; then he had taken out his gun.

Herschel was just a little older than my sister Barbara.

The Nazis' revenge was brutal. Their supporters looted thousands of Jewish shops and businesses, from tiny news-stands to big department stores; they killed a hundred or so Jews – among them some who merely looked Jewish – and arrested well over 20,000 more. A collective fine of one billion marks was then levied on Jews to pay for the damage.

The Nazis did not want to make mistakes, so each of the premises they were to attack had a big red 'J' daubed on the front together with a Star of David. Many Js sprouted overnight like mushrooms.

Early one morning we noticed one on a café next door to our school. By the time we were let out again in the afternoon, the owner had painted a swastika next to the red 'J' with a message in big, bold capitals: 'MISTAKE! PURE ARYAN PROPRIETOR!' Scrubbing out the 'J' itself was more than he had dared to do. It was, after all, a legal notice.

This thuggery was still going on when I walked home. I stood open-mouthed as a number of men, wielding wooden clubs, shattered the front of a shoe shop on the other side of the road. The glass splintered with a shrill clatter. I was horrified. I remembered the punishment I was given for pitching a ball through our kitchen window a year before. This was a lot worse. It would surely mean bad trouble for them. The men stepped in and out through the broken glass, wrecked displays, loaded piles of shoes into a waiting van, then moved on to other shops before crossing the road. I knew it was very wrong indeed of them. Apart from anything else it was stealing, something I had been taught never to do.

As I stood wondering whether I should call the police, a man suddenly appeared from a doorway almost next to me. He was unkempt and carried a small suitcase. He was in a frantic hurry. A taxi was waiting for him. A metal plaque fixed to a tree outside the premises showed his name and profession. The sign was yellow, like the one outside our own home, indicating a Jewish business. He wrenched the metal sign off its backing, crumpled it between his hands as though it was just paper, and threw it on the ground. He got into the taxi, immediately stepped out again, picked up the buckled metal, smoothed it out and laid it face up on the ground to show his defiance.

For once I actually felt concerned for somebody's plight other than my own. With one quick glance at the storm troopers relentlessly coming towards him, the man got back in the taxi.

I cheered him on silently, hoping he would escape. The taxi pulled away fast. I breathed a sigh of relief and quickly recovered my old self. What a story I could boast of to my school friends!

As a child I found this turmoil exciting as well as frightening, and I wasn't enchanted at the prospect of having to leave Germany, but it was soon to be. It might be too soon for me, but millions who desperately wanted to leave would find it impossible to do so.

We had permission to ship one container out of the country. Furniture, china, glass and cutlery, books, kitchenware, linen and soft furnishings were allowed, as was an insignificant amount of cash. Significant amounts were not. Nor were investments, jewels and most other articles of value.

Did that include my precious toys? I wondered anxiously.

After the removal men had packed up and taken away our goods, and the lease to our apartment was surrendered, our home was bare and Father's office ceased to exist. We three children were farmed out to some of Mother's relatives who were not Jewish.

When the day of our exodus arrived and all the suitcases we could manage were packed, I was more or less reconciled to leaving, and a bit excited, even. After all, it meant a train ride all the way to Hamburg. There was also the prospect of meeting an old school friend of my mother's, who would see us safely off and might give us a farewell present if we behaved ourselves. Auntie Mimi, as we called her, must have been very rich. She took us shopping to three shops for three presents for three children. I chose a fancy jeweller's to buy a watch. It took me a long time to choose, but I finally settled on one in gold-coloured metal with a luminous dial.

Afterwards, she treated us to coffee and cream cakes and followed that with a sightseeing boat trip around the harbour to see the big ships. We drew up alongside the SS *Manhattan*, a huge American liner that was the ship we were to board for Southampton. I was even allowed to touch its hull with my bare hand.

When the time came for the 'All ashore that's going ashore' call, Auntie Mimi hugged and kissed us. We stayed on deck for a long time watching Germany get smaller and then disappear into the distance. It had been one of the most exciting days of my life.

Only years later did I even begin to consider what my mother's feelings would have been that day. She was leaving behind brothers, sisters, nephews and nieces, aunts, uncles, both her parents, many close friends and a tragic number of her in-law relatives. She had lost her home and was now facing an unknown future in a foreign land. Yet her instinctive resilience, her refusal to despair and her gratitude for even the smallest blessings never deserted her. On that day she would certainly have appreciated the fact that – unlike millions of others in the coming years – she had escaped the Nazis with her husband alive and well, with three children she could surround with love, and with her own health and strength intact.

CHAPTER 2

Shredded Wheat

On her way to England, the SS *Manhattan* stopped at Le Havre. I tried to persuade my mother this gave me time to take a look around France. Her answer was a firm '*Nein!*' Once off the ship, I might be kidnapped and sent straight back to Berlin. I wouldn't have minded particularly, but as a good German boy who obeyed orders without question, I knew my duty. She offered a sweetener: there would be an on-board film show that evening starring cowboys from Hollywood in glorious color (colour without a 'u', that is – real American!).

Mother must have breathed a huge sigh of relief when we took our first grateful steps on British soil. Well, British concrete, really – it was only Southampton docks. We spent the night in a modest hotel. I was still queasy from a choppy Channel crossing and relieved to get to bed. We were sharing a room. The others went to have dinner, leaving me alone.

It was pitch dark when a knock on the door woke me. A second knock jerked me into a sitting position. Panic nudged. Who was there? Or worse – *what* was there? I tried a timid

'*Ja, bitte schön*...?' to no effect. Where was Mutti? Why wasn't she here? Was she now abandoning me altogether? It wasn't fair. I slid under the blanket and swore never, ever to forgive her. I hated her for making me cry and stuff, and I hated my Vati for running away to London without me and stuff ... and things and stuff ... and – and so on. Halfway through this major whinge, I suddenly remembered the awards given to me, a mongrel, earlier that year. Perhaps I was Mongrel of the Year! Yes – I had been judged an invincible *mischling* of man/dog! Surrender was not an option. My tears turned to tears of gratitude for the omniscient, omnipresent, omnipotent Führer who never lets a good German down. But my high spirits crumbled almost at once. Hadn't I stupidly switched allegiance to cuddly Uncle Joseph?

Again there seemed no hope of sleep except... except! A few days earlier I had been taught a single sentence parrot fashion in the awesome gibberish called English. These words were to be used if I got into any kind of trouble. The effect could even be enhanced by simple repetition of the message, only louder.

Imminent confrontation with a life-threatening creature outside the bedroom reminded me of the sacred mantra. Still clutching the blanket, I directed my voice bravely in the direction of the keyhole and declaimed with all the confidence I could manage: 'I am sorry I do not understand you I am a little German boy.'

There was no response. What now? Had the magic failed? I tried again a little louder as advised. Then a lot louder. A minute went by with still nothing. Was the danger over or not?

I never found out. The chambermaid, if the chambermaid

it was, had given up and probably gone home, while I, alone and lonely, put a pillow over my head and went on cursing my mother, cursing the English, cursing their so-called language, and cursing my failure to find freedom at Le Havre.

I awoke next morning happy, refreshed and fond of my mum again but facing a second hurdle as we all sat down to breakfast. In front of each of us was a china bowl containing a 10 x 6 cm mound of dull-coloured, fibrous material compressed into an oblong slab with a rounded top.

'What, please, this is?' Mother asked an approaching waitress.

'Breakfast,' she muttered rudely. (She could have been working at Fawlty Towers given her attitude.)

At least we now knew the aggregate of unknown origin was food rather than a pan scourer, as my brother had thought possible. We looked at each other and took a daring bite from our portions, not realising Shredded Wheat can become almost edible when combined with milk and sugar. The experiment did us no harm. It served instead as a useful introduction to the culinary standards of the nation, which turned out to be no more discouraging than German menus, where tradition dictated that food for the masses was fuel, not fun.

On the whole, we managed quite easily to adapt to the new regime. Shredded Wheat became my brother's favourite cereal, while I preferred the puffed variety and, later, in an effort to be grown-up, went for tough guy's porridge without sugar.

None of these breakfasts could compare with our mother's love-filled and heaven-sent variation on Dr Bircher-Benner's muesli. This was real food of spiritual delight, in no way comparable to the fake stuff supermarkets sell, which gums up the molars with cavity-filling grit, and where the only skill involved in preparing it is adding milk and, then, cramming the hydrated gunge down into the stomach.

Mum loved the cuisine of the Tyrol – where her father had been born – and it wasn't hard to teach us to love it. Apart from the muesli, she was a dab hand at delicacies like *kalbsgulasch*, *zillertaler krapfen*, *kaiserschmarren*, *topfenknödel*, *zwetschenknödel*, *oberösterreichische fleischknödel* and some *knödel* with names even longer than those, all dishes that made our little mouths water and our little tongues twist.

My favourite was *schweizer reis*, a heap of boiled white rice turned golden yellow by vanilla, eggs, cream and almonds, plus Mutti's inimitable love-touch, all topped off with a generous sprinkling of cinnamon and sugar. Yellow and cinnamon brown are still among my favourite colour combinations for everything, from shirts to wallpaper.

Father had also become a fan of Tyrol's mountain landscape and its people – especially his wife – and would tell us unlikely tales of children having to scramble down dangerous cliffs at dawn to get to school, then run up them again twice as fast at dusk, desperate for their *knödel*. He told us there is no such word as 'obesity' in Tyrolese. These man-mountain men and women ate only to beef up their muscles, especially those padding the stomach area. This explained their nation's world-renowned sense of balance. Vati would then become unstoppable. The Tyrolese needed their calories because they often had to rush out into the snow, hurl themselves over a crevasse that could swallow them, and hunt the famous chamois, a tasty mountain goat ideal for spit-roasting outdoors in a blizzard as a snack between meals.

Delicious! Profitable, too, for the hides of the chamois could be turned into fine polishing cloths for window cleaners throughout the world. This would typically be the moment for our mother to order her husband to bed without supper.

We loved his fables and fantasies, whatever she thought of them. Why, he could do anything – even write poems that rhymed properly and sometimes even made sense.

After we had finished breakfast, we took the train to London. Vati met us at Waterloo Station. There were happy hugs all round, marred only by an embarrassing amount of kissing between the two grown-ups. I was pleased we were reunited, but what was especially exciting was seeing motorcars and taxis driving in and out of the station. In Berlin I was used to seeing them only on roads. I was keen to learn what other revelations lay in store, and was getting fed up with all the soppy stuff going on right next to me.

Brother Tom smugly dismissed my reaction to indoor traffic as being pathetically ignorant. He claimed to know everything there was to know about London, having researched the subject thoroughly in Berlin. His all-knowingness came largely from one volume in our parents' library. It was his bad luck that this book was his beloved *Adventures of Sherlock Holmes*.

The London of 1938 was very different from Holmes's late Victorian London. In line with his 'facts' from 700 pages of his stupid fiction, Tom had expected London to be packed with hansom cabs and horses, 'bobbies' with truncheons and helmets, and thick fog. His own pathetic ignorance had made him step into the wrong century! Oh boy, did I gloat.

Our superior, older and hated but brainy sister Barbara called us both 'fatheads', using a recently learned English word, and then topped it off with a quotation from Schiller (another stupid author): '*Mit der Dummheit kämpfen Götter selbst vergebens*' – 'Even God cannot battle against stupidity.'

The family was reunited, but only to be separated again almost immediately; our parents left for furnished rooms close to where Father worked, while we children were whisked off to charitable acquaintances in far-flung areas of London. We had to wait until our family possessions arrived from Germany and we could move into a house that Father had rented for us.

The house was small, the furniture big. The biggest object of all was the bookcase, a solid-oak affair especially designed for Father. It stretched to the ceiling in one direction and almost to Birmingham in the other, and was made up of five bookcases – two double ones, with a fifth single one set neatly between them. On the front of each case there was a plate-glass door set above five lockable drawers. The contents arrived in tea chests, which were stacked wherever there was any space. More crates were packed with clothes, bed linen, kitchenware, toys and everything else a family of five might have acquired over the years. Well, not quite everything. Before we left Berlin, we had parted with those of our possessions, including books, that could be suspected of contravening the Reich's export regulations. Still, we had sneaked several forbidden but valued authors through. On the other hand, too many of our allowed and delicate antique pieces and treasured china and glassware had smashed in transit.

None of us could bear to see our mother cry. A single broken saucer could bring on the tears. Now, she could not bear seeing a dozen fragments of her beloved Limoges dinner service at the bottom of a tea chest, or examining pieces of a shattered Dresden candlestick. And what was too much for her was too much for us, too.

Father had also refused to leave his beloved cello behind. He had learned to play as a boy and joined a part-time chamber group. In our later days in Germany he played less and less because it was so hard to relax when Jews were always on edge. So I, as the youngest in the family, had only heard him infrequently. But they were treasured moments. I judged him to be probably the greatest cello player in the world and the instrument became, and still is, my favourite one, next to a mouth organ.

With him off early every morning and back late every evening, trying to scratch a meagre living, the rest of us had to buckle down and make a home out of a house on the outskirts of London: a precious little semi-detached Englishman's castle in Hatch End.

Our clever father's foresight relating to furniture design came into its own. In our final Berlin flat, the bookcases had stood as a harmonious unit against one wall, with room to spare on either side. No chance of that in Hatch End. With the help of a couple of brawny neighbours, two sections were moved laboriously into two rooms, and the third, one of the doubles, was dragged all the way up groaning stairs and converted into wardrobes. This left books still in piles with nowhere to park them, until an Anderson air raid shelter was delivered later that year. The shelter eventually would also house illiterate tadpoles and newts.

The turmoil of unpacking and arranging went on for days, if not weeks, sometimes while air raid sirens were blaring. I didn't have that much interest in the furniture, and I became more and more of a nuisance until, one day, my mother lost her temper and told me to get out of the house. My ghastly sister added I shouldn't come back. This was my chance to feel sorry for myself and make a tragic exit.

It was my first foray alone into undiscovered territory. I stepped through the front door into six inches of snow. It was reassuring to learn that thick snow fell every winter in England, as it did in Berlin. So England was going to be fun! It took years before I forgave the winter of 1938 for deceiving me so badly. Snow was then, as it still is today, an event in weather-obsessed England.

Once on the pavement I held up a wet finger to determine the direction I should take: downwind, of course, in case of dangerous beasts on the prowl. Or should that have been upwind? Whichever it was, I nodded confidently and turned left. There was no one and nothing about. Just the silent sound of falling snow. Lovely.

A few minutes later, I spotted a man standing by a lamp post, wearing what looked like a uniform and a helmet with a badge on the front. Men in uniform had never been a welcome sight in Berlin and were best approached, if at all necessary, with eyes down and with care. Keeping a steady pace and showing no sign of fear was the best policy. He was a big, round man, and looked at me carefully as I got closer. A *Polizist* of some kind? Possibly, but his uniform was hardly smart enough compared to the policemen I was used to, and the helmet was more silly than threatening. He wore no shiny leather coat, so he was not a member of the SS. Nevertheless, better to be safe than sorry. I rounded my shoulders and lowered my eyes in the accepted racial tradition, but not before casting one furtive glance in his direction.

To my astonishment, he was smiling at me – a very nice, open smile; something quite unexpected from a member of the ruling class.

Then he spoke. I had no idea what he was saying and stared at him dumbly. He repeated his message louder and slower, so at least I knew he was English. My heart began to beat more gently. Was it worth trying my rescue sentence, even though it hadn't worked in Southampton and I still didn't know what the words meant anyway? Well, it was worth another go.

'I am sorry I do not understand you I am a little German boy.'

He looked surprised. His smile turned into a laugh and he tousled my hair. I moved smartly back. I hated people who went round tousling children all over the place. But still smiling and nodding benignly, he asked me the simplest question he could think of, giving it a slight foreign twang to put me at ease.

'Ah! *Englisch* ... not...'

What was that supposed to mean? I understood the words, but couldn't work out how to respond. Was it a question or a statement? If I said 'No', that would be the truth, meaning, 'No, you're right, I'm not English,' but it could also mean, 'Yes, you're right, I am English,' which I wasn't; and if I said 'Yes' to him I would want it to mean, 'Yes, you're right. I'm not English,' which would again be the truth, but it could also mean, 'No, you're wrong, you are English.' Or something equally confusing that might be another lie. Then again, he might be talking of English as a language rather than a nationality, so how could I give the right answer? It was all too much for my little foreign brain. My mouth started turning down at both ends and my eyes were desperate to do babyish things.

'No, no, *nein*!' he said, in an effort to comfort me. He produced a shiny whistle, put it to his lips and made a sound soft enough to calm a neurotic burglar bungling a break-in. He had my interest immediately. He tried to hand me the whistle. I supposed he wanted me to blow it, but that wasn't on. It could have been poisoned, so I declined with a thin smile and a '*Danke schön.*'

He smiled back and pointed at me, raising his eyebrows invitingly. 'Name?' he asked. 'Your name?'

I understood that all right. The word is the same in German: *Name*, only pronounced as two syllables. But I got scared. Why did he want to know my name? Was he going to demand my papers? I didn't have any papers!

His smile – maybe it wasn't friendly at all but more like the one I imagined Himmler might smile. Everyone knew he wasn't a nice man.

In fact, our local bobby on his beat, for that was what he turned out to be, pointed at himself and said, with all the caring and sharing he could summon, 'Me, Reginald. Uncle Reginald ... Say "Reginald"?' The raised eyebrows again.

I thought I had better do as I was told. 'Regiland,' I murmured.

He smiled again, shook his head as well and raised his eyebrows for the third time. 'Reg-i-nald,' he repeated, separating each syllable with a pause in between. This time I got it right. Then he went on. 'Your name, please?'

Another little stab of panic, but there was no way out.

'Andreas,' I said, as softly as possible, hoping I would not be arrested, but he simply went on with, 'I shprekke Doitsh.'

That was a surprise. He could almost say it, but I knew he wouldn't be able to spell it.

He pointed to the road. 'Shtrahssa,' he said proudly.

His English 'r' could not be ignored. I became more assertive. '*Strrrasse!*' I said, giving the 'r' a triple roll.

'Ya! Goot! Goot! Dunkershoan.'

Before I could correct him again, he pointed to the lamp post. 'Strasslumper. Ya?'

I was flattered by his keenness to tap my superior knowledge.

'No,' I replied in perfect English, which isn't difficult with a word like 'no'. '*Straa-ssen-lahmp-er,*' I said, with shorter pauses between syllables to please him, and in an effort not to show this nice man up with more triple r's.

Our linguistic exchanges continued for some minutes and, by the time he had escorted me home, we had become friends. He took his weird helmet off to greet my law-abiding mother and siblings and, before leaving, gave her his whistle to pass on to me. We were all amazed by the strange thought that in strange England, a policeman's lot could indeed be a happy one.

At about this time my parents underhandedly, behind my

back, without asking, arranged an interview with the headmaster of the local junior school. Although he spoke even less German than I did English, he accepted me as a pupil on the basis of a glowing account from my parents. I was highly intelligent, had good manners, was totally devoted to duty, highly sensitive and those were only my most obvious qualities. Yet all the headmaster could come up with on my first term report was a scribbled 'Charming smile'. I thought that was really daft, but worthy of further practice in front of a mirror.

One or two other misgivings about my new hosts surfaced during those first weeks. I had been taught in Berlin, for instance, that a trip to the seaside was possible in only one direction – north. In Britain, however, they were trying to tell me you could get to the sea in any direction you chose. It seemed to me as just as well these *dummkopf* Englanders never laid claim to membership of the master race.

When I eventually understood the meaning of 'island', I went straight to our family atlas and made a resolve (never resolved) to write letters of condolence to the Hungarians, Swiss, Czechoslovaks, Afghans, Paraguayans and several other nationalities who had no access to the seaside, and were thus deprived of one of the supposedly great British joys of life – looking at water.

I still prefer looking at mountains.

My daily walks to school were fun and, if I had the time, I would stop at a patch of water: a stagnant pond in a little wood a few paces off the road. It turned out to be a spellbinding hothouse of life, with an impressive variety of exotic larvae, pond skaters, water boatmen, dragonflies, frogs, toads and newts. And not just the common newt, either, but the other one that looks like a miniature iguana: the crested newt. It is a beautiful animal and it is a shame it's such a rare sight now. Even the one I adopted finally became surplus to national requirements. The pond survived the war, but not the concrete that eventually covered it.

I was forever hoping to catch a glimpse of that rare creature, the *bufo calamita*, otherwise known as the natterjack toad. But I never did. Had I been prepared to tell lies at the time, it would have made a mighty attention-grabbing boast to my friends then, and an even better one these days.

At the age of nine, when I saw myself as the Charles Darwin of Hatch End, I was forever imagining coming across natterjack toads in my secret nature reserve. I sensed even then that they were under threat. I only realised recently that my long-held soft spot for natterjack toads is because I, like them, was also a member of an endangered species, rather than being due to the influence of fairy stories about frogs turning into princes and getting the girls.

Well, whichever it is, dear, aptly named *bufo calamita*, we have something in common, and you are much cherished.

One of the shocks I had to suffer on starting school was the disgraceful number of hours we had to stay in class. In Berlin, we had got home at the beginning of the afternoon, not at the end of it. In England, though, the school day seemed to go on for ever. I could only assume that my classmates had learning difficulties and needed longer to cope with the mysteries of their language and every other quirk of their culture.

One teacher did speak some German. At our first meeting, Miss Taylor had me recite all the English I knew. It wasn't much but it did, of course, include my one complete parroted sentence. I was horrified when she translated it for me and I got to know the meaning of 'little'. She came to my defence before I could.

'"Little" is not right, surely!' she protested. 'I think of you as a big boy, don't you?'

I knew at once this was a woman I could do business with. To be understood by a grown-up official was overwhelming. And that was only the beginning. During those first months, Miss Taylor played an important part in getting me to learn English without actually having to make an effort. I have no memory of agonising over rules of grammar or syntax, or having to cram words with impossible spellings into my brain. English was taking root almost as though it were my mother tongue. By the end of my second term, I could make myself reasonably well understood. Well enough, I decided, to express a grievance about our working hours to the lovely Miss Taylor.

There was an explanation behind my untypical flash of assertiveness that had nothing to do with language. Young refugees like me weren't aware that along with breathing the clean air (as well as the smoke and fog) of London, we also absorbed another quite different atmosphere; one that exposed us to novel ideas. In Germany, I had always accepted that an adult – any adult, even one without a uniform – was fault-free and protected by divine right from criticism. Miss Taylor should have fitted comfortably into that category. In Germany, I wouldn't have dared even think of defying an adult... But in Hatch End I wasn't afraid.

Miss Taylor listened attentively and then asked me to compare the hours spent in an English school with those in Germany. I was to answer in English only, please, armed with some new words from the dictionary: addition, subtraction, division, comparison and result. I did well and was proudly able to confirm that German schools worked fewer hours than English ones.

Miss Taylor smiled graciously at my triumph and shook my hand. I was just about to leave the room when she asked, all innocent, 'Those hours are of course for a five-day week, are they not?'

My smugness faltered. 'Five-day?' I stuttered. 'Yes, I mean no, I mean I forgot…'

'I only ask because I may have read somewhere – do correct me if I'm wrong – that in Germany you have classes on Saturdays as well? Making it one day more than here?'

I went bright red and tried to nod in agreement. 'Well, perhaps, but only in the mornings. I forgot…'

'Oh, yes, that was it. Of course. I wasn't sure. Do forgive me. Well, no harm done. Thank you for letting me know. So, in the end, it works out at more or less the same number of hours in both countries. Would you agree?'

I nodded again, muttering something about thinking Saturdays wouldn't count because it's the weekend. I hadn't meant to offend her. I felt terrible in case I had done just that. Miss Taylor and I had just shared a really good lesson with no sign of superiority from her, no frowns and not one harsh word. Teachers can dazzle children.

She took up a pen and said, 'Before you go, I have four new English words for you, quite difficult ones actually, but I think you're ready for them.' She wrote them down. 'You will find them frightfully important in this country, Andreas. So I want you to learn their meanings when you get home and perhaps pay particular attention to the fourth word. Will you do that?'

I nodded enthusiastically.

'Good. Do ask your parents if you need help.' She tucked the paper into my pocket. 'We'll talk again tomorrow. Meanwhile, one final, general point I'm sure you will be interested in. You have made excellent progress today, and I believe your studies are advanced enough to tackle a really tricky point of grammar that even British people find hard to grasp.'

Miss Taylor then gave me a clear and concise explanation of the difference between 'less hours' and 'fewer hours', confident that her little Hun would embrace pedantry of this kind more easily than her native-born charges.

Once again she took my hand. 'We've had a lovely time, haven't we?' she said. 'Thank you so much.'

At home that evening, Mother and I honoured Miss Taylor's request. With the help of a dictionary we translated 'free speech', 'tolerance' and 'democracy' nicely into *redefreiheit*, *toleranz* and *demokratie*, though I was actually none the wiser about what they meant, but her final word, 'honesty', hit home at once and didn't even need translating. It was the gentlest but clearest of reprimands from this dear woman. I was ready to die for her. I wanted to live up to my middle name of Siegfried and slay a dragon to prove my love for her. I even thought of marrying her, until just a few short weeks later, when sex reared its ugly head and caused embarrassment.

My classmates had readily accepted the freaky foreigner in their midst, and we got on together well with a minimum of words and maximum of noise and confusion. Groups of us would leave school together, chatting along the way. One of my occasional companions was a girl. She had pigtails, so I didn't like her. I had better explain that I hated pigtails because my sister had one long one hanging down her back and wouldn't let me pull it hard even when I needed to. This creepy little female had two of them lapping along behind her ears. One day, an evil stinker from another class chalked a message on the pavement just outside school. It read for all to see: 'Andraiss lovs Synnthiai.' It was an illiterate lie and, anyway, I considered myself too manly for love and ugly pavement scrawls so I didn't walk with her again. And I changed my name to Andrew.

The streets of London turned out to be more dangerous for me than those of Hitler's Germany. On a homeward jaunt from school one day with my friend Mac, we hauled ourselves up on a brick wall; we were fooling about. Mac threw himself off with a Highland battle cry and landed on his feet. I tried the same and landed on my stomach, with my right arm getting in the way. I was in agony and found it hard to breathe. Mac helped me to my feet and suggested this might be a good time to meet his mum.

When we got to his home, she made a pot of tea. I was still in pain and so the three of us caught a bus to the doctor. When we got to the surgery, I was told to count to 100 so they could gas me to oblivion. Even though I'd only just managed up to fifty for Miss Taylor, I was determined not to let myself down now. I got to about seven and went under. I came to again to find my right arm securely packaged in a wooden splint and covered with a heroic amount of white bandage.

Mac and his mum took me home and I received a gratifying amount of tearful fuss from my mum and, later that evening, a jar of boiled sweets from my dad. The next day they took me to hospital for the splint to be replaced by a plaster cast. They let me keep the wooden splint but not the bandages. Never mind, I had quite enough booty to impress the school with, and space enough for many autographs on the plaster, which turned out to be my introduction to fan mail.

Miss Taylor's sympathetic tut-tutting later that day was particularly appreciated. She asked me if I had profited from the experience. I was desperate to reply with something that would impress and offered her two important English words I had learned at the doctor's: radius and ulna. Both secured a good reaction from her.

There were more silver linings to my broken arm. Inspired by my calamitous injury, Mac's generously proportioned mother had actually honoured me with a starting insight in one of the great British traditions. I got the first inkling that tea is to the English what chicken soup is to Jews. Even more: as a Presbyterian Scot, my pal's mother was neither English nor Jewish. But she was apparently still British, and therefore as much in thrall to the mystical powers of Darjeeling, Assam, Earl Grey and PG Tips as everyone else from Land's End to John O'Groats.

I learned something else – fooling about on walls can be dangerous but gets much easier if you practise. The same principle applies to almost everything else, from arithmetic to zoology. The best gain of all, though, was the exhilaration I felt at being the centre of attention. I began to wonder whether there might be some way of achieving that on a more regular basis, preferably without breaking bones – except as a last resort. I was determined to investigate the possibilities as soon as I could.

Meanwhile, I continued to explore the stagnant pond and named it 'the Darwin Nature Reserve'. Special school friends were invited to share its mysteries, and to benefit from my wisdom. Spring and summer were the best times, watching swarms of living mini-miracles doing their dedicated bits for the environment.

Pond-skaters for instance: little insects that walk on water and never get their feet wet. And they manage this not just on a mere two legs like Jesus, but on six. And at breakneck speed without ever tripping up. If that wasn't a miracle, I didn't know what was. Then there were the beetles and bugs, the frogs, toads and newts … and leeches.

Leeches were good news. With luck, one or two of them might stick to our wellies as we waded. If we went in too deep and let the water in, they would stick to our socks. If we took our socks off first, they were supposed to drink our blood, though we never found one that did, try as we might. But we did catch a few of them to sell at school – and got into trouble.

Miss Taylor made me look up obscure words like 'invertebrate' and 'arthropod' and 'chrysalis' and 'annelid', so I reckoned she must have heard about our misdemeanour (another word I learned that day) but she never told me off. I loved her even more.

The year 1939 was one of tension, anxiety and change for the rest of the family, too, and, indeed, for the whole country and the world. The question of whether there was to be a war was on everyone's mind but I was still too young to grasp what was happening. Instead, I was worried by what seemed to me more important matters, especially that our father never seemed to be at home except on Sundays and sometimes not even then. We missed him. I was getting desperate to take him to the pond and teach him all about annelids and other aquatics. But he never came. The boiled sweets he gave me from time to time did not make up for all that absence.

He was at work. Always at work. We had hoped our new life in England would mean our troubles would be over, but there were still many challenges to deal with, particularly for him. On most days he left home early in the morning and returned after our bedtime. He was studying hard to familiarise himself with the way insurance worked in Britain, which was different from the way it did in Germany. If he had not had a good command of English, we would probably not even have seen him on a Sunday. We had to understand that family togetherness for the time being was rationed. I wasn't much help. As the baby of the brood, I was a spoilt little brat, as my horrid sister quite rightly put it, with my endless *knatsch*-ing if I didn't get my way, driving everyone mad. *Knatschen*, by the way, means whining or bleating, as in 'You spoilt little brat, stop your *knatschen*.' When delivered properly, the word produces an effect better than any

English equivalent. Success depends on some vocal dexterity regarding the first three letters. An irresistible 'k' (as in 'key' but not as in 'knot') needs to explode against an immovable 'n' (as in 'nose' but not as in … whatever) powerfully enough to project the 'a' (as in 'aardvark' but not as in 'anteater') with enough momentum for a haze of unpleasant nasal matter to be sprayed at the target's face. Very satisfying for the *knatsch*-er knaturally, but less so for the target.

Our parents never *knatsch*-ed and, on the whole, we children needed little guidance from them to find ways of curbing our whiny self-pity. In most respects we were good kids and glad beyond glad that our Vati had escaped from Berlin just five days before the horror of *Kristallnacht*.

It was not until some years later that I took a more mature interest in events prior to the declaration of the Second World War – and began to realise what my parents had been forced to endure. I didn't know it then but they illustrated perfectly the stoic English attitude, 'Mustn't grumble', though they had so much they could grumble about.

Even before we left Berlin, the *Eintritt Verboten* signs for Jews on restaurants and other areas had spread to include theatres, cinemas and concert halls. Soon afterwards, Jews were banned from German colleges and forbidden to drive a car. A 20 per cent tax on all Jewish property worth over 5,000 marks was imposed, and jewellery was confiscated.

It went on getting worse. At least our immediate family was now no longer subject to these Nazi 'laws', but our parents must have been torn between their concern for those left behind, and a deep gratitude – quite possibly tinged with guilt – for not being among them.

That summer, while I was busy monitoring molluscs at my Darwin Reserve, Mother travelled back to the Tyrol for her much loved father's funeral. She returned via Berlin and brought back, or more likely smuggled back, the rest of her jewellery, which had been left with her family. We might be able to sell it in London.

Then, just before September, Adolf Hitler, in his desire for friendship and peace, guaranteed the frontiers of Yugoslavia, signed a non-aggression pact with Denmark and invaded Poland. Britain declared war. The Führer, disappointed but not surprised by this act of Allied treachery, reassured Holland and Belgium of his true friendship. Then, as Christmas approached, Hitler asked his respected comrade Adolf Eichmann to begin clearing out the Jews from the territories he had so generously liberated, or was about to liberate. These included surely his next target (Father must have paled at the thought): England. Hitler then went to greet his troops on the Western front, to give them his heartfelt wishes for a Merry Christmas and a prosperous New War... I mean, of course, New Year. Sorry once again.

And Fate smiled upon him, for the time being.

CHAPTER 3

War

We were eager to celebrate our first family Christmas in our new home, though we would do that in a more modest style than we were used to. Celebrations in Germany always began in the midnight hours of 6 December, the feast of St Nicholas, when the patron saint of children arrived on his donkey to offer a modest heap of goodies for believers – and even for pretend believers. The only condition St Nicholas seemed to insist on was that we left a shoe with a carrot and a few sugar lumps in it outside the bedroom door.

Next morning, lo and behold, our donkey treats would have been replaced with tastier ones for us. There was no sign of St Nicholas himself, of course, although faint traces of hoofmarks on the stairs were certainly proof of his visit. The event was always the perfect start to our festive season. No wonder, with a resident Jewish saint in the house doing the honours.

Later, a well-worn collection of special kitchen equipment, as much part of our family as we were, would be brought out. The ancient, half-corroded metal shapes were scrubbed, buffed, polished and then used for cutting out stars, birds, hearts and fish. We used them to make tray after tray of *pfeffernüsse* – the traditional brown, cardamom-spiced, fiercely crisp, yummy biscuits. After kneading the dough and flattening it enough to cover a table top, Tom and I dealt with the geometric niceties of ensuring a regulation 4mm thickness that allowed the creative work to begin. We all contributed our own designs: flower blossoms and snowflakes and other female stuff from Barbara (rubbish), bug-eyed flatworms from me (excellent) and miniature roller skates from Tom (hopeless). When our little masterpieces came out of the oven and cooled, they were stored in airtight containers that kept them fresh for weeks and as brittle as the English version of muesli, minus the toothache.

After dark on Christmas Eve of 1939, our mother unlocked the living room door while we stood in awed silence to take in the spectacle: the lights low, the candles lit and a small branch of smouldering pine needles lying on a silver tray, scenting the air. Decorated pine branches hung at ceiling height in the corners of the room and around picture frames. The tree itself, miraculously hidden from us until that evening, was the biggest our parents could afford. It was simply but elegantly decorated with coloured glass balls and many strands of silver tinsel. A dozen or more fragile candleholders, inherited from ancient relatives, supported the flickering candles. Underneath were our presents, beautifully wrapped.

Out of sight but well within reach was a be-ribboned metal bucket full of cold water and a wet towel … just in case.

But best of all, oh yes, the very best of all, was our father, right there, seated by the side of the tree, playing his cello and encouraging us to join in: '*Stille nacht, heilige nacht, alles schläft, einsam wacht*' – 'Silent Night'.

A week later came *Sylvesterabend* or New Year's Eve. Hot, homemade doughnuts, pancakes and other calories were on the table, plus small lumps of lead. These would be melted in spoons each of us held with trembling hands; once molten, each spoon was carefully tipped downwards and the now liquid lead sizzled dramatically into a pan of cold water and promptly solidified into random shapes. These shapes would predict our fortunes for the coming year – supposedly. Inventing largely meaningless interpretations provided us with a noisy half-hour's debate, argument and insult. Real fun.

The evening ended with a beginning: a toast to the New Year. We children were allowed an allegedly alcoholic champagne-type fizzy drink; our parents had a rare shot of schnapps. We wished health, happiness and peace for everyone we knew, as well as those we didn't – with notable exceptions for the villains in the Third Reich, of course – and declared our growing affection for the strange but welcoming new hosts we were learning to adapt to.

Not long into the New Year, however, the war involved us in a particularly unwelcome way. It turned out we were living in a buffer zone set up hurriedly to protect a military air base in the middle of it. All foreigners within the zone had to leave the district at short notice.

We three children had to leave the area, as did our parents, but we could not stay together. I was shunted off to a fellow refugee's unthreatened home and got to learn something of the English countryside, the Grand Union Canal and the local ice-cream parlour. I had plenty of opportunities for merry japes with trees, lock gates and tuppenny cornets, and I only had occasional domestic duties to dampen my spirits. On top of that, I had the joy of all those school-free days.

When I got back a few months later to my nearest and dearest, it was to a new home: a couple of top-floor furnished rooms in Kilburn with a kitchenette and share of a bathroom two floors down. It was a bit grim but it would do temporarily as my parents searched for somewhere big enough to house the five of us more comfortably. We brought only the barest necessities with us. There was hardly space for more. The rest of our belongings were put in store.

I had to move school and found that tougher to come to terms with. Was there a pond? Would I have to lose touch with Miss Taylor? If Tom and Barbara could stay at their own school, why not me? It wasn't fair. They can't make me, and I'll never stop *knatschen* for the rest of my life unless...

But nobody was listening.

Our new address was in a busy part of London, well placed to be flattened by the *Luftwaffe*'s air raids. Our landlady resented having to squeeze all her tenants into the basement whenever an air raid warning sounded. Going down five flights of stairs seemed daft to me, and I told my family so. Much better stay upstairs, I said. I had now decided I was an expert on how to survive bombs. If there was a direct hit, I told my family, we could hang on to a falling beam, drop on top of all the debris and stay alive. If we were in the basement, however, we had every chance of being crushed to death. I proved it to them by explaining how Isaac Newton saw the proverbial apple fall and discovered gravity. As usual, nobody listened.

Sixty and more years on, it is easy to forget the small irritations which loomed large at the time. The horrible landlady once complained to my mother that Tom's hair had stained her basement wallpaper with Brylcreem as he leant against it during the raids, but we thought she put it there herself because we were enemy aliens which, in her warped mind, was the same as being Nazi spies. I suspected she was an alien herself because she never once made us a cup of tea like British people did. I found some good definitions for her in the dictionary, like 'saboteur', 'fifth-columnist' and 'traitor', all superior show-off words to add to my growing stock of insults. Tom believed the offending smudge wasn't Brylcreem at all, but black-market lard.

Then, Churchill barked his famous order – 'Collar the lot' – and all aliens who had come from enemy countries were to be interned. It didn't matter if they were Jews who had escaped from the Nazis. We were told the British wanted to make sure there were no Nazi infiltrators.

Tom and I could see their point once we had looked up 'infiltrators', but it would take them weeks, if not months, to sort out. Fortunately, Mutti and we children avoided internment but Vati couldn't. How could we manage without him? He was our Vati, for heaven's sake! It was no comfort for us to know he was one of thousands of others to have their status as bona fide refugees investigated. The British, who, incidentally, had invented the concentration camp during the Boer War, set up a number of camps, including one on the Isle of Man. It became famous because the internees included great artists like Kurt Schwitters, the future members of the Amadeus String Quartet and Andre Deutsch, who became a successful publisher. One of the internees had an unusual profession for a Jew: he was a lion tamer. Maybe it wasn't so unusual, if one remembers the heroics of Daniel in the Bible. 'Collar the lot' did not apply, however, to lion tamers; he was one of the first internees to be released, as his wife could not handle the lions by herself.

In our childish way, Tom and I came up with a solution which would allow our hosts to decide who they had to intern. We were back to an obsession with Jewish noses, which, I suspect, was a way of deflecting our fears. The British just had to measure every alien's nose with a ruler as we imagined they were doing in Germany. That would separate the Jews from the Nazi spies straight away. Vati and the innocent refugees could then be sent home by the weekend, leaving the short-nosed Nazis locked up in the camps.

Barbara rubbished our idea but couldn't come up with a better one so, because of her, we had to wait months before Vati came home. I didn't like that at all. It wasn't long before I succumbed to episodes of misery like realising I was alone, friendless and nobody loved me. Without a pond there seemed little point in being Charles Darwin any more, so I shaved off my imaginary flowing beard and bushy eyebrows and stopped wanting to ride giant tortoises on the Galapagos Islands. At this time, rude words were starting to pass through my mind and, inevitably, over my lips.

I hated my new school. Every meal was rotten. They made custard with water instead of milk, didn't wash the plates and cutlery properly, and wiped the greasy bits onto last week's tea towels to be boiled up for the next day's soup. There had never been an air raid in Hatch End, but the *Luftwaffe* seemed bent on blowing Kilburn into tiny bits. Half our playground at the school was given over to air raid shelters made of bricks that would have collapsed with a hefty kick from a sparrow. Every time the air raid warning went off, we had to pile into these death traps with a barley sugar and carry on with lessons while the bombs fell and the ack-ack guns cracked the walls with their rotten row.

On my ten-minute walk to school I used to pass through the only bit of greenery in London that I knew of at the time. Queen's Park was a square-shaped excuse for a park with a few benches, one or two retired trees and a public lavatory. It had no pond teeming with animal life, only rain puddles on selected days. But there were some swings and see-saws. Others from the school were sometimes there as well ... and one or two who never went to school at all.

Thus began my life of crime, with my father away in a camp and not around to keep me on the straight and narrow. My mother would have thought at least two of these new friends 'common', but I thought them heroic enough for me to consider juvenile delinquency as a career option. They kindly offered starter tips in the art of truancy. You had to learn to lie convincingly to teachers and/or parents, and study the art of forgery. Our library might be vast but it did not include books which offered useful advice to the apprentice criminal.

At the playground, we held our delinquent conferences on a roundabout which we kept on the move. An hour of perpetual circular 360-degree motion often made me want to puke up breakfast. To keep my mind off my nausea, my friends taught me interesting new words that weren't in the dictionary but had a certain poetry about them, like 'luvaduck', 'cor blimey', 'wotcher, mate' and 'shitabrick'.

My 'tutors' were quite sensitive to my stomach upset, and I showed my appreciation by offering the only word I knew that might prove useful to them: *sitzpinkler*, a pejorative term to describe a boy or man who pees sitting down. There is no translation into English – which made me wonder if no Englishman had ever peed sitting down. Did they win the Empire because they always peed standing up?

Over the next few weeks, I spent several hours at the playground instead of school and got away with it each time, but it wasn't long before I realised that regular classes and watery custard were a lesser evil than boredom, rain and puking. I gave up playing truant. However, the experience did teach me to seek a better direction in life in which I could flourish – like shoplifting.

There were three possible targets in nearby Kilburn High Road: Marks & Spencer, British Home Stores and Woolworths. M&S was useless as it was full of stupid clothes and I had enough socks and underpants already. BHS sold better stuff like pens and glue, but Woolworths was best. They had a very good jewellery department. My favourite items were small-scale replicas of military insignia designed to be worn by wives and sweethearts in honour of their heroic menfolk fighting in the war. There were pairs of wings with the RAF emblem in the middle, Royal Navy and Merchant Navy badges, Household Cavalry, Royal Armoured Corps, Artillery, Royal Engineers and the Parachute Regiment. Each one was made from brightly coloured enamels, beautiful diamonds and genuine gold, like my watch. Each was mounted on a piece of shiny cardboard and cost two shillings and threepence if I remember right, which was a lot more than my pocket money.

I was clever enough to pocket never more than two at a time, and probably no more than a dozen over a couple of months. I was never caught, a further confirmation of my aptitude for theft. Nothing would stop me now. If my mother had had any idea of what was going on in her little angel's life, I would be ready to schmooze my way out of trouble. But she suspected nothing – another tribute to my skill. Needless to say, things would have been very different had my father been home. One look at my shifty eyes would have given the game away and put an immediate stop to my villainy. But he wasn't. I was too young to blame Churchill. I just thought my father had let me down by not being there, so it was his fault I was led astray.

While all this was going on, I couldn't understand why, from time to time, I would feel my familiar syndrome of lip tremble, eye damp, downward pitch at either end of lips and throat lump. Did it signify anger, frustration, the tears of a sissy or something more obvious to anyone but me? Like 'Heeelp!'? I didn't bother to reason it out. Who cares about reason when there's fun to be had?

My brother was stupid enough to believe that my jewel heists had been dumped in the Woolworths dustbins as 'export rejects'. So I gave him a brooch with a tank on it as a sly reminder of his *Panzerkraftwagen* debacle on the Baltic. Hee hee. I never did anything at all with the rest of the baubles except fling them down a kerbside drain, once they had fulfilled their purpose as training exercises to sharpen my faculties.

I now find myself faced with a difficult choice. In revisiting my childhood, it seems I have unwittingly dragged myself into a major dilemma, and must pause for a few moments to consider the next step. Should I simply (a) delete all reference to that part of my darker self as described above, or (b) continue to reveal all, no matter how painful?

I recorded earlier my regret for wrongly challenging the undeserving Miss Taylor. Before I can conclude with the final and worst episode in this sorry chain of events, there is one other misdemeanour to reveal: a vile crime I committed at an even earlier age.

The scene is Vomp, a small village in the Tyrol. We were paying a farewell visit to my mother's parents in the summer of 1938. My first cousin Jörg lived there with his mother, my aunt Maria. It was there that I climbed my first mountain.

STOP! Forgive me. Honesty above all. I did not climb. It was more like ambling. We were on a family outing; an overwhelming experience of giddy heights, thick shoes and thin air, which was even more overwhelming for Tom when he blundered off the path and rolled ten metres down towards a raging torrent. Mother screamed; Tom howled like the oaf he was. He was hauled back up and we continued with him limping behind until we got high enough to encounter the magnificent, and not easy to find, *edelweiss*.

Edelweiss is the shy alpine plant of legend. It is the subject of one of the most touching songs in *The Sound of Music*. It was sacrosanct and anyone who plucked or stole it would be thrown into a crevasse by marauding gangs of mountain peasantry who, for once, had international law on their side.

Back in the valley later that afternoon, my cousin Jörg had something to show me. There was a market gardener's establishment not far from his house. Among the rows of vegetables and fruit were some flower beds that included the precious, but here curiously plentiful, *edelweiss*. I was amazed, shocked, horrified and pleased all at once. Jörg explained they were not the wild kind that was *verboten* to pick, but legal ones cultivated here in the lower altitudes and sold to customers.

After making sure we were not observed, we sneaked away clutching several of the plants we had from Mother Earth 'untimely ripp'd' – as Macduff was from his mother's womb. We showed them to Aunt Maria, having agreed on convincing lies to her inevitable questions. We had found them on the mountain: they had been stolen by a robber who was escaping from a policeman and who panicked and dropped them. They were lying on their sides, dying of thirst, and so we thought it only right to bring them home as a gift for you, Aunt Maria, hoping you could save their lives because you are so good with plants.

Aunt Maria was no fool. She accused us of stealing. How she knew, we couldn't work out. We feared serious punishment. But she was famous for spoiling every child she came across. We relaxed and she then explained how the market gardener, Herr Hoffman, was a good neighbour and friend, and how wrong it was to take something from him without paying. 'But this unhappy affair need never be revealed to anyone,' she went on. 'What is said in this room, stays in this room, you understand. So we will forget all about it this time, but you must promise never, ever again.'

How I loved my auntie Maria then. Kisses all round. She decided to serve our favourite dinner in fifteen minutes: 'Just time enough to pop the *edelweiss* back to Herr Hoffman, pay for it and for you to tell him how sorry you both are. Good. Off you go.' She left the room.

We stayed rooted to the spot with this Hammer Horror hammer blow, but there was nothing for it. If we wanted dinner, we would have to go through with it. The curious thing was we had a sneaking feeling we ought to do it anyway, dinner or no. So we did. It was a galling experience.

Confession is good for the soul, they say, so I will continue my catalogue of crime to tell of the final event when I, quite off the rails, pocketed a ten-shilling note. This was proper stealing – and from my own saintly mother. It was not a good time for her. She had three hungry children packed into poky lodgings; her husband was confined in a camp unable to earn a living. There was never any cash to spare. Yet somehow she managed to scrape together farthings, ha'pennies and pennies.

One afternoon, when I was alone in our top-floor eyrie, I went on a sightseeing tour around family belongings that were none of my business; I opened a drawer and found tucked up small in the far, right-hand corner – I can see it clearly even now – a ten-shilling note. Time stopped while my brain disengaged. This was several days' worth of Mother's household budget, which had magically fallen into my hands. Making sure to smooth down the contents of the drawer so she would never notice, I took the ten shillings. I left the room on tiptoe, even though there was no one at home.

It was some days before Mother discovered her loss. It took less than two minutes for her to grasp the shocking possibility of my involvement.

The moment I rang the front doorbell on my return from school I knew something was seriously wrong. She took a long time coming down to let me in. She was crying and looked dreadful. My heart sank. I couldn't move my feet. She closed the door behind me, then climbed wearily back up the four flights in silence – and without looking back. I followed two steps behind, fighting back my own tears, my eyes fixed on the stair carpet.

She poured me a glass of milk and sat down, folding and unfolding the crumpled handkerchief in her hand. She may have been looking at me but I don't know; I couldn't meet her eyes. She wiped her tears again, and still said nothing. All her strength seemed to have left her.

I sipped my milk, hoping she would break the silence. Was she waiting for me to own up without being asked? But that would be impossible. Why didn't she just accuse me straight away and get it over with… Please?

At last, she sighed and, with her head still bowed, asked me if I would like to know why she was so sad. I managed to produce a little mumble and nodded. She must have understood it was as much as she could hope for from me at that moment, and quietly began to tell me what I already knew: that her ten shillings were missing. She blamed herself for leaving the money where it could be found so easily by any of a dozen people living in the house. Then she started to cry again. There was no hint of any suspicion directed at me.

Alone without Vati, she went on, only her children could give her the strength to carry on. She was being even kinder than Miss Taylor, and I loved her even more, but continued to sit stupidly looking at my milk until, at last, she provided me with a little opportunity.

'Can you think of anyone who might have taken it?' she said.

I mumbled again and shrugged.

She sighed, shaking her head slowly. 'No. I suppose it would take a little courage to admit it if they had.'

I supposed so, I nodded.

'I mean, if someone like *you* had taken it, I know you would have the courage to tell me.'

How could I possibly respond to that? I struggled and struggled and only managed another nod.

'But of course, if you had not taken it, that wouldn't need any courage at all to tell me.'

I managed a whispered 'No'.

'Well,' she said, 'I wonder which it is, then.'

She leant forward and gave me an encouraging little kiss, then sat back again and concentrated on her handkerchief. By this time

I was in total confusion. The longest pause in my life followed before I finally managed an almost voiceless: 'It was me...'

But she hadn't heard. And I had to say it again, only louder to cut through my uncontrollable sobbing. She put her arms around me and patted my back.

'Very good,' she said, before joining in the sobbing.

Then a miracle happened. After a few more moments, she got up and made a pot of tea. It was confirmation to me that everything in England turns out well in the end. And it did – after reparations had been arranged.

I can't now remember what actually happened to the money itself, but I must have spent it. I had nothing to give back except a promise to return every penny from any pocket money due.

She shook her head. 'I can't afford to give you any pocket money at the moment. I'm sorry,' she said gently.

I felt even worse now. But not for long. Together we devised a plan. She suggested I could work off the debt by doing little jobs for her like running errands, drying dishes and laying the table. Each chore would reduce my debt by a penny. She would also teach me to darn socks at the rate of another penny per hole. Polishing my own shoes would be equivalent to two pennies, one for each shoe. I begged to be allowed to polish Bossy Barbara's shoes as well, and even Tom's smelly ones, to make a grand total of sixpence per session. So two sessions alone would be worth twelve pence or one whole shilling! That left only a hundred and eight chores to reach my final target. I worked with fanatical energy. And it brought its reward. When I reached my hundredth chore a fortnight later, Mother was so proud she let me off the other twenty.

I should have felt proud too, but niggling at my conscience was that empty right-hand corner of the drawer. I made a secret vow that I would spend not a penny on myself from any future pocket money until I could arrange for another ten-shilling note to be found in its original hiding place.

Fortunately for me, both my parents had always enjoyed a smoke, and as long ago as our Berlin days I had been collecting the cards that came with the packets. There was a set of motor cars of the world, featuring exotic masterpieces from Rolls-Royce, Mercedes-Benz, Fiat, Duesenberg, DKW, Bugatti, Hotchkiss, Armstrong Siddeley, Railton, Packard and many others. There was another set illustrating the Berlin Olympic Games of 1936, and one of famous film stars from Germany and Hollywood, which included Emil Jannings, a distant relative of ours and therefore extra precious. I was prepared to sacrifice the lot with no qualms – except perhaps for the photograph of our Uncle Emil. Emil had true claims to fame. He was the first actor to win an Oscar and he had starred with Marlene Dietrich in *Der blaue Engel*. I had no doubt they would bring in a fortune, well above my target sum.

But wartime markets are notoriously fickle. The information on the back of the cards was in German and therefore much less attractive to my schoolmates than I had hoped. No amount of persuasion, bargaining, wheeler-dealing, cajoling, even bribing with unrationed cough drops, could raise enough money for my needs. Nevertheless, it was a beginning. I gritted my teeth and let the treasures go at rock-bottom prices. There was little else to sell except a first dozen cards from a series on freshwater pond life which no one was interested in except me, and a few miscellaneous other cards with only small potential value.

However, help was at hand from an unexpected source. Cricket. I had never managed to understand its rules, but I had twenty or so cards that featured great cricketers down the ages. One of the ironies of sporting history is that the son of George II, Frederick, an immigrant like me, became a devoted cricket fan and even a reasonable player. He tried to introduce the game into Germany but failed, which is just as well as the thought of Germany beating England at cricket is awful (and how Mr Fawlty would have reacted is ghastly to contemplate).

The set of cricket cards, incomplete though it was, caused enough of a stir for an impromptu auction to take place. The bidding ended at three shillings and sixpence – one shilling and ninepence more than the amount I was aiming for! A happy miracle. But the new owner of the cards was one of the Queen's Park truant gang on the roundabouts.

And even reparation has its problems. I worried about whether to accept his no doubt ill-gotten gains. Fortunately, my conscience reassured me that it was his business where the money came from, not mine. So that was all right.

Next day, I managed to lure my mother with the utmost cunning into opening the drawer, and could hardly contain myself as she uncovered a crisp new banknote. She didn't exactly cry with relief nor did she want to accept the money. But I was firm with her, oh yes, very firm, until she did. It was a major moment in my life when I felt honestly good about myself.

From the fateful day I had rung our doorbell to the moment I was able to return the money was two months. But I must have grown ten years.

CHAPTER 4

Oppidans Road

Once, sometimes twice, a week, we would receive an envelope, the size of a postcard, with a printed form inside, completed in our father's neat hand. My memory is not perfect, but the following example can't be far off the truth.

Date

Dear

The weather is:

I am well/not well. Specify:

I would like to receive: tea/toiletries/clothing/food/writing material/books/other. Specify:

Personal message:

Signed: Vati

Warning: All replies are subject to censorship and/or confiscation.

The forms gave us no clue as to where Vati's internment camp was located. I think it was in Wales, but I have never been entirely sure. In writing this, I have looked at what conditions in those camps were like. The Isle of Man camp is the best-known, and inspired a Jewish joke. One of the local Manx specialities was kippers, so every day was Yom Kippur, the Jewish Day of Atonement. More seriously, many internees were frustrated and depressed, as being interned without trial was far too similar to what the Jews were suffering in Germany. There was little sign of Miss Taylor's tolerance here.

One story struck me in particular. The artist Kurt Schwitters became so depressed that he suffered a relapse into the epilepsy he had had in childhood. He also tended to sleep under his bed and periodically barked like a dog. As there was no plaster of Paris available, Schwitters was driven to sculpt with cereal. He made three Dadaist sculptures, which made his room stink because the porridge developed mildew and became cosy for bacteria; the statues were covered with greenish hair and bluish bacteria excrement. Some art historians even claim the camp saw one of the earliest examples of performance art as, while he was interned, Schwitters performed *Ursonate*, a pre-linguistic sound poem.

After three months, Mr Churchill kindly took the collar off and Father could return home. When he did, the way we lived had to change. Unless we were to sleep standing up, there was no way our top-floor hovel could house the five of us, so we had to find roomier lodgings – though our family budget could barely cope with survival, let alone a higher rent.

Mother took up the daunting challenge with her customary vigour. Strapping on her sturdy seven-league boots, she went walkabout, talkabout, writeabout, phoneabout and wheedleabout for days on end through the terror incognita of bomb-blasted London.

She found nothing remotely affordable. Terror incognita was very expensive but her resourcefulness was magnificent. She was trudging home one day, distraught, deep in gloomy thoughts and the algebra of rationing. Were there enough points in her ration book for a teatime treat? Yes. Did she have money in her purse for buns? Yes. At least her children would enjoy picking out the currants and arguing if the total could not be divided by three. She walked into the nearest shop and looked around, blankly.

A gaunt English gentleman in a pinstriped suit came forward. 'Good afternoon, madam,' he said. 'How may I be of assistance?'

'I want some b … some buns…' She stopped. 'This is not a cake shop, is it?'

'Might I suggest a little sit-down, madam, if you care to … with a glass of water?'

'*Danke, nein.* I am sorry…'

'Or would you perhaps prefer a drop of herbal tea? Only a pale imitation of the real thing, I'm afraid, but it has the blessing of being unrationed.'

She shook her head a second time. 'I am making mistake.'

He smiled consolingly. 'Very easily done, madam. A little turn, as we call it in this country, is not at all unusual nowadays. One of the inevitable problems of war.'

Business was snail slow and he was obviously glad to have someone to talk to. He sat down at his desk and indicated the chair facing him. 'Do sit down. But I must admit buns are not really my strong point.'

She sat down at last. *'Vielen dank.* I thank you. You are very kind.'

'Oh, please!' he said modestly. 'I think we could both do with a little pick-me-up, don't you? I shall put the kettle on.'

He moved to a corner of the office. 'Let me introduce myself. I am Rupert Fellowes of Fellowes & Danby Limited. We are estate agents, madam. That's what we do. Or at least try to do,' he added with a brave giggle. 'We buy and sell houses and apartments.'

She smiled back. 'I am sorry. I have make mistake.'

But had she? Later she told us her confusion perhaps expressed a need to share her distressing problems with someone, anyone, who might be in a comparable situation. Many estate agents were struggling to survive in the autumn of 1940. The Battle of Britain was raging; the *Luftwaffe* was dropping bombs day and night. House owners were desperate to sell up and move to safer locations; but who would want to buy property, even at a bargain price, when it might be reduced to rubble overnight? Fellowes & Danby had not seen a single would-be customer for a fortnight. The depressed estate agent and the depressed refugee had all the time in the world to commiserate with each other.

Finally, Mr Fellowes took down Mother's name and address, 'Just in case we come across anything for you, madam. I'm frightfully pleased to know you. Please do call again, won't you?'

On her journey home her mind was buzzing. In the course of their shared lamenting, Mr Fellowes had spoken of a house that was proving exceptionally difficult to shift. It was just off Primrose Hill, a historic and fashionable park as he described it, famous for its panoramic views of London.

In peacetime.

The war had changed Primrose Hill. Its gentle eastern slope, ideal for children to sledge down in winter and roll down in summer, had become a scarred acreage of vegetable allotments. The government urged people to 'Dig for Victory', i.e. plant potatoes, carrots and suchlike. Allotments, however, were not gardens beautiful and were hardly attractive selling points for potential buyers. The top of the hill itself was barred to the public altogether. Half a dozen huge anti-aircraft guns sat there ready, day and night, to attack enemy bombers and local eardrums. Their vibrations shook nearby buildings. Chimneys jittered and juddered and sometimes fell down, and frightened moggies could be decapitated by a dive-bombing slate.

The owner of the house the estate agent had despaired of had moved to America shortly before the war. He had decided to sell it soon after but wartime travel restrictions meant he could not return home to do so.

A tiny bell had tinkled in Mother's mind on hearing the owner's name. She had been a librarian, after all. She began to form not a cunning plan but a possibility, a dream. A few days later, without telling anyone, she went to the property itself. Looking through windows and the letterbox, she expected to see nothing but floorboards, bare walls and empty space, but instead the house was furnished! It looked as if someone lived there. She rang the doorbell several times, but there was no response.

She made her way to Messrs Fellowes & Danby again. Lance Corporal Trevelyan de Vere Danby of the Home Guard was also present this time. As pinstriped and urbane as his partner but unpatriotically rotund rather than gaunt, he was introduced to *Frau* Saish. There followed the English weather ceremony, the 'how are you' ceremony, where it would have been very bad manners to actually describe how you are, followed by the English tea ceremony. The ceremony did not impress all foreigners who had taken refuge in Britain. In the classic *How to Be an Alien*, for example, George Mikes accused the English of ruining tea by insisting on serving it with milk, a barbarity unheard of in his native Hungary.

Some way into the English tea ceremony, the estate agents confirmed the property was indeed unoccupied. Mother admitted she was worried the building looked abandoned, with little more security than a Yale lock on the front door.

'Oh, by no means abandoned, Mrs Sashs,' they both protested, almost in unison. 'The property is inspected at regular intervals by our local man. He keeps us informed of any problems and Mr Malinowski's representative in this country is also available.'

Mother's lips began to tremble. She was a humble foreigner who was about to make an outrageous suggestion which was, in fact, a magnificent example of chutzpah. She now found the courage to point out their client's true title and that he was, in fact, a professor. 'Forgive me, sirs, many apologies,' she continued in her charming English. 'I can only speak as a woman and I feel so muchly for the professor and his work, desperate, desperate...'

She produced a handkerchief and paused to calm herself. The two gentlemen, curious at her reaction, apologised and withdrew a few paces from this unsettling display of Continental emotion. To calm their stiff upper lips and to lift the lady's spirits, they decided to sacrifice some of their precious Darjeeling – at present locked in a steel cabinet. They could not but admire her touching concern on behalf of an apparent stranger. It should be realised how progressive these men were for 1939 as they appear to have been able to put a kettle on, produce milk and make a pot of tea by themselves without female help.

Mother apologised again. Perhaps, she explained, her hosts were not aware their client was actually the famous Professor Malinowski?

No, indeed. They were not.

This gave her the confidence to continue with a carefully researched – and rehearsed – CV of Bronisław Malinowski, the great anthropologist, world renowned for his investigations into primitive life in remote areas of the South Seas; the author of *Coral Gardens and their Magic* (two volumes), *Sex and Repression in Savage Society* and many other important books. She spoke of his influential work in mathematics, physics and psychology, and of how famous he was as the originator of modern methods of ethnographic fieldwork. Her attentive admirers were impressed. The tea ceremony continued in total harmony.

She felt bold enough to enquire politely whether, in the light of this new information, they still considered the house safe and secure, especially as the professor's unique archive material was just protected by that one Yale lock on the front door.

Given the news that Malinowski was nearly as famous as Freud, of whom the estate agents *had* heard, they had no alternative but to say they were eager to do what they could to protect his property – depending, of course, on the cost.

Various options were discussed. The transfer of all important items to a secure bank vault had to be rejected for financial reasons. A more modest scheme of additional locks, chains and bars on all doors and entrances also did not seem that practical. Any anthropological burglar who wanted to get their hands on Malinowski's archive only had to fling a brick through a window to get in; the loss to science would be incalculable. They could hire a 24-hour professional watchman but that was judged to be the most expensive of all, and also dismissed.

The triumvirate pondered in silence for a few moments, until Mother coughed demurely and spoke. 'I have a solution, perhaps?'

'Please…' they offered graciously.

'You know I have not found yet anywhere for my family to be living,' she began. 'Perhaps, perhaps, if that is possible, we can be allowed to take care of the house with great care, and we need not many rooms. And we have trust and honesty in our family. And my children are angels. Really. And my husband is cultured and can mend windows and put out incendiary bombs and when the house is sold, we are pleased to find somewhere else.' Her voice tailed off.

The partners paused, nodded, grunted in a genteel manner, and began to consider the benefits. Certain arrangements would have to be agreed, of course. Professor (as they now knew him to be) Malinowski would have to agree. Duties and responsibilities would have to be decided, and first-class references received.

'Your scheme seems well worth investigating, Mrs Satch,' said the partners to her with a smile. And cheap, thought the partners to themselves with a similar smile.

Mother made her way back to Kilburn with a spring in her step. She was desperate to share her hopes with us, but kept her audacious plan to herself for a fortnight in case it went wrong. Then the estate agents told her it could work.

To mark the occasion, she bought a precious Mars bar from her own sweet ration and dissected it with a razor blade into eight equal slices, with the two end pieces cut into three narrow strips each. We had no idea why. Two slices and two strips were then artistically distributed on to three saucers and presented to her three angels as if they were the finest *knödel* in Tyrol. We still had no idea why we were being offered chocolate nirvana.

Then, with a genteel lick of a finger, Mother vacuumed the leftover crumbs onto her own tongue as a reward to herself for Outstanding Chutzpah in Property Dealing. Only after everyone had licked the last chocolatey veneer from the plate did she break her silence.

It was to be good riddance to the Black Hole of Kilburn and to the Wicked Witch of the West landlady who ran it, and 'Hello!' to a famous professor's exclusive residence in Oppidans Road, which offered six bedrooms, four receptions on several floors, all the mod cons, was lovingly maintained, boasted many original features, and was close to Primrose Hill. We were, as the English, would say 'lucky ducks', a phrase not echoed in other languages.

(The French don't speak of *le canard fortune*, the Germans speak of *viel Glück*, and if you're a Peking duck, you're wrapped in a kind of pancake and served with lettuce, which isn't lucky at all.)

'What?!' we cried, eyes popping, jaws dropping and the three of us all jabbering together. 'We're going to buy a big house? With my own bedroom please – please – at last. I want a garden, will I have to sleep in the basement, can we get all our stuff out of store today? I want a guinea pig…' and so on.

Mother's reply was shorter. 'Don't be ridiculous!' she said. She was right, of course.

Barbara inevitably had an objection. 'But Mother! We can't become caretakers! That's for working-class people.'

Tom mumbled something about three moves in a row and griped we might as well have stayed in Berlin.

And I said, 'What is he famous for?' referring to Malinowski.

Mutti must have sometimes wondered why she wanted children rather than dogs, but she answered patiently, 'He is an anthropologist.' She knew I wouldn't know what it meant. But I was willing to guess.

Could it be to do with monkeys? I asked myself. But no, that was *anthropoid*, something I did know all about. Before I could leave the room to look it up, she caught my sleeve and reminded me that most of our books were locked in a shed in Wembley, but would be with us again once we moved to Oppidans Road. 'He is also a writer of books and an explorer, and a psychologist as well!' she added, knowing I knew what those words meant, apart from 'psychologist'.

My memory of exactly how and when we made the move

to Primrose Hill is vague. But Dad was back and we were a whole family again, which was good. I was gradually calling him 'Dad'. I had decided 'Daddy' was too babyish; 'Father' was nice and respectful, but sounded too posh – I had already absorbed some sense of the English class system and knew that was too formal. Vati sounded a bit rude when you consider a German 'v' is pronounced like an English 'f', and the 'a' is like 'aah'. As for Mutti, that survived a bit longer, especially in private, but gradually turned to 'Mum', with an occasional 'Mummy' when I felt pathetic.

People these days tell you that moving house is very stressful. It did not feel like that. It felt like freedom. But not perfect freedom, as I had to move from one rotten school to yet another rotten school which also served watery custard cold as a puddle.

But 6 Oppidans Road turned out to be a real treat. At first sight it was gloomy, like most of the surrounding houses, with windows blown out by the earth-quaking racket from ack-ack guns a hundred times more ear-splitting than a diva shattering her wine glass. The empty windows had been replaced by do-it-yourself sheets of old plywood or planks and cardboard that often let in the rain. But it was also mysterious, in that certain rooms were out of bounds to us children. We were given strict orders not to trespass into the private areas, and certainly never to root among the treasures of a famous man kind enough to allow us in his home. That made rooting around more tempting, of course, but we obeyed without question like the good little children we were.

Unlike 6 Oppidans Road, Haverstock Hill School could never

be described as a des res. It stood, massive and unsmiling, bang opposite Chalk Farm tube station. For five days a week, between hours that seemed longer than a whole day, we were separated from life by an endless wall as hard to scale as the one in China.

One morning, as we whining schoolboys crept like snails unwillingly to school, we found a small part of this wall had collapsed by the pavement. A bomb further up the hill the previous night was to blame. There were cheers all round from us, of course, combined with the hope of a direct hit next time. The damaged wall hung precariously over the pavement for weeks. Despite a frail wooden barrier and a 'Keep clear' sign, it soon became a dumping ground for rubbish: soggy newspapers, a gas mask split in two, odd shoes, a scooter with one wheel and a pram with none, and so on – all useless except for the empty beer bottles good for a penny a time on return.

Despite hating the new school, I made a friend of sorts from another class. His real name was Cyril but he liked to be called 'Coop' after a famous film star. I didn't like him much until one day I managed to make him laugh a bit, which naturally revised my opinion of him. He was one of the few boys still collected sometimes from school by one parent or another. That made him a sissy to the rest of us, including me.

'Your mum sounds nice,' I said to him one day, to cheer him up.

'Huh! Better'n me dad,' he said.

'Don't you like your dad?'

'Nah,' he said, with a sneer.

Thus began the first of three quick-fire shocks to my system. Since both my parents were perfect, the possibility that one of

LEFT My maternal grandfather, Hans. He gave my mother her love of writing and I'd like to think a little rubbed off on me.

MIDDLE AND LEFT My wonderful mother, Katarina. To us she was a heroine and she certainly guided me through my early life with love and care.

My father, Hans Sachs, born in 1885. He was awarded the Iron Cross in the First World War but it was not enough to save a Jew from persecution by the Nazis.

My school in Berlin, where Ralph and I (front row, I'm first from left, Ralph next to me) were assigned our patriotic metal-collecting duties. We were encouraged all the way by our teacher Herr Plischert (seated second row from the back).

Märchen der Brüder Grimm

Mit 100 Bildern nach Aquarellen von
Ruth Kofer-Michaëls

ABOVE LEFT My wise and beloved Vati shortly before he left Germany for England.

ABOVE RIGHT My first week at school, aged six.

LEFT *Märchen der Brüder Grimm*: one of the many books on Vati's bookcase. The book was beautifully illustrated by my aunt.

Army days. I was in the tank regiment but managed to spend two years of National Service never getting in a tank!

Me and Melody – the quick-change artists – on our wedding day, 1962. We just got there in time.

LEFT With Stephen Moore as the Ugly Sisters in *Cinderella*, 1966.

BELOW On holiday in Brixham with Billy, John and Kate, 1969.

Handling a snake in South Africa. Despite the smile, not one of my most relaxed moments.

Albert Einstein in an Anglo-American TV documentary from 1972. Thanks to a brilliant British make-up artist, I look more like Einstein than myself.

No Sex Please, We're British, 1971. Catching this huge stack of books on stage was not fun (at least for me) following the *Fawlty Towers* fire!

LEFT Family portrait: Connie Booth, John Cleese, Prunella Scales and me in our *Fawlty Towers* get-up.

BELOW Torquay tender. This banknote may be faulty!

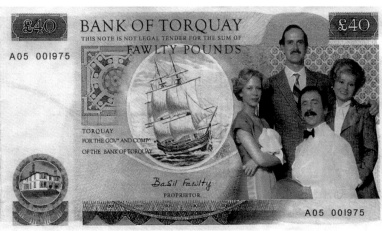

£40 **BANK OF TORQUAY** £40
THIS NOTE IS NOT LEGAL TENDER FOR THE SUM OF
A05 001975 FAWLTY POUNDS

TORQUAY
FOR THE GOV" AND COMP"
OF THE BANK OF TORQUAY

Basil Fawlty
PROPRIETOR

A05 001975

Manuel asks his favourite question, '*¿Que?*'

them could be less so than the other had never occurred to me. I couldn't think what to say to him. He saved me the trouble.

'He's dead, anyway.'

Shock number two. I had always assumed parents to be immortal and that only very old people, and sometimes children like my friend Buschi, could die.

'Oh!' was all I could manage.

'Yeah,' he sniffed. 'Murdered.'

Another jaw-dropping shock. 'Oh' was on the tip of my tongue again, but I didn't want to repeat myself.

'Good fuckin' riddance, that's what me mum says.'

What? I could not believe my ears. I knew that expletives of that kind were sometimes heard in Chalk Farm and Kilburn, but that a *lady* could even be aware of the word's existence, let alone allow it to pass across her lips, was a startling shock.

It has to be remembered that it took years after the grey days of war before technicolor obscenities began to trip off the tongue like nursery rhymes, as they do today. My enthusiasm for the English language, thanks to Miss Taylor, was way above a mere need to learn the basics. Under her guidance, dictionaries had become trusted companions and played a major part in my progress. Yet not one of those I ever had access to even hinted at the existence of this F-word. Even if I had not moved school, I would not have been able to consult Miss Taylor to help me out. Any research into forbidden words would have to be empirical. *Empirical* was another recent acquisition, like *anthropologist*.

I felt the time was right for me to create a secret code in mirror writing and start a personal archive entitled 'Rude Words'. It was filling up nicely with entertaining little gems like piss, shit, arsehole and tart, and was also open to further examples from fellow enthusiasts in my class. The empirical verification process that followed regularly offered many a furtive giggle in remote corners of the playground.

I did realise, though, that the F-word (even now I can hardly bring myself to spell it in full) was in a special category, tucked into an even more secure niche at the back of the back of my head pending further investigation.

Teenagers have always tussled with the question of how you find out just what rude words mean. I couldn't ask, so I had to seek. I set off courageously to eavesdrop on a gang of swaggering toughs in the neighbourhood, and only just avoided grievous bodily harm by running faster than they did when they realised I was listening to them. I ran like the clappers. They lost my trail when I ducked into a local dustbin.

The following may sound incredible but I have promised not to tell lies while giving myself some licence in the matter of recorded dialogue.

The scene is not a wooden O as at the start of Shakespeare's *Henry V*, but the dustbin where I inserted myself to catch my breath and escape the angry toughs. The said dustbin also afforded rest and recreation. (And, since I hadn't yet decided to become an actor, I was unaware that at the same time Samuel Beckett was dreaming up *Endgame*, featuring two characters who live in dustbins.)

My dustbin also turned out to be erudite as it contained a dog-eared copy of *Teach Yourself Good English*. I was quickly engrossed in a section that defined a certain group of words as being uniquely versatile, and gross. I was convinced my four-letter one would certainly qualify had it been familiar to the authors.

According to *Teach Yourself Good English*, all words in this particular group could function equally well as adverbs, or nouns, or verbs transitive and intransitive, and verbs future, past, present, active passive, subjunctive, imperative and f— knows what else. In other words, my word was a wonderful, multi-functioning bundle of almost unlimited meanings, or possibly none; indispensable for some, forbidden to others, and unknown to lexicographers, philologists and linguists throughout this f... oolish world. What a mystery.

It was about this time that examples of a different kind – perhaps inspired by the F-word, who knows – joined my list of taboo words, which had up to now been largely lavatorial. The new additions were words actually paraded openly in dictionaries and reference books galore! And they were all apparently fit for use in polite society.

Fit, that is, until obnoxious little cherubs like us got hold of them as a foretaste to the approaching murky mire of adolescence. Then we, and our words, and most other things, became gloriously filthy, exciting, mysterious, embarrassing and grown-up – and, I'm sorry to say, even more infantile than before. We almost wet ourselves with definitions of prostitute, breast, intercourse, brothel, vagina, French letters and VD. Even 'duck' found a place because it rhymed with the F-word. Our list was endless, thrillingly educational and far more inspiring than long division and custard.

Coop was not a member of our cult. As far as I could make out, his interest in language was confined to usage rather than meaning. I hoped I would never have to meet his foul-mouthed mother. On the other hand, I couldn't help but feel some concern for the poor woman – and her murdered husband.

Once I got my breath back after Coop's shocking revelations, all I could manage to come up with was, 'That's very sad, isn't it?'

He sneered again. 'Nah, 'e 'addicomindinnee?'

His usage this time was beyond me. I pretended to understand. 'Did you ... I mean, have you ... did they find out who did it?'

'Me mum.'

'Your mum found out?'

'Nah. Memumdunni'dinnshe?'

Was this still English? The time for 'I'm sorry I do not understand you I am a little German...' etc., was long gone, so I resorted to a few 'Pardons?' in a horrified whisper.

'Your mum killed your father?'

'Beat me to it, mate.'

It was coming thick, fast and macabre now. But no, it couldn't be, shouldn't be, *wasn't* true, was it?

'And the police, they haven't found out?'

He wagged a finger at me. 'Don't you never let on, mate. Gorrit?'

I was certainly beginning to gorrit; the gist of it anyway.

He went on, finger wagging more dramatically now. 'You're my best mate. Right, mate?'

I nodded firmly. It was not a time to argue.

'So if you wanna stay my fuckin' mate, you don' say fuck all to no fucker. Gorrit?'

This was amazing! Adjective, adverb and noun all in one sentence.

'Gorrit!' I said, and nodded immediately. He was bigger than me. 'Oh, yes, Coop. I gorrit. Oh, my goodness fucking hell, I have,' I said, with only the slightest German accent.

That day I dragged myself home, carrying a secret I could share with no one, and hoping against hope my mother wouldn't ask me the usual questions like, 'Have you made any nice friends today?'

Before she had a chance to ask, I decided to have a bad stomach ache. It triggered her immediate concern, followed by all the comfort I could hope for, but a dose of castor oil as well.

Sleep did not come easily that night. I was in turmoil. I decided to keep my distance from Coop. He was nearly always on his own anyway so I didn't think he would mind very much. Or even notice.

I managed to avoid him over the next days, except for impersonal nods now and then. And it was true, he didn't seem to notice. But one afternoon I happened to be going through the main gate on a day he was being collected – this time by a big, beefy man as well as his criminal mother.

Coop called to me. 'Come 'ere!'

I had no choice. I walked towards them, calm on the outside, and was introduced to his mother.

'Me mate,' Coop mumbled, nodding in my direction.

'Oh!' said his criminal mother with raised eyebrows and a smile. 'Luvly! Pleased to meet ya, sweetheart. I've 'eard all abaht ya.'

I managed a half-smile.

She turned to the big man. 'It's Cyril's best friend.'

'Oh yeah?' he said brightly, looking me over. 'The little Jew boy, eh?' He grabbed my hand and shook it hard. 'Pleased to meet ya!'

I winced.

'Sorry, mate. Don't know me own strength. Don't worry, you're safe wiv me, even if you are a Kraut, eh? 'Ere, Cyril, why doncha bring 'im back for tea?'

'Yeah, lovely!' Coop said. 'Is that all right, Mumsie?'

'Yeah, luvly, darling,' she said, and turned to me proudly. 'We got a canary.'

I wondered if it would be served on toast, given the family's violent tendencies.

I had a brainwave and excused myself on account of an urgent date with a dentist.

Coop's mother understood. 'I get ya. Anuvver time then, eh?'

Never! I thought. 'Yes, please,' I said eagerly.

'Like termorrer?'

'Er…'

'Or whenever, eh? Luvly.'

'Ta-ra, Jew boy!' the man said, and they left.

Twenty-four hours later, Coop collared me.

'Me mum thinks you're great.'

He didn't move. I wondered what to do next. 'I … who was that man yesterday?'

'Eh? Me dad, wannit.'

Was I hearing right? 'Your dad?'

'Yeah.'

Something was not quite as it should be. I had expected perhaps 'uncle' or 'neighbour', but certainly not 'father'. It took a moment to sink in.

'But he's dead,' I said.

'Yeah.'

'So he's not dead?'

'Nah, worse luck.' Coop shrugged. 'He got better.'

'You said he was dead!'

He snarled menacingly. 'Any day now.'

I started backing away.

'Where ya goin'?'

'D-dentist.'

'Right,' he said. 'See ya termorrer.'

I held out for over a week until he greeted me with what one might almost class as a charming smile.

I tried to smile back and show at least one friendly tooth.

'You got a sister, ain't ya?' he said.

At once, I was on my guard and needed time to think before opening my mouth.

'I got summink for 'er.' He nodded mysteriously, tapping his nose with a finger. 'See ya after.'

He moved off, enjoying his moment. My heart sank an inch or two. Was he going to share some other family drama even worse than murder?

Every hour of that day was eighty minutes long before the final bell sounded. Coop and I approached each other as arranged. This time his expression was even more brightly mysterious, and I was even more wary.

'Your sister. Wassername?'

So far I could cope. 'Barbara.'

'She's a girl, right?'

'Ye-es.'

'So she could do wiv a doll, coonshe?'

'A doll?' I managed.

'I fahnd a big one for 'er. She'll go effin' mad abahdit.'

My sister was fifteen by now. I felt an 'oh' would be enough for the moment.

'Come on then. Foller me.'

We walked a few paces along the pavement to the collapsed section of the bombed wall, and hopped over.

'Have a gander in there, mate.'

I put my face close to where he was pointing. Darkly, in a recess among the debris and trash, lay a scruffy doll with tangled hair, dirty legs, one shoe and a worn-out summer dress.

'Effin' scrub up lovely that will.' He was animated in a way I had not seen before. 'You don't get many o' them for a fiver, tell your effin' sister.'

I nodded in imitation of gratitude and started withdrawing my head to gain time for a suitable reply.

'But you're me bes' mate, so I'll give it ya fer nuffin',' he said grandly.

'It looks nice and real,' I managed.

''Course it is. Pull i' aht, pal. It's yours.'

He was hovering behind me. What could I do? I reached in and took hold of the doll's arm, but had to let go again. I was expecting china or Bakelite like the dolls Barbara used to play with when she was little. This one was not like them at all. It was more like, more like…

Through the deep shadows of the bombed wall I could see now what it was more like. I withdrew my hand calmly, methodically, without panic, and stood up swaying and as pale as the baby itself.

'I think it's dead,' I said.

'Do wha'?'

'It's a dead baby. A real one.'

Coop looked into the darkness. 'Effin' 'ell. You sure?'

There were the remains of an umbrella lying nearby. I picked it up and gently prodded a forearm. The skin dented unlike any cuddly toy. It definitely was – had been – a baby. I now noticed one cheek was bruised and one eye had remained half open.

Coop and I stared at each other. He pulled himself together before I could. 'Come on – scarper!'

He jumped over the wall and ran five paces before hissing back at me. 'Get ahta there, mate. They'll string us up for bloody murder!'

He started running again, and stopped again. With one possible killer in the family already, I could understand he wouldn't want to meet the police.

'No. I can't!' I called, hoping the baby might somehow still be alive. 'We've got to get help.'

'You talk abaht this and I'll have yer guts for garters!' and he panicked off into the distance, trying to look casual.

My first instinct was to get help from the school, but that would leave the baby on its own. No, I would have to stay where I was, just in case.

There were not many people on the street. But eventually, cold and trembling now despite the warm afternoon sun, I was able to get someone's attention. A short, stocky man ambled over and peered into the recess for a few moments, and then took charge.

'You stay where you are, lad. What's your name?'

I told him.

'At the school here?'

I nodded.

'Right, I'll phone the police. Don't you move. They may want to talk to you.'

My heart sank. 'I want to go home.'

'You will, son. Don't worry.' He patted my shoulder.

Twenty minutes later a police car arrived from further up the hill. They took the body away in a hessian sack. They didn't need me.

Walking home I relived the tragedy again and again, while at the same time rehearsing it into an attention-grabbing entertainment for my schoolmates the next day. Soon, however, shock took over; shock not so much from the terrible event itself as from shame at my readiness to transform a real-life tragedy into something that would entertain my classmates the next day.

I never wanted to do that again.

CHAPTER 5

Of Mice and Zoos

I turned the corner into Oppidans Road that afternoon and saw a pigeon that had been hit by a car. The bird was leaving a little trail of blood behind as it fluttered its life away. Not knowing what to do, I brought it to the kerbside and sat watching it die. I then laid it under a shrub in the nearest front garden.

I started crying, and couldn't stop all the way home.

Barbara opened the front door and sighed. 'Oh dear, what have you done this time? Mother!' she called. It was one of those rare occasions when we were all at home. Dad persuaded me to get whatever was on my mind, off my mind. It was difficult but a dead pigeon would be easier to talk about than a dead baby, so I took a deep breath and reported the little drama simply, without making myself its main character.

Tom offered to collect the pigeon and dig a proper grave for it in our garden, but, in the end, we agreed to let it rest in peace where it was. For a few moments, no one said anything more until Vati broke the silence.

'And that is what made you cry so very much?'

I nodded.

'Hm. Just the pigeon?'

I nodded again.

'I wonder, there is nothing more to tell us?'

Well, of course there was, but again I really didn't want to, when suddenly the local artillery roared into action and saved my bacon. The house shook. The doors rattled. Teacups panicked on their saucers and a butter knife flung itself under the table for cover.

When relative peace returned at last, Vati continued: 'You were trying to say something.'

For the second time, my words somehow came out without me thinking of playing up the tragedy to impress my audience. My only problem was Coop. How could I describe him, his behaviour, and, above all, his language, to my parents? I couldn't, so I demoted him from his starring role as arch-hooligan to a walk-on (but definitely not talk-on) appearance as a 'school friend'.

No one spoke when I finished, and I started crying again. I was relapsing into childish, pathetic mode. I even addressed my parents as Mutti and Vati instead of Mum and Dad.

But I had recovered by the next morning, which saw me bouncing up and down on the mattress making King Kong noises and beating my chest with both fists. I was all Man again. Back at school, I never mentioned the dead baby to anyone.

I avoided Coop over the next few days, but he caught up with me in the end.

'Here, Saxie, you comin' back for tea, then?' He grinned, as though nothing had happened.

I searched for an excuse as he went on. 'We got a canary, you know. Lovely little fucker.'

All I could think of was, 'I have to go to the dentist again.'

His mood changed. 'Piss off! 'Course you ain't,' he said. 'You're a fuckin' liar, ain't ya?' and added mournfully, 'Same as every other fucker.'

'No, I really have.'

'What's the matter with people arahnd 'ere? Fuckin' fuckers,' and he shambled off without waiting for an answer.

After that we hardly spoke to each other again. I tried once or twice but we never really made it up.

Haverstock Hill Primary, my third school in England, was even less stimulating than the Kilburn one. Fortunately, I discovered that Oppidans Road and the surrounding area could offer me all the education and inspiration I needed.

Tom and I still shared a room but at least we had beds of our own with enough space in between for battles. He was also getting to be quite human at times, in my opinion, and I found myself to be reasonably tolerant of his inferiority. As for Barbara, Tom and I both agreed she had become unacceptably adolescent and should leave home after assigning her bedroom to one of us.

Our parents continued to be above criticism, even when they insisted on treating us like children, or were mean, unfair, selfish, cruel or just unavailable. They were, in other words, almost perfect. I did have one or two reservations about them, however. I was their third child instead of their only child; they sometimes lapsed into speaking German in public; and they walked too fast, could make me cry, and didn't always laugh at my jokes.

All those petty quibbles were forgotten the day I was given permission to have a mouse. (Those who seek to find continuing themes in a life will conclude it was inevitable that I should find myself devoted to a hamster and sharing major scenes with a rodent in *Fawlty Towers* some thirty years later.)

In 1943, my rodent starter pack included a roomy cage with an exercise treadmill; a book of instructions called the *Happy Rodent Manual*; and the little creature itself. My father raised an index finger I found altogether too Prussian for comfort, and commanded, 'Andreas, my boy, this expensive privilege you are being granted will, most importantly, include Duty and Responsibility. Do you understand that?'

I nodded solemnly. 'I do.'

'And you are prepared to give a contribution from your pocket money.'

For a mouse of my own I was prepared to say yes to anything. 'I am.'

'Will you make it four pennies?'

This was a tough one, especially as being allowed a mouse was less a reward for good behaviour than a bribe to stop bad behaviour. Three times over the past fortnight I had been caught, long after bedtime, organising a bread and cheese soirée in the kitchen for a family of squatters: unwanted, untameable house mice.

My excuse each time was that 'I only did it because I want to be a zoologist'. There was actually a glimmer of truth in this.

Earlier in the year I had been invited to join a next-door neighbour's family walk across Primrose Hill. I didn't realise we were going to the world-famous Regent's Park Zoological Gardens, only a few minutes' stroll from Oppidans Road! I can still recall the happy delirium of that Sunday afternoon.

My first visit (how could it be even more inspiring than my Darwin Reserve, but it was) made me want to keep returning for the rest of my life. I started going to the zoo as often as I could. There was only one problem: it cost sixpence to get in – officially, that is.

After I had promised to contribute the four pennies, Mother and I went off to the local pet shop with the budget for our one-mouse starter pack. My father had been characteristically thorough in his research and had discovered that a mousetrap was highly recommended for any mouse owner. The Micky Come Home, unlike the spine-snapping murder machines that start with a gurgling scream and end with twitching limbs, was a welcoming box with an entrance that allowed no exit, but a removable viewing panel that did. When baited with morsels of whiffy food, it offered a 99 per cent guarantee for the return of any runaway *Mus musculus*, the Houdini of the animal world.

'These lovely little things live together in groups,' the salesman told us. 'Playing together, eating together, having a bit of a giggle together – very like humans, really. Otherwise I'm afraid they tend to wither away rather quickly. So two mice is the very minimum we recommend.'

He sounded convincing, but how could Mum justify increasing

the budget? 'I am very sad,' she said at last. 'But I must come back and discuss with my husband perhaps next week.'

The salesman was used to resistance and suddenly offered the rodent bargain of the year. 'Three mice for the price of two,' he said encouragingly. 'How does that sound?'

'Oh yes, very good,' I said, even though he wasn't talking to me. It was an unmissable bargain. I had it all worked out. Once we were back home, the three mice could do a bit of four-letter word stuff and there would be millions of baby mice in no time, at not a penny extra! A little persuasion from me, and Mum would melt and agree and I would get my way.

Dead easy. Oh yes.

'Thank you, sir, but I see my husband first.'

Oh no!

'In that case I am sorry, but you may have a problem as the offer has to cease today. From tomorrow, you see, because of the wartime conditions, we are forced to increase the price of mice by three pence per mouse i.e. from one and ten pence ha'penny to two and a ha'penny. Therefore, three mice will cost six shillings and four pence ha'penny as against our bargain of only three shillings and nine pence today! A massive saving of two shillings, seven pence ha'penny!'

My dear mother was now confused. She had come from a land where financial calculations were based on a simple formula of one hundred *pfennigs* to one *mark*. England might mean tolerance and democracy, but it also meant having to struggle with a currency designed by Anglebert the Improvident, Inglebert the Untidy and Ethelbert the Confused. So, 240 pence made one pound, twenty shillings also made one pound, and twelve pennies made one shilling. Four farthings made a penny and there were 480 farthings to a pound. Dentists and doctors were usually paid in guineas, which was twenty-one shillings.

My mother's eyes glazed over. Her mind went numb. Her limbs were weak. I was biting my lip, hoping against hope I would win out.

The salesman realised this was not going to be an easy sell. After a well-timed pause, he offered, 'I will include three packets – free – of our special MouseMunch with added vitamins, normally priced at thruppence-ha'penny per packet. No, make that four packets. A grand saving of another one and tuppence. I can't say fairer than that, can I?'

Even my eyes were glazing over now but I hung on to the gist of it: it sounded like three mice for three pence, or something. Anyway, it was surely the bargain he said it was. The salesman gave Mum another winning smile. I followed suit, and added a touch of anticipation, longing, innocence and modesty all garnished with a few moist eye-blinks for extra emotional impact. It won her over. My dear mother was ready to sacrifice that extra amount, whatever it was, to make me, the little shit, happy.

Then came the time to choose my three-for-the-price-of-two mice. Here she was not to be moved. Any type or colour I liked, but definitely no breeding from any of them.

'Very wise,' said the salesman. 'In that case, our best option would be ladies only. Gentlemen mice without the ladies tend to get a bit pugnacious, if I may use that word.'

He picked one up and examined the area under its tail. 'Have a look here, sonny. You see this? This is a lady mouse, or doe, as we call them in the trade.'

I blushed. This was ever so rude.

He lifted another one by the tail. 'And this one is a gentleman, or buck. Notice the difference?'

This was even ruder because 'buck' rhymed with... you know.

He took the tail off a dozen or more until I got my three: a snow-white beauty with pink eyes, a piebald pin-up girl with black eyes and a chocolate-brown one even lovelier than an unsliced Mars bar. How they managed to breed them in all those colours was a mystery to me when I knew they had all started off as plain grey when they were in their wild state.

Mother paid and I was allowed to carry the hutch that held my happiness.

As we were walking home I glanced at her, hoping she was no longer upset. After a few minutes, she started to smile. I breathed a sigh of relief. She was actually finding pleasure in giving me pleasure!

Why did I feel ill at ease, though? At first they were a joy but then ... my three mice turned into ten. There were seven newborn, strictly forbidden babies. How could it have happened?

'I know how,' said Tom. 'You swapped one of yours at school so you could make babies when you're not supposed to!'

'Don't be more stupid than you are,' I hissed back. 'I know everything about mice! It takes three weeks to do that and we've only had them for two.'

'You have to tell Mum, or I will!'

I tried to hit him, but he dodged out of the way.

'I know exactly what happened,' I said. 'It was that rotten man. He sold us a female that was already going to have babies.'

'Well, you can't keep them,' Tom said smugly. 'So what are you going to do?'

'I don't know,' I shouted.

As it turned out, Mum was wonderful. It took only one question from her and she knew I was innocent. When Dad came home that night, he did three things. He shook his head while wagging his Prussian finger at me; he suggested I offer a further tuppence a week from my pocket money to help pay for extra animal upkeep; and he gave me a boiled sweet. So that was all right.

I felt pretty good. From one mouse to three mice to ten mice in a matter of days was better than any interest offered by a bank. However, I was to learn quickly that the value of investments can go down as well as up.

One of my toddler mice then went missing. It must have been small enough to squeeze through the allegedly impenetrable mesh at the front of the hutch. Tom and I searched the room and discovered a tiny space by one of the floorboards, hardly big enough for a spider, let alone a mouse. We plugged the hole immediately and hoped the escapee would be homesick and find its way back home by the time we returned from school.

This moment was when I realised that my brother had some intelligence, something I had not cared to admit since I was three. 'We will have to unplug the hole first otherwise it can't get back in,' he said.

I nodded. 'Exactly. I was wondering how long it would take you to think of that,' I bluffed.

Unfortunately, Big Ears Barbara had overheard our panic from the hallway and marched straight into the kitchen to betray us. We heard her demanding a key to lock her own bedroom door against rodent insurgents. Tom and I enjoyed reminding her that keys, like iron railings and old bicycles, were scrap metal and had been taken away by the government to make guns. Tom was even more brilliant. He offered her some of his discarded chewing gum to stick into the keyhole and make it mouse-proof. She didn't speak to us for a long time after that, which was nice.

By the time I got back from school that day, every one of the other mini-mice had gone. They must have squeezed through the unplugged hole. Only our three adults were left. I knew exactly what to do for Operation Micky Come Home. First, I needed bait. But Mum was in the kitchen. I would confess everything to her. I played it beautifully, keeping cool, calm and collected. So much so that Mum quizzed me on the strategic positioning of the Micky Come Home and sorted out a few whiffy morsels, with a stern reminder that Professor Malinowski's private area must remain strictly out of bounds.

Of course. Didn't need to be said. Understood.

So I left the kitchen and made for Professor Malinowski's strictly out-of-bounds private area. Hear me out before you condemn me.

More than once I had stared longingly through a window at

the back of the house, where there was a gap in the curtains, and dimly made out the professor's inner sanctum.

Since my mice had done a forbidden thing by escaping, it was obvious they were now on the slippery slope to even worse forbidden things, like gnawing the professor's papers to destruction. In the name of the proper study of mankind, this was something I simply could not allow. I saw it as my responsibility to place the trap cunningly among his documents to save them for future generations. On the other hand, I also knew I should obey my mother. I tussled with my conscience for some time, then decided to enter the taboo premises through the unlocked door (the government had requisitioned the key to make Spitfires). It was not my fault I had to disobey Mum.

I placed the mousetrap in an ideal spot and cautiously backed away, making sure to avert my gaze from all anthropological treasures to avoid the sin of trespass. As luck would have it, there was a dusty book lying on a desk, written by the professor himself. Try as I might, I could not avoid reading the title: *The Sexual Life of Savages*. I simply had to open it, didn't I? With a title like that, how could I not?

For the next twenty minutes, nothing existed for me but my laudable quest for knowledge. That I could make out only a fraction of the complicated text was neither here nor there: the accompanying illustrations were mind-boggling. Some were photographs of naked people; some were naked women and you could actually see their naked breasts. And all the other people in the pictures were smiling!

Whew! This was one rude book all right.

I tore myself away at last, determined to – big breath – extend my understanding of the naked savages and their sexual lives on the far away Trobriand Islands of Melanesia in the South Seas off the eastern coast of tropical New Guinea.

I had picked up some geography as well in my first study session. Not bad, eh?

The Micky Come Home contraption turned out to be rubbish. None of the mice ever returned. Sadly though, while searching our gloomy basement one day, I did come across one of them half dead, which is a gentler way of saying I came across half of one of them, dead. The poor thing was in the process of being reduced to whiffy morsels by a cabal of vampire maggots.

The next day a friend of mine took me to visit his grandfather, who had a famous collection of goldfish. Mr Arnold told me I should think seriously about breeding goldfish rather than mice. Like him, I could breed fish of all kinds of colours and shapes that customers might pay a lot of money for. Some might call that monkeying about with nature if one can monkey with fish.

A few days later, all thought of breeding fish was quickly forgotten when Dad announced we had to leave Oppidans Road and find yet another home as it was taking him too long to get to work. Barbara at sixteen, and the cleverest of the three of us, was solidly on her way to the sixth form and a Nobel Prize and wanted no change of school. Tom was happy to move, provided he could leave school and join the merchant navy. I suggested we were more like gypsies than refugees so we should have stayed in Berlin.

Barbara got quite fierce about that. 'Gypsies in Germany are as "subhuman" as you are,' she said. 'They're dying to come to England, and they're dying if they don't. So shut up and be grateful.' That put me in my place all right.

A few minutes after Mum had stopped crying at the thought of moving again, she armed herself with a pencil and a cup of tea to plan the next house hunt. It didn't take her long to find a nice top-floor flat only a couple of miles away. The location meant Dad would be able to get to work more easily, but Barbara could stay on at her school and so could Tom.

So at the end of term I would have to wave goodbye to Haverstock Hill Primary, which was good, but I would then have to start at a secondary school, where I would hate the teachers and wouldn't know anyone and would probably be bullied, which was bad.

The rear windows of the new flat looked out over London, but I still had to share a bedroom with Tom. I was given a bicycle in more or less working condition two weeks before the move, which was good, but no pets were allowed once we moved which was, er, well, by this time I didn't mind too much either way, but I was determined to find a nice home for the mice in a maggot-free environment, with a stipulation that no fancy-breed mouse designers need apply.

Unfortunately, no one I approved of seemed to want my three beauties. Then Barbara came up with a typically stupid idea that was brilliant but I couldn't let on, of course. 'If you had any brains you'd give them to the zoo,' she said, in that superior voice of hers.

The following Saturday the panniers of my bike were loaded with a well-thumbed *Happy Rodent Manual*, a spare packet of MouseMunch, the rest of the starter pack and the Micky Come Home doing something useful for once – carrying my livestock. I set off for Regent's Park having polished my boots, combed my hair, brushed my teeth twice and washed behind my ears as a mark of respect for the world-renowned Zoological Society of London. My generous gift of three mice might even be rewarded with an FZS after my name like the famous men I would no doubt encounter that morning.

The first zoologist I met was, rather surprisingly, an ordinary-looking woman behind a reception desk who asked if she could be of assistance. 'I've come to donate some animals,' I said.

I knew that 'donate' rather than 'give' was the right word to use in these matters. Each exhibit at the zoo had a label on its enclosure with a short description of species, habitat, date of birth or arrival, followed quite often by the words 'Donated by' or 'Adopted by' with a person's name added. I wanted to be classed as a donator myself and, later perhaps, as an adopter.

She smiled at me. 'Please excuse me while I find someone to attend to you.' She disappeared through a door, leaving me on my own.

I sat on a bench and looked around this temple of living history where world-famous zoologists had been coming for a hundred years. Charles Darwin might have been here to donate a giant tortoise from the Galapagos; explorers like Stanley and

Livingstone would have brought a lion or two from Africa with them. I might meet a famous living explorer like the great Frank Buck, who trapped animals for zoos around the world and whose terrific book *Bring 'em Back Alive* I was reading. I knew it was more likely he was thousands of miles away in deepest Malaya trapping orang-utans and giant tapirs but oh, how I wished I could do that sort of thing. What a hero! One day, perhaps.

A bearded man I naturally assumed was a famous zoologist shocked me back to reality. 'I understand you would like to donate some mice?'

I sprang up from my seat. 'Yes, sir,' I said. Did I hear the word 'donate'? I could already see my name on the label.

'What species are they?'

'Species? Er, really nice ones,' I said, and handed him the Micky Come Home.

'Ah,' he said. 'Tame mice! Well, that would be a first.' He looked straight at me. 'I wonder, is this your first visit to a zoo?'

'Oh no, sir. I come here all the time. Like today. I've got my sixpence.' I pulled it out of my pocket to show him. 'Because I'm going to be a zoologist.'

'Are you indeed?' He smiled. 'Well then, you must have noticed we don't really deal with pet animals here.'

I swallowed hard. This was not going too well. 'Yes, sir. But, but pets are not allowed where we're moving to, and there's no one else who will have them. And they're very nice. And I want to be a zoologist.'

He nodded again. 'I think you had better sit down.' We both

did so. 'You come here expecting me to find a home for three pet mice nobody wants. But you don't tell me how, you don't tell me where. Heaven help me. You give me no option, do you?' He rose to his feet with a big sigh. 'Leave them with me then.'

He pointed a warning finger at me, just like Dad. 'It's just this once, mind.'

'Oh yes, sir. Thank you very much, sir.'

I was so grateful I offered him the Micky Come Home as well, 'Just in case one of them might escape, sir. You never know.'

'Very kind but no thanks, you've given me enough to cope with,' he said. 'Are you planning to spend your sixpence here this morning?'

'Yes sir.'

'Well, don't. Put it away and follow me.'

He led me through doors that opened straight into the zoo itself. Then, without any tousling of my hair, which I hated, he put his hands on my shoulders and said very nicely, 'I wish you all the luck in the world for your chosen profession. It's a pleasure to see someone taking such care. Now go and enjoy yourself.'

'Thank you very much, sir,' I said again, and watched him walk back through the doors.

I couldn't believe my luck. He had made me a donator and saved me sixpence, and I didn't even know his name! As far as I was concerned, he was more famous than any other zoologist in the world.

There was no way I could wait a whole week before locating my donator label with my name on it, even though it would mean having to borrow more money from Tom. I had by then spent the original sixpence on something else. My dear brother was at his meanest: repayment in cash plus four sweet coupons as interest this time. Or, no repayment at all (sounded good) but eight – yes eight! – sweet coupons interest. It was evil. With no sweets for weeks I could starve to death. But I had to agree.

Two days later I set off on my mission after school. By the time the zoo closed, I had found neither label nor mouse. It had been a depressing waste of coupons, money, time and trouble. I limped home a broken man.

Mum was sympathetic. 'Perhaps they need more time to arrange a nice place for them. Perhaps you will find them at the weekend?'

Barbara showed no mercy. 'Pointless,' she said. 'They'll have been fed to some starving carnivore by now – there's a war on, you know.'

Mum was deeply shocked at this and told her so. Even Tom disapproved. I had what was probably my last major howl of childhood and swore never, ever to speak to my sister again as long as I lived. And I didn't for a whole week. But the nagging suspicion that she might just be right launched me on a noble quest for truth. Siegfried was not my middle name for nothing!

I was duty bound to continue scouring every corner of the zoo in case the mice should turn up and prove Barbara wrong. I owed it to the Zoological Society of London to root out any zookeepers who were traitors to my cause. Naturally my noble principles also demanded that not a single silver coin should ever again subsidise the zoo's evil deeds, if proved.

Do I hear you ask how I would scour the zoo successfully without cash? Child's play, if you were a child. There were seven foot-high turnstiles at various points around the zoo's perimeter; they allowed visitors to get out, but not to go in. They were set in a cast iron frame, which was capped at the top with more iron, but there was just enough space in between to allow a short, determined and bendable little miscreant to squeeze through. I could then clamber down, almost head first, to the ground. I had no qualms about trespassing in this way and if caught, was quite prepared to be martyred.

But I never did see my white, piebald and Mars bar-brown beauties again. So the outcome was both negative and positive: I had lost my hope of star billing on an official label but my suspicions were confirmed. The innocent creatures had indeed been butchered.

I now had no choice but to confront the zoo's mouse murderers and have it out with them, man to man. I was especially set on confronting that unctuous assassin with the face fungus to whom I had entrusted them in good faith. As a further gesture of defiance I cancelled my choice of profession.

The zoologist harpy behind the reception desk greeted me with a big smile. 'Hello!' she said before I could attack. 'I'm glad you've turned up again because I wanted a word with you.'

'Oh yes?' I asked suspiciously.

'Well, I'm afraid we couldn't accommodate your mice after all – there are quite strict rules about such things here – but instead, I've been allowed to take them home with me! So let me tell you they are now being treated like kings – or queens, I should say – and are making my own children very happy indeed.'

What could I say to that? I managed a 'Good', with a smile designed to reveal none of my shame at drawing the wrong conclusions.

I was then shepherded through the doors straight into the zoo again. And in a confidential whisper this good woman said: 'I have permission from my superior – that's the bearded gentleman you first met, you remember? He was so impressed by you that I'm allowed to offer you free entry at any time you find yourself short of sixpence. Do keep that to yourself though, won't you?'

On my way home I wiped the slate clean and un-cancelled my cancellation.

I stupidly left both the main hutch and the Micky Come Home in Oppidans Road when we finally moved, and I rather missed them. But the enemy didn't. Sometime later, they and the house itself were crushed to pieces by a V2 rocket. I am not sure how many of Malinowski's notes survived.

CHAPTER 6

Rule Britannia

Our move from Oppidans Road to Daleham Gardens went smoothly. We now had more space (having occupied only a few rooms in Malinowski's house), which allowed us to retrieve belongings that had been in storage since we reached England. The bookcases were emptied of bric-a-brac, towels, the vacuum cleaner and other household paraphernalia, and generally smartened up to welcome back the actual books.

After Tom and I promised Dad that we had discarded our theory concerning thickness between covers as a measure of a book's merits as infantile, we were granted the privilege of restocking the shelves, but we had to stick to alphabetical order. We were now not only speaking and writing instinctively in English but thinking and dreaming in it too. It didn't take us long to regard English as our first language and German as the foreign one. Barbara, on the other hand, managed to straddle both languages equally well. It was quite annoying to have to admit she was cleverer than either of us, despite being a girl. In the end, Tom and I graciously accepted her character flaw as one from which she was unlikely to recover.

Refugees like us felt a patriotic need to stick to English. German was the language of the enemy. It might also be dangerous to speak it near good English folk who might mistake us for spies and have us shot. Despite that, we remained faithful to the German books that first started us reading. My own favourites, some heavily graffitied with restless crayons, are still on my shelves and still in decent condition: the collected *Märchen der Brüder Grimm*, for instance, containing over a hundred favourite tales like *Rumpelstilzchen*, *Hansel und Gretel*, *Rapunzel* and *Schneewittchen und die sieben Zwerge*, all beautifully illustrated; some other children's books and poems with delicate watercolours by one of our aunts, who let us watch her at work and gave us biscuits; three great adventure stories by Erich Kastner, the author of *Emil und die Detektive*; and ten of my grandfather's novels that, I'm ashamed to say, I have only briefly glanced at. My excuse is that he wrote in the Tyrolean dialect, which is as remote from standard German as broad Glaswegian is from Queen's English.

Our family library had an encyclopaedia, *Brehm's Thierleben*, literally 'Brehm's Life of Animals', which covered every animal species known to man at the time – except man himself. It was first published in a mighty ten volumes in 1870, and our edition from 1879 had been mercifully edited to three still hefty tomes. It took Schwarzenegger-like biceps to lift one off a shelf. I still have them in my study. There are over 2,500 pages and almost 1,300 detailed engravings that often owe more to the imagination than fact. Some pictures are also highly dramatic, such as one which gives an immediate grasp of what a bear eating his dinner would look like, when said dinner was a deer. I would pore over these illustrations and painstakingly copy some of the more dangerous beasts, like lions and tigers, into my sketchbook, fancying I was dicing with death in the jungle with only a pencil to defend me.

The scholarly text was less easy to tackle. I had no problem with the stylish Gothic typeface and the obscure Latin names didn't worry me – they came with German equivalents anyway – but making sense of what Brehm meant was not always easy. As a writer he often lacked clarity. I was always intrigued by the mysteries of natural history and eventually became aware of many anomalies in the volumes.

The nice-looking passenger pigeon, for example, is recorded in *Brehm* as the world's most abundant bird species, with an estimated population of four or even five *billion*. The arrival of the first European settlers in North America meant curtains for the birds, however. Their numbers diminished rapidly for two main reasons: the pigeons raided the crops, which wasn't nice of them; and they were good to eat, which was. Brehm seemed to miss the fact the passenger pigeon was becoming extinct. It shows how interested I was in natural history that I discovered later that a few captive individuals survived, until one o'clock on 1 September 1914 in Cincinnati Zoo, Ohio when Martha, the very last of her kind, fell off her perch.

My interest in natural history also taught me that formerly unknown species come to light from time to time. One of the most remarkable is the okapi, a glamorous relative of the giraffe, about the size and shape of a horse, with a beautiful velvety reddish-brown pelt and startling stripes on its legs like a zebra's. The length of its neck could never compete with that of a giraffe, but the okapi compensates with a tongue that reaches far enough into its ears to clean them inside and out. Very hygienic.

I had to wait until well after the war before an okapi arrived at London Zoo and I could greet it face to face. It was a significant moment, which took me right back to the age of twelve and the pride I felt – for no good reason – in my astounding observation that the Brehm of 1879 did not mention okapis at all. It was only in 1900 that Sir Harry Hamilton Johnston, GCMG, KCB, colonial administrator, famous explorer and British to the core (hurrah, hurrah!) 'discovered' the okapi and was awarded the honour of joint billing as *Okapia johnstoni*. Discovered? Well, yes, unless you lived in the African jungle where your family and forebears had been living happily among their long-tongued neighbours for generations.

Perhaps on those special occasions when Sir Harry came visiting – quite possible, as he was respected by the pygmy tribes as one of their benefactors – they might well have invited an okapi to join them for a festive dinner. Or more likely to *be* the main course. The okapi was fascinating but distant; there were other fascinations closer to home.

At the rear of my new secondary school, a waist-high gate led in and out of the playground. This was an open sesame to 1,800 acres of green wonderland called Hampstead Heath. For townies like me, it was soon to prove what I had always suspected – that trees offer more opportunities for adventure than lamp posts. The heath boasted a famous lido where show-offs dived from the top board, hoping not to crack their heads open, while we sissies in the shallow end hoped for nothing better. There was a sports ground next to the lido. Beneath the pitches, it was rumoured, lay an underground warren of bombproof shelters for VIPs like His Majesty the King, Winston Churchill and our headmaster.

My daily walk to school took about twenty minutes if I was late and had to run, and a lot longer if there was time to look for spoils of war. It was usual to see children and even adults, shoulders hunched, eyes resolutely down, scouring the ground inch by inch in search of shrapnel – the jagged pieces of crumpled metal that dropped to earth from exploded anti-aircraft shells, or, better still, from German bombs or even bombers. The bigger the piece and more exotic its origin, the more respect its finder received when showing it off at our playground supermarket. A really hefty lump marked with some form of identifying inscription turned up on rare occasions. It would be displayed for sale or exchange, or simply to make others envious.

Even the tiniest piece of shrapnel brought its rewards. On rare occasions, my mates and I earned ourselves enough coupons to be able to refuse school dinners in favour of overdosing on a better class of vomit potential from a local sweet shop. Having had our fill, we would eventually wobble off, grey-faced, to the local snack bar for slices of bread and dripping with scrunchy bits that were guaranteed to upset our insides. The gritty dripping alone was a bargain at a penny a time. All in all, our new school was a pretty good place to be. It was certainly better than any of the others I had experienced.

Yet all was not what it seemed.

In common with many other citizens living in vulnerable areas of the country, the pupils and staff of William Ellis School had been evacuated earlier in the war to the relative safety of Leighton Buzzard in Bedfordshire. The vacant building was then renamed the North London Emergency Secondary School and filled by those of us who, for one reason or another, had to stay in the capital.

School was becoming harder as we had to grapple with new and unfamiliar subjects. Physics, for example, was horrendously horrible. Chemistry was very dramatic, especially when we found out that dropping calcium carbide into an inkwell produced a stink that could clear a classroom. Doing it risked detention, but it was worth it. French: hmm, let's wait and see. Latin: ditto. English, OK but old hat; and English literature: very, very interesting but I was doing all right on my own, thank you, trying to make sure I could keep up with my brother. I had begun with shorter works of quality such as the *Dandy*, *Beano*, *Hotspur* and *Rover* before moving on to longer ones. One of these was an omnibus edition of four novels which some of my friends at school had recommended. They turned out to be rather ridiculous adventure stories and I was about to discard them when I began to suspect they might not be the cheap fiction I had first assumed, but a coded introduction to the real character of my new country, the character that exemplified the Great in Great Britain. I found that more than very, very, very interesting.

We now live in a multicultural society that has decided that the old motto 'When in Rome do as the Romans do' is insensitive and even morally wrong. It was very different in the 1940s if you were an immigrant to Britain. There were no multicultural sensitivities. As a child I desperately wanted to fit in and understand the mores of my new country so I was very much taken with patriotic books that featured unscrupulous villains who sought to stop Britons (who never, never shall be slaves, thanks be to the King) from protecting the world from anarchists, Bolsheviks and crime barons of low breeding. At the time, just having a foreign accent was enough to make anyone suspect. If you think I'm exaggerating, read Agatha Christie. Her detective, Hercule Poirot, who was no Jew but a Belgian, was always having to deal with snubs and sneers because he was foreign even though Scotland Yard called on his 'little grey cells' to solve baffling murders.

Enter, luckily for civilisation, a writer, a genius using his codename of 'Sapper'. His powers of persuasion seemed to me infinite. Sapper's mission was to inspire the nation with the self-evident truth that Britain Knows Best, and to do so in the guise of entertainment so the public could absorb his message without realising they were being brainwashed in favour of Britannia. Sapper's eloquence was inspiring and his characters became some of the most influential role models for our generation. Sapper's hero was a veteran of the First World War: the redoubtable Captain Hugh Drummond DSO MC, late of His Majesty's Royal Loamshire Regiment, who was a scourge to his enemies and represented everything that is best and noble in our sceptred isle. Hugh 'Bulldog' Drummond *was* Great Britain.

Once I was aware of the real significance of the books, I

became a fervent disciple. I wanted desperately to be one of Bulldog Drummond's band of frightfully decent chaps; to do their deeds, walk their walk and talk their talk. I was realistic enough to accept the first of those ambitions would have to wait until I left school but the second was possible as long as I got my parents's permission on a Saturday to go up to the West End on my own in a bus. My secret mission was to investigate Drummond's haunts: Berkeley Square, Belgravia, Knightsbridge, Piccadilly, and the famous gentlemen's clubs of Pall Mall and St James's, whose magical names I could roll around my tongue in a would-be posh accent: The Athenaeum, Reform, White's, Savage, RAC, Boodles... Could Captain Drummond be a member of all of them? I wondered. I would gaze, star-struck, at each one and dream of the extreme Englishness behind their imposing facades.

One day I plucked up enough courage to approach the commissionaire of one of these temples of culture. I was going to ask if Captain Drummond was a member but my nerve failed me and I only managed something embarrassing about how much it would cost to join. I know now the commissionaire was only a doorman, but to me then he seemed a glamorous, glittering and probably titled being. This Englishman of power listened attentively to me, shook his noble head in silence and turned his back with an overwhelming elegance. I was grateful he had even noticed me. Membership, I guessed, might require more than the few pennies I could scrape together.

Mayfair became my hunting ground. Those who don't know London may not realise it is the most elegant district of the city.

(Now only rich Arabs and Russian oligarchs can afford to live there, it seems.) Bulldog Drummond lived on the very short and very select Half Moon Street. The name alone conjured up breathtaking romance and mystery. In the hope of getting closer to my idol, I wandered up and down it for hours, my heart beating fast inside, but all suave confidence and a don't-mess-with-me look on the outside.

In the books, Drummond himself gives his address as No. 60A so why didn't I ring the doorbell? Another question arises: is Half Moon Street even long enough to number into the sixties? For a moment, some years ago, I considered revisiting the street to find out for myself, but my inner voice pulled me up with a sneering 'Act your age, Sachs' (I was nearing sixty at the time). I'm ashamed to say the desire to make sure still lingers. The phone number is more easily explained. It was listed as 123 Mayfair. That might have been so in the 1920s, but by the 1940s it would probably have changed to MAYfair 1234. Today there are no more MAYfair or AMBassador or REGent exchanges. They are all strings of numbers.

When I am logical I realise that Sapper must have died long ago, but I was not the only boy at school to be so obsessed. A select few of us at school founded an inner circle of Bulldog devotion. We trained ourselves to be fluent in Sapper-speak, often referring to each other as 'my dear old bean', or 'my dear old flick' or 'my dear old bird', or even 'Say! You priceless old stuffed tomato.' This was especially odd as English cuisine at the time did not stretch to stuffed tomatoes.

Homework became either 'deuced awkward' or 'most fearfully

jolly'. Teachers we approved of were 'all-round good eggs', while the rest were sentenced to be 'foully done to death with animal fury'. Our smiles were mocking, infectious or devil-may-care as required. Sometimes we pretended to be international criminals, snarling thickly and uttering guttural chuckles. We also became terrific at improvising scenes. Choosing a period of relative silence, for example, we would alert the playground rabble with an ear-catching startler such as: 'Dash it all, Algy Longworth, old fruit, a hooded cobra is not a pleasing pet, don't you know.'

Timed right, it could turn heads in our direction and grab an interested audience. So we carried on with such priceless lines as: 'I remember it well, Drummond old flick. Tricky devils and no mistake. What say you, Toby, old bean?'

'You had a dashed close shave that time and no mistake.'

'That ghastly cad Carl Peterson was behind it, of course.'

'Who else!'

'Algy saved my life.'

'Always a good'un, spot-on feller.'

'Hear, hear!'

'Least I could do, old sport.'

'You sucked the venom from my foot. Shan't forget it.'

'Nor I.'

'Left one, I think.'

'Right, I thought.'

'As you say.'

'Frightful taste, cobra venom. Like custard made with water.'

We would only stop when the school bell rang to haul us all back to reality. But, try as we might, it wasn't long before our fickle public started drifting off with murmurs of 'Heard it all before' and 'Rubbish!' or 'Boring!'

When I think about it, it is odd that the little immigrant boy who was so inspired by Bulldog Drummond's love of England should play a Spanish waiter who is also starry-eyed about Britannia. Manuel wrote a touching ode to England. As a poet, Manuel would like to stress that to get the full beauty of the verses, they must be read aloud with a Barcelona accent:

> Of all the countries in the world
> There's only one for me
> Where a man can live, werk and play
> The country of the free!
> I speak of Ingland's green and pleasant land
> Juss next door to Franz
> I been here a long time now
> Not days, not weeks but munts
> Sometimes is not so hot as Barcelona
> The summer before is here is oready gonna
> But the winta with the snowings
> And the springtime with the flowers
> When little burds ar olways sing
> Togetha in one chowrus.

Kipling probably is not fearing for his reputation.

I felt, along with the select few, that the North London Emergency Secondary School boys should be inspired by Bulldog Drummond and his Britain Knows Best crusade. For we did know best. We *were* best. Certainly better than those deserters in remote Leighton Buzzard skulking away from the ravages of the *Luftwaffe*, while we bravely coped on the front line – as cannon fodder.

Our first resolution was to sever all connection with the demeaning title of North London Emergency etc. and stake a claim that we few, we happy few, were the only true Elysians worthy of the name. Let the Bedfordshire dogs cower in shame while we fought on the beaches in the field of human conflict. *England Über Alles!*

Back home, my mini-swagger alerted the family to the suspicion that a little *Gauleiter* was joining them for dinner. A few carefully chosen words from Dad suggested that I might be clever enough to revise my cock-eyed pronouncements about the Bedfordshire dogs. School, he suggested, was for learning, not proselytising. I considered this carefully. Would I get a boiled sweet if I found out what the word meant?

There was a short pause. Possibly, he indicated.

And another one if I learned how to spell it?

A single raised eyebrow from him needed no 'Don't push your luck, son' to make his meaning clear. It was a moment of British sophistication worthy of Drummond himself, and I loved my father all the more for it. He then went on to ask if I would consider taking some time to define the difference between a fan and a fanatic, using the '3 Cs' as a guide.

I knew what was expected of me. 'What are the 3 Cs, please?' I asked dutifully.

'Cool, Calm and Collected.'

By the next meeting of the Drummond stalwarts, I had worked out a Cool, Calm and Collected plan of action. Our performances in the playground, I declared, were no more than childish entertainment for a stupid audience. We should, therefore, stop trying to recruit others to our cause and go underground to consider our priorities at some more convenient time before surfacing again twice as dedicated.

Had I been entirely straight with my friends? No: the truth was that I simply couldn't bear the ghastly shame I felt at losing our playground fans. We had gone from loud cheers to louder boos in less than a fortnight! It was extreme humiliation of a kind that could only, I supposed, be tolerated by professional actors well-schooled in suffering. A calling I would never sink to, thank you very much. I'd rather be a film star.

And where had that idea suddenly come from? I knew virtually nothing about the world of cinema. True, if my hands were reasonably clean, Barbara sometimes let me peep at her copies of *Picturegoer*, a magazine of sepia-tinted photographs packed into a reduced number of pages because of the war, dedicated to keeping up the nation's spirits with facts about glamorous film stars, their rise to fame and fortune from humble beginnings, their true romances and top-class talent for divorce and other exotic scandals. It seemed an interesting world to explore.

The first film I had ever seen was on board the SS *Manhattan* on our way to Southampton. The second one was *Snow White and the Seven Dwarfs*, in a fancy cinema in the West End. It was our first outing as a whole family since *Zirkus Krone* in Berlin. Snow White herself was exactly as I imagined her, except she could now sing as well. And so could the seven dwarfs, who had each been given a name they didn't have in my treasured *Märchen der Brüder Grimm*, but I generously accepted one might have to allow for mistakes in translation, and anyway it was an interesting surprise. The film was going magically well until the wicked witch made my hair stand on end and reminded me of Buschi's blood-poisoned death. He hadn't been on my mind for a long while but now I was really upset and started to cry a little.

When we left the cinema, my mum launched into a tirade against Walt Disney and all of Hollywood for corrupting her precious boy with their irresponsible and immoral goings-on. She was inspiring. I dried my tears in sympathy and agreed with every word she said, even the ones I couldn't understand.

My first step in following Mum's good example would be to reassess my growing interest in *Picturegoer*. I would confine my future cinema study to the revelations and lovely pictures of Hollywood's purest, unsullied stars like Lana Turner, Hedy Lamarr and Rita Hayworth.

Ah, Rita Hayworth…

It occurred to me that I was embarking on a spiritual crusade I had best keep to myself. Unshared. Private. I was searching for perfection, talent, charisma, and I chose wisely. Bette Davis, for example, great actress though she might be, scored low for her silly short back-and-sides and the neurotic way she smoked cigarettes. Katharine Hepburn and Ingrid Bergman also failed because they seemed so intelligent – and I was a teenage boy who was not so interested in female intellect. *Picturegoer* introduced me to immaculate women, a select number of whom I hoped one day to conquer and slay dragons for.

Through all this, Dad realised, I think, that I wanted more attention from him. A few weekends later, when he actually had a day off work, he offered me a special outing to the Odeon Swiss Cottage where, by coincidence, a Bulldog Drummond film was showing. It starred a famous actor called Ronald Colman.

I was popping with excitement. What was skulking hopelessly up and down Half Moon Street against the certainty now on offer? My excessive joy was excessive.

Dad was not so enthusiastic, of course, but backtracking on a deal would not have been in his nature. So, he dug deep into his purse and we parked in the ninepenny stalls. I sat open-mouthed, eyes glued to the screen but otherwise giving not much away, while he monitored my every reaction with sneaky looks.

On our walk back to Daleham Gardens, I guessed he would want me to offer a verdict on the film. But I was in difficulties. During the performance, my mood had changed for reasons I couldn't quite figure out. All I managed were a few hopefully profound but actually meaningless nods until he eventually raised an eyebrow and asked me straight out, 'So what did you think of it?'

Another token nod from me before managing a 'Very good' and adding, 'Oh yes. Good, all right.'

He raised both eyebrows this time. 'But not special?' he ventured.

'Oh yes, special all right,' I said, and added, 'Oh yes, I'm hungry.'

The afternoon had certainly been special, but not for any reason to do with the film. It was special for having my father to myself for once. I think he hoped I would not think the film that special as, for an educated man, a member of whose family had starred with Marlene Dietrich, Bulldog Drummond was rather crude and melodramatic.

In fairness, I did enjoy the film. It was fun to hate the foreign crooks but some things had been plain wrong. Like Algy Longworth, for instance, who looked different from the real one – by which I mean, of course, from the way I imagined the 'real one'. Some of the other characters in the film were not in the books, which was stupid.

I wish I could have been a bit more responsive to please Dad, but I was grappling with a major upset. The only man I have ever been truly in love with – apart from my father that is – was Bulldog Drummond. But in close-up after close-up on that fateful afternoon, the truth hit home. Robin Coalmin, or whatever they called him, actually didn't look anything like the real Bulldog Drummond in the books. Only I could claim that honour, so it just wasn't fair. In the film, my hero had turned out to be little more than a devious impostor, fit only to fade away like any other old soldier.

Little did I realise that my abrupt shunt towards reality marked only the first of my many skids on the banana skin of adolescence. Worst of all, my dear dad did nothing to ease my confusion. Nothing. I see in retrospect that I found it easy to feel that everyone in the world had deserted me – even my poor dad. I was determined never to speak to him again as long as I lived and only postponed telling him this because of the happy smile on his face.

The following day was a Sunday, when he got his boiled egg for breakfast and I, as the baby of the family, could expect the top 10 per cent section of white-plus-hint-of-yellow when he sliced it off. It was a treat I couldn't afford to miss, much heightened by the barely concealed snarls of resentment coming from my brother and sister. Oh, joy.

But my joy would not last long.

CHAPTER 7

Growing Pains

J oy was premature. Joy was about to disappear.

That evening after dinner, Vati fell sick. It wasn't the first time. I, the child medical expert, didn't think it was serious, but our mother went into a surprising flurry of worry. If Father had to stay off work for however short a period, it could spell disaster. I shook my wise head. What had happened to Cool, Calm and Collected, I wondered.

Managing to keep just the right side of panic, Mother sent her husband off to bed, straight away, no arguments. She took his temperature and pulse, summoned the doctor, ladled medicine, nursed him devotedly, and did anything else that might save us from starving to death by the weekend.

Even Barbara seemed concerned, which was a real surprise because she never bothered herself when her little brother was ill. She didn't care if I had measles, mumps, scarlet fever, chicken pox, whooping cough or any of the other awful maladies children then had to take in their stride. Neither she nor my mother seemed to understand that real men like my father were tough and brave, not namby-pamby weaklings too scared to climb a mountain or write poetry. My father could do both – and bring up his dinner without fuss if he needed to. I knew he would be off to work early next morning as usual, fit as a fiddle and ready to keep us all alive and fed. And so it turned out.

Vati still looked a bit grey when he came home that evening, and he wasn't much help with my homework for a few days, but my philosophy was that anything was better than toothache. Then came an unwelcome surprise, a change to my Sunday breakfast routine. Mother explained that Uncle Manasse, our family doctor of long standing, had diagnosed Dad with 'a touch of tummy trouble', as she put it. 'It is very important to build up his energy again,' she told me, 'so Mr Churchill has been kind enough to arrange that the Ministry of Food put special coupons in his ration book for white meat like chicken and veal, which will make him better soon. So that is nice of him, isn't it, *liebling*?'

Now at secondary school, I was old enough to remind my dear mother that I was no longer a child, so I took her to task. Chicken and veal did qualify as white meat, I explained, but was she aware that veal came from murdered baby cows whose mothers despaired and died of grief? Dad would never approve of anything so cruel. 'Forget veal,' I advised, 'and go for the humane choice: cod and chips.' I said it twice, but she wasn't listening so I gave up. I had to accept that veal might be immoral but at least it wasn't as deadly as our Thursday school dinners of bangers made from leftover donkeys and sawdust.

Nice Mr Churchill then doubled Dad's weekly egg ration. Terrific! There would be something in it for me then.

No, there wasn't. My contribution was to be brave and give up my Sunday egg treat altogether.

This was a blow. Why me? It wasn't fair! Or did I hear Mother say 'very brave'? 'Well, we are concerned about Vati, of course, so maybe you should try being very brave.' Yes, of course, I decided, mutating into my current idol (I was far too attached to Bulldog to let one shoddy film destroy my faith in him). Bulldog would have said, 'Frightfully jolly don't you know Mater, old bean!' So I directed a heroic, Drummond-like, Cool, Calm and Collected smile lovingly at my mum. What a deep moment of pride it was for me when she praised my magnanimous sacrifice! Even better were the following moments when she offered me two unexpected slices of Mars bar in gratitude for my selflessness. And – heavens, wasn't I wonderful! – I even continued to glow with humble pride and the same sweet smile despite having to stomach the sudden, sadistic, slimy, sneaky smirks of my two subhuman siblings. Talk about *Schadenfreude*!

I was on a roll. After a short, though quite difficult, moment of hesitation, I managed to indicate to my dear sister and brother that selflessness brings its own reward, and offered them both my slices of Mars bar. It was a truly biblical event I would luxuriate in for a whole minute, and regret for the rest of my life. Oh Lord, let them be foully done to death with animal fury, as Bulldog would say.

But my filial duty had been done. Vati's health could now be safely left to others and, once he returned to work, I presumed he had recovered from his stomach problems.

I continued to study film stars – the most fabulous creatures during the war. The enchantments of *Picturegoer* were a world away from the women you saw in wartime London. They were mainly a sorry bunch in drab clothing-coupon dresses, gas masks on string slung across a shoulder while struggling with heavy cans of paraffin in one hand and pushing squeaky babies in squeaky prams. Oh dearie me! Some of these poor souls were even uglier than our physics teacher. Bette Davis might chain smoke, but she had some nice frocks and was rich.

Too many of the women in London had let themselves go, displaying unsightly blemishes and bandy legs, embarrassing acne, cold sores, moles, boils, crusty warts and false teeth that clattered. It would not have surprised me to learn they had hair growing from their armpits like men. If these ladies expected more than a 'Good Morning' from me, they would have to conform more to my standards. I look back on what I thought and think '*Oy vey*' and 'What vanity on my part!'

Glamour was certainly hard to come by in those battered streets, and eventually even *Picturegoer* was beginning to show its wrinkles. It was time to move on.

But where to? Hollywood was 6,000 miles away and an impossible dream. The Odeon Swiss Cottage was only ten minutes away, but seemed sometimes just as hard to reach. I would have welcomed it if my parents had said, 'God speed, my boy, and follow your stars, you deserve the best and here is a golden sovereign,' but it wasn't going to be so easy. Gaining access to the starlit Swiss Cottage movie palace would be fraught with multiple conditions, like approved 'U' certificate films only, weekend afternoons only and never on school days; fully completed homework only; cost of tickets from own pocket money; and proper use of bathroom at all times involving soap, toothpaste and okapi-quality ear-ablutions. To wangle permission to go to the cinema I would have to rival Shakespeare in eloquence and how could I ever reach those heights? Probably never, even if I practised – and I did, for days and days, with growing frustration and diminishing confidence until I packed it in and kicked the furniture. It wasn't fair. The world was against me. No point in living. Heavy sighs, moan, groan and bilingual *knatschen*.

A force-7 wallow in self-pity can, on rare occasions (but don't bank on it), morph into a rosy puff of good fortune and, lo and behold, my life took a turn for the better. Better in one way – not so nice in another.

Let me explain in a way I couldn't at the time – and am still a little hesitant to try now.

I came back from school one afternoon to find my father sitting in his favourite chair holding his wife's hand and look-ing very pleased to be where he was. What a miracle. The best treat imaginable. Normally it would be rare for him to get home before bedtime, let alone teatime. His daily routine was to catch an early morning bus at about the time that I was staggering out of bed, and make his way to Messrs Leroi, Flesch and Co., where he worked six days a week, often until late into the even-ing and sometimes even through the night, when he took his turn fire-watching on the roof of their office building.

On this occasion he had apparently fallen sick shortly after arriving at work, and Mr Leroi and Mr Flesch had insisted he went straight back home and stayed there until he recovered. I looked forward to seeing a lot more of him. My happier than happy eyes registered every precious detail of that afternoon – apart, that is, from his pallid complexion and sheer exhaustion which, I'm ashamed to say, I failed to spot immediately.

We all rallied round the next few days and gave Father the best of good care and concern. Tom, always desperate to put school behind him, postponed his ambition to join the merchant navy in favour of getting a job – any job – to contribute to the housekeeping. But he wasn't allowed to do so. Barbara was due to leave school that year and was already taking time out at home to help her mother and spoil her father. In fact, the very next morning she presented him with a banana. Another miracle! Bananas had become extinct in Britain after 1939.

'I got it from a good friend,' she said proudly, and passed it to him.

'Good friend be buggered. Dirty Yankee sailor friend more like,' Tom whispered. I sniggered for about half an hour because I knew what that implied. I was growing up fast.

Leaving school at the age of thirteen was not an option, of course. I was enjoying it too much anyway, the best part being my daily wander back for tea, when time became meaningless and I could dream my impossible dreams. But now Vati was home I made sure I got home faster: no dawdling, no Drummond escapades, no shrapnel searching – just straight back and a brief review of the day with Dad. I was always ready to keep him company whenever he felt fit enough, and sometimes when he didn't.

In retrospect, I think I may have been more of a burden than a joy. We would play a game, or I would recite a bit of a poem I had to learn anyway or, alternatively, not complain about algebra and related hardships. Sometimes he dozed off without warning; at others he just looked at his cello for a long time, which was a bit sad.

I could tell, though, that he was getting better once he started smiling again, felt like checking my homework and told me he hoped I would go on to university and learn to play an instrument. After a few days, he went back to work and I missed him straight away. But his full recovery this time was taking longer than expected.

Finally, despite his protests, Mr Leroi and Mr Flesch decided to limit his workload to five days a week instead of six, until he was truly fit. They were good people and happy to help care for an old friend. Mother got herself in another tizzy, fearing we would all starve to death, until she learned that his salary would not be affected. She was overwhelmed with gratitude and cried a lot before going back to the battle with his 'tummy trouble'. It was her cosy way of dealing with unfriendly medical jargon. Euphemisms didn't fool me. My generation knew all there was to know about 'tummy trouble', a routine hazard in wartime, when we had to cope with toxic menus at school, egg-starvation and castor oil at home, and a sweet ration that wouldn't keep a flea alive. Tummy trouble? Forget it. We called it what it was: throwing up, puking, retching, Vomit for Victory, face-down-the-loo-spew and, for the really talented among us, the much-envied skill of getting yourself sent home from school. All these expressions were quite unacceptable in polite society, of course, a society that also did not permit doom-laden words like 'cancer' to be uttered.

Despite Father being home more, the time he and I spent together was sometimes less rewarding than I hoped. In the past he would often have found time to talk, read, play games or discuss any school problems I might have. We did so less frequently now. Even more frustrating was his bad habit of countering a question of mine with one of his, which delayed my getting on with more interesting things. He was also no longer endlessly patient should my grasshopper brain start skipping into attention deficit. When I complained once that he made me feel stupid because *he* never got anything wrong, he paused a moment, then confessed to being even more mystified by the deadly subject of physics than I was. I found that remarkably encouraging and forgave him.

My father was my hero in all ways, and the perfect supplement to teachers: they told me what to learn; he taught me how to learn. The gift of two whole days at home after a busy week was a godsend for him, as well as for the rest of us. I did all I could to monopolise his attention, but soon came unstuck with a churlish 'Don't you ever think of anybody but yourself?' from my sister, who couldn't mind her own business. Unfortunately, her complaint was supported by my misguided, indeed treacherous, mother, who decided to ban me from my own home on Saturday mornings to stop me cheering up my father.

It took no more than one of those Saturdays, moping resentfully along damp streets with no friend for company, to realise that this new-found freedom had one major positive.

In common with most cinemas in the land at that time, the doors of the Odeon Swiss Cottage were flung open once a week to hordes of eager children bent on mayhem under the alibi of 'Saturday Morning Pictures'. Quite unexpectedly I was allowed to go with virtually no maternal conditions imposed on me apart from returning home by lunchtime, preferably in one piece. I wasn't asked to complete any outstanding homework or tackle extra chores. Even the price of a ticket (or bribe, as my sister snarled) was no stumbling block. The real management i.e. my dear, dear mother, pressed a weekly sixpenny piece into my hand just to get me out of the house. It was an offer I couldn't refuse.

I had no delusions that our local silver screen might further my investigations into the beautiful ladies of talent and glamour that I found so inspiring. The only real purpose of Saturday morning pictures was to grant a few hours of serenity for exhausted parents at home, a few hours off the lead for their unbearable offspring and a life sentence of hell for the cinema staff.

We, the little ruffians, were shown a main feature that more often than not involved cowboys and Indians using double Dutch dialogue: for example, 'Gid aada tahn boy else aah blow ya heed orf afore ya hoss noze ya left the sadl,' and doing the usual nasty things to each other in black and white. Fitted in somewhere would be a couple of equally violent shorts and cartoons, including *Tom and Jerry*.

At some point during the Saturday morning film show, a mighty Wurlitzer would rise up in neon-lit splendour from the region of the tube station beneath our boots. The twitchy organist sat ready to torture us with his four hysterical limbs going hell for leather through an endless sing-along with a bouncy ball. St Vitus, as we called him with no affection, put up with all the rowdy abuse with a frozen smile that never faltered. We reckoned he was actually deaf.

Towards the end of the morning, we would be shown a serial with a cliff-hanger ending, designed to get another sixpence from us the following Saturday. All the noisy while, the sweating manager and his thugs, who were technically ushers and usherettes, would stride up and down the aisles with canes, ready to swish our tender bodies whenever crowd control required a bit of GBH. I usually managed to avoid the worst of any havoc by mounting the back of my seat and stepping adroitly from one row to the next like a tightrope walker, until I reached the rear stalls. I wasn't the only one who had the balancing skills, but I did claim to be the fastest and most agile. I never caused major injury to any ears, eyes or scruffy scalps that got in the way.

In the end, the many distractions and constant struggle to decode the on-screen gibberish began to sap my enthusiasm for those juvenile Saturday mornings. It was time to get to grips again with my more mature researches – only by this time, a major change was taking place at home.

I came home from school one Friday to be given the shocking news that my father had to go into hospital for an operation the following Monday. My reaction was predictable and loud. 'Why am I always the last to hear about everything?' I complained, without waiting for an answer. Because I was only the baby of the family and always would be, so I could be ignored. I might as well go and live somewhere else because I didn't matter to anyone here. Nobody cared about me, and so on and on, with more of the usual guff.

Barbara stopped me in mid-flow. 'How clever of you, little brother!' she said. 'You are quite right, you don't matter here and no one does care about you because we're too busy caring about our Vati, who does matter. So go to live in hell for all we care. I'll lend you the bus fare.'

I spluttered some more, red in the face, and stamped my foot on the lino like my mother sometimes did when she lost her temper. This wasn't the first time Barbara had called my bluff. She was managing to be deadly accurate about me more and more often. I hated it. There was no getting away from it; my sister was hateful and smart.

She hadn't finished. 'Come to think of it, I doubt they'll let you in. Even Satan has his standards. Only don't come snivelling back here, will you, at least not until you turn human. Now go away and good riddance – and don't bang the door!'

With her last words ringing in my ears, I fell over myself, tried to look dignified, and banged the front door behind me. Hard. The uncarpeted landing retaliated and banged against my bum just as hard. Actually, I think it was more of a suicide attempt than a fall because I was now struggling with an attack of growing pains and anxiety about my father's health. When I saw him later, he appreciated the extra-special hug I gave him, though, oddly enough, he hardly seemed to notice my genuine, but also clever, look of penitence. I was so self-centred, I'm ashamed to remember, that I realised almost at once that

I needed more rehearsal. After sparing a moment to bless the genius who invented mirrors, I returned defiantly to the family. And managed to do so without banging any bit of my anatomy.

Our mother was by her very nature strong and positive, yet she couldn't hold back the tears once Dad left the room to freshen up for dinner. Tom took refuge behind one of his deadpan looks that stopped all emotion leaking out. You could never tell what he thought – or even if he thought. The true surprise was our hard-as-nails sister, who rushed in and out of her bedroom constantly, crying buckets. It was unnerving.

It was left to me, as the only sensible one, to bring a bit of balance into the proceedings. I tried to persuade Tom, Barbara and Mother that operations were ten a penny these days. Everybody had one sooner or later to make them better, so we should just jolly well get on with it. 'And our father isn't just anyone,' I went on. I was getting into my stride now, and they were paying attention finally. 'Let's remember he was a hero in the last war, never mind this one, with an Iron Cross and every-thing to prove it, and he got pneumonia and they operated that clean away. So how can he not get better this time? Easy.'

And for a final touch, I added, 'Let us not make a mountain in a molehill.'

Brilliant – but only Tom was left in the room. The other two had found better things to do in the kitchen.

Supper that Friday turned out to be surprisingly animated. Our father was usually exhausted after a day at work and had recently got in the habit of changing into a dressing gown, ready for an early exit to bed if he felt too tired. This night was different. To our delight, because we all watched him, he managed to eat more than half his meal and keep it down. He clearly wanted to enjoy himself so we took our cue and followed his mood – as was, no doubt, his intention. The talk was lively and covered the current war situation – always a must in those days – but he also started talking about other subjects. By the end of the meal our cares had been magically forgotten, as they were the following evening – until he began talking calmly about his condition and calling it by its proper name. After the initial shock of hearing the word 'cancer', and a few more tears from Mother, she relaxed and held his hand and he smiled.

Barbara and Tom already knew the dreaded word, but to me 'cancer' was just a sign of the zodiac. I looked it up and there it was, though nowhere near his birthday, or mine. He was born in Aquarius and I was next door but one from him in Aries. However, it said both of us were brave and then I really knew I was just like him.

On the Sunday before going to hospital, Father went to bed early, even earlier than my own bedtime. For the first, and I think the only, time in my life, I went to tuck him into bed instead of the other way round. I told him a funny story I had learned at school, and he followed up with one from his early days that I hadn't heard before and was even funnier. When we finally said our good nights, I patted him on his back for encouragement like he always did me, and tiptoed out.

Later on, in bed, I was just dropping off myself when Tom came clumping into the room – never mind the noise – and threw himself on his bed with a splutter that sounded like crying. Oh no! Not another one to cheer up, I thought, but he didn't want to know. He flung himself round to turn his back on me and hit the wall hard. Serve him right, I thought. Five minutes later his snivelling changed to snoring that grew louder than a doodle-bug and kept me awake half the night. I wondered if every family was as crazy.

Hospital Monday finally came. Tom and I hugged our father good luck after breakfast and left for school, while Mother and Barbara fussed over him until well after he was comfortably settled in his hospital bed, enjoying an inevitable cup of tea, and ready for the next day, when a team of doctors would cut away half his stomach.

CHAPTER 8

Vati

The first information we had after his operation confirmed that it had been a success, but Vati would need a spell of intensive care before he could leave hospital. Then he would need a substantial period of convalescence. The news was quite good enough to cheer us all up.

Mother hardly moved from his bedside during those early days, and often stayed late into the evenings, hoping he would be awake for periods when they could take comfort in each other's presence. Tom and I were usually in bed by the time she came home, and on our way to school again before she got up the next morning.

Barbara took charge in the crisis. Tom and I were recruited as her underlings and, somehow, an unfamiliar truce blossomed between the three of us. We were more than ready to do her bidding without argument or even raised voices. Spooky.

I had only one complaint. The two of them had been allowed to visit Vati in hospital almost at once as a priority. So why not me, I *knatsch*-ed. It wasn't fair. I was given stupid excuses like 'only two visitors at a time', which was rubbish because Mum was always there as well and that made three. Or 'children aren't allowed', when I had already established that, at thirteen, I was not a child; or 'you might get upset'. Well, of course I might. I was!

Direct action was my only option. Mother agreed to take a postcard to him in a sealed envelope marked Private & Confidential, pleading my rights and enclosing a free gift to help him decide: this was a personally signed drawing of a polecat, expertly traced from *Brehm's Thierleben*, volume one. The drawing would impress him with my skill as an artist with a future.

It worked! Vati must have ordered his wife to obey him immediately, for the very next day the two of us set off by bus. As usual, I charged ahead to claim front seats on the upper deck to get the best views en route to the Royal Homoeopathic Hospital in Great Ormond Street. However, I soon realised my fascinating commentary on the London scene on the way didn't fascinate my mother. She was worried about the visit and worried by the fact that I'd been stupid and showed no sign of understanding the ordeal Vati had had to endure over the past months. I realise now what I could not realise then – how afraid both my parents were.

Somehow, I binned all further irrelevant drivel from my mind and offered her what she most needed: my full attention. The top deck was empty so we lapsed into our comfortable Germlish – the two-in-one family patois. We had a nice cuddle and I willed her to go on for as long as she needed. And she did, movingly.

She spoke, not for the first time, of Vati's love for his children, of her love for Vati and especially of the extra support he now needed from each one of us until, God willing, he would be well again. She held my hand all the way until we got off the bus, and then thanked me. I couldn't make out why exactly; perhaps it was because I had understood for once and had listened with my heart as well as my head – though, admittedly, with one eye still tracking the sights on the Euston Road.

We mounted a grand staircase at the hospital as she continued to remind me – we were back to her best English – not to expect too much from him; to pretend not to notice that he looked a little weaker than before the operation; that he might be asleep; not to be too lively or try to make him laugh, but just look pleased to see him and make him feel good. I now see this was the anxious chatter of those who love and who fear the worst for those they love.

I was already fully in tune with her anxieties. At home we talked of little else but our father. Fortunately, I could empathise perfectly with him because of my own past ordeals: my broken arm, the unpleasantness of mumps and tonsillitis, sprained ankles, unwarranted GBH from dentists, frequent bread-and-dripping attacks, physics – my list was long.

When we reached the top of the staircase, an impressively designed plaque directed us to 'VAUGHAN MORGAN WARD'. It instantly grabbed my attention for a lot longer than it took to read. Without knowing why, I suddenly fell into a curious panic. Nothing existed for me at that moment but the name on the plaque. The other visitors passing into the ward,

Mother standing right next to me, Vati who was supposed to be my overriding priority, all of them flashed out of my mind, obliterated from my consciousness. I saw nothing but that name. I became helplessly, hopelessly obsessed and found myself shouting the name on the plaque aloud.

And in my anxiety, I did not even shout it correctly!

'FORGAN MORGAN!' I blurted out against my will, turning heads and turning puce. It sounded ugly and wrong so I tried again, anxious this time to keep the volume down, but 'VAWN MAWN!' brought no relief.

Mother, no stranger to my occasional bouts of insanity, nudged my arm. I managed somehow to hurl myself back to reality and give her a big smile.

'FORGAN *GUTEN MORGAN FRAU SACHS*,' I said with a German accent, hoping for a laugh. But her mind was elsewhere.

It was all unnerving, and indeed embarrassing. Here I was on this very special day, with my poor mother opening her heart to me, and all I could manage was to indulge in some half-witted verbal gymnastics. As we passed through the door to the ward, she remained calm enough to point Vati out for me among two endless rows of beds.

'*Da ist er!*' she said, pointing.

I took a moment to focus. 'Oh, no!' I groaned. 'He's asleep. Will they let us wake him up?'

She pointed again. 'No, *Liebchen*, not that one. Vati is…' and she counted: '*Eins, zwei, drei, weiter noch* – further, you see? Come.'

I shook my head. 'No. That's not him – where is he?'

'Is Vati, Anderle [the diminutive of Andreas, my German

name], sure! Is Vati,' she said again and nudged my reluctant body in his direction. 'You pretend, yes?' she whispered urgently.

Pretend? How could I pretend such a lie to some unknown stranger? And yet she was right! I was looking at my father, but not a father I had ever seen before. His face was grey and skeletal, his sunken eyes opened hardly wide enough to see us at the door. He tried to raise himself on his pillow with a hand of skin and bone too weak to wave in our direction. I realised I looked shocked. And, worse, maybe he saw me looking shocked. I calculated it would take ten to twelve seconds to reach his bed, without rushing. Ten seconds in which to abandon my unconvincing plea of 'That's not him' and become my father's son again. Ten seconds in which to pretend as I had never pretended before.

Swallowing hard to push back a lump in my throat that was about to launch a thousand baby tears, I gurned my face into a look of pleasure – as though I had only seen him at that very moment – offered a glittering smile that highlighted my eyes and teeth to best effect, raised two hands in a merry wave, and strode jauntily towards him. When I reached his bedside, I gave him a loving but careful embrace.

That first visit to the hospital turned out to be my only one. Mother confessed later she should have realised I might have been too upset to cope – and guess who tried to comfort her with a predictable 'Too deranged, you mean'? Barbara was being her usual self.

When I look back on my father's illness and my ridiculous 'Forgan Morgan' moment, I realise that humankind cannot bear too much reality, as T. S. Eliot put it. We all seek escape. Showbiz is escape, the fairy-tale world where reality is no match for fantasy. And so it became in my case. I didn't need some Hollywood talent scout to confirm that my performance had been a master class in overacting of Oscar-winning potential. If I could be shocked one moment and a doting son the next, I had what it takes. Soon I'd be pitched to fame and fortune as a star who had even more fans than King Kong.

The day arrived at last for Vati's homecoming. Three preferred members of my family were to collect him that afternoon. I, of course, was excluded from that pilgrimage – no surprise there – but was graciously considered to have recovered enough from my paranoid-like spat caused by feeling excluded to accept a really exciting challenge: the responsibility of putting the kettle on to boil the moment they walked through the front door. How lucky can one get?

They took forever to arrive. I supposed that it being wartime, Dad, being walking wounded rather than stretcher case, would not have been entitled to a ride in an ambulance, and a taxi was most likely beyond our means. Apart from an impossible walk home, it only left the underground or a bus – long and uncomfortable trips for someone in his condition. When they did finally make it, I was much less shocked by his appearance than I had been when I saw him in hospital.

Once he had got his breath back and caught sight of the boiling kettle, his eyes lit up and sparkled into the brightest of smiles with a happy, 'Ah, cup of tea, yes!'

My knees buckled in gratitude. I was witnessing a miracle!

My father, a mere foreign enemy alien refugee, had been magi-cally elevated to the ranks of the God-selected breed of true Englishmen by cracking their secret code of ah-cup-of-tea-yes! If true – and I knew it was – his baptism into the real super-race would include all his family, and carry with it a guarantee that everything would work out jolly well top-notch OK in the end. With a helping hand to get him into his slippers, dressing gown, favourite armchair and that nice cuppa in his hand, we celebrated his homecoming; we were happy, relieved, and we jumped for joy.

The time Dad needed to recover meant he could not work and so our income diminished. We realised it would be a long time before he could return to work. Barbara, meanwhile, had put her ambitions for further education on hold and taken a secretarial job in a construction company world-famous for reinforced, or was it pre-stressed – who knows, who cares? – concrete.

Tom and I had been persuaded to give up our pocket money pro tem. Tom left school at last to his great delight, decided to become an apprentice at a local tool-manufacturing outfit for a low wage (probably not much more than his surrendered pocket money), 60 per cent of which he tinkled ostentatiously into the household treasury jar. It was very noble of him. I was still held in custody at school, and could do little more than apologise for my inability to contribute to the family coffers – but just wait until I joined the real world, when I'd show people what I was made of.

Being work-shy in those wartime years was nowhere near as popular as it is nowadays, but I managed all right – until Mum, my supposedly best friend and normally a pushover where her favourite little munchkin was concerned, rented me out as slave labour to the local population. I became a garden weeder, dog walker, potato peeler, shopping carrier. If I'd been small enough she'd have hired me out as a chimney sweeper, too. Fortunately I had learned the meaning of duty from Capt. Drummond, not to mention 'By jingo', as a proper English boy would say, and doing what you must do if you are one of the 'noblest English whose blood is fet from fathers of war-proof'. So I was soon earning more than my pocket money and making a healthy profit of more than several shillings. I tinkled modestly into that jar. No way was I going to have a rotten brother nobler than me.

Even Mum was part of our family workforce. She got herself involved in the evenings, crocheting little bags and purses for a ladies' wholesale outfitters. It involved scraping together the bus fare to the West End to collect the raw materials and scraping together another bus fare later to deliver the skilfully finished articles. It was the most boring job in the world but she never complained.

Meanwhile Dad was busy doing all the right things to recover and maintain his energies, with regular medical checks, plenty of rest, careful diet and exercise, and eventually returning to work part-time, to start with, for the ever-supportive Messrs Leroi and Flesch.

With all our comings and goings, it became quite an event for the entire family to get together, and I missed the easy access I was used to with my dad. It was more like an appointment system now. If I was free, he might be at a hospital appointment, and when he was free, I could be polishing somebody's silver. I certainly missed his expert guidance in dealing with some aspects of homework. On the other hand, that guidance became a lot less welcome when he chose discipline, or even worse, self-discipline, as a subject he deemed relevant. He was still very ill so we certainly didn't have the same amount of fun and good stories as of old. Sometimes I got a bit fed up with the lack of laughs and generally not being appreciated by anyone. Poor me.

Teenagers can be very selfish. At the time my father was so ill, I became interested in roller skates I didn't have, in black magic with Dennis Wheatley, and in messing about with shifty mates on the Heath. Or without them. I dawdled home from school on my own, kicking empty milk bottles and even ignoring potential shrapnel benefits. On top of that, I cultivated a growing disenchantment with virtually every subject I was being taught at school, as well as with nine out of ten of the teachers themselves. That was the worst of all. The best of all was falling asleep during physics and not being found out. But at least I never played truant again.

My sister got it about right when she said (in my presence, would you believe!), 'Have you noticed, Mother dear, that your little darling is growing sideways instead of up?'

Being disenchanted with school led to a drama. It was inevitable that sooner or later a confidential document from my shockingly disloyal school would inform my parents of their son's unaccountable academic decline. The document included a hefty folder of revision studies to be completed over the summer holidays. It fell into my mother's hands a day or so before I brought my report home. The similarity between the two accounts was uncanny.

My mother made me sit down. Oh boy, was she angry! I had never experienced anything like it. I was wilting under her onslaught, knowing that every complaint she was making was true. She was agonising whether or not to share the dreadful news with her husband. Did I have any idea of the damage it would cause if he knew his own son was letting him down so badly? We owed him our full support as never before, she went on. Without it, he might one day just give up and not even *want* to get well again. And then he could die. That possibility had never occurred to me.

I couldn't speak. It took long moments just to get my breath back, I was holding back tears. My mother did not cry. She was just determined her husband should stay as proud of his children now as he had always been.

'So what do you say?'

I was beyond saying anything. All I could do was stare at the floor and snivel pathetically. She took that as a positive response. 'Good. But you understand, don't you, that taking up the biggest challenge of your life will mean putting your heart and soul into getting better marks than ever, so that Vati never need be told of what can stay our little secret?' She smiled and handed me the deadly folder and added, 'I know you can do it, yes?'

I half nodded in reply, more in hope than confidence.

'So the sooner you start, the better it will be, yes?' I nodded again, and she added, 'Like now!'

Another 'Yes' and another nod. Things were getting tougher by the minute.

'This minute, yes?'

Oh no! That made three nods and four yes's! What about my holidays? What was she doing to me?

'And in your spare moments, which I will make sure you have between your studies, there will be time to spend with Vati and do whatever he asks and cheer each other up until both of you have fully recovered, his body and your mind – you understand what I mean. And, most important of all: never, ever, trouble him with your revisings. Ask somebody else. And meanwhile, no more loafing around. Good! I shall keep in very close attention with your work, as I'm sure you want me to.'

She folded her hands in front of her, looked fondly at her repentant son and said, 'So, let us look forward to the end of this week when we will see the good results of your first efforts.'

I slumped further into my chair while she, with the happiest smile I had seen on her face for a long time, went off, only to bring me – after all that – two sherbet dabs.

I think it would be fair to say that I did have enough sense, if not enough sensitivity, to understand what had gone wrong and to try to make amends. I tackled previously neglected school-work well enough to impress my mother a few days later. Only physics remained too ghastly to contemplate. Otherwise, I was back on course and proud of succeeding without asking for help from anyone, most of the time.

Dad's health, too, continued to improve. He was putting on weight again, while peace, quiet and rest were still a high priority for him – always monitored nicely by Mum. The time he could spend with his children was understandably rationed. It was an eye-opener for me to find I was not my father's favourite child at all – just one of three. Accepting that demotion was tough, oh it was, but with my amazing generosity I quickly learned not to bear a grudge. All right, so I was not his top little treasure, but he was, and always would be, my top big one.

Only once during my brain-warping studies did I allow myself a minor slip by asking him for the help my mother had so strictly ordered to be *verboten*. He was 100 per cent unco-operative. I eventually learned that my mother had gone back on our arrangement by revealing to him quite early on the full content of the treacherous report that had brought about my fall from grace. It seemed I had lost the 'favourite' label with my only other parent as well.

I had a lot to learn.

It took years.

CHAPTER 9

A Wounded Bird

One weekend in September 1943, I came home and made my way up our stairs for an urgent visit to the loo. Coming out again, I noticed what looked like a scrap of rubbish flapping about between the two panes of the open sash window. It turned out to be a forlorn little bird caught in the narrow space and struggling feebly to haul itself out. My hand and fingers were too clumsy to attempt a rescue. Dad was the only one at home and, although it was not one of his best days, he was more than ready to help.

After fetching my book on birds from my bedroom, we tiptoed back into the toilet. The poor thing was still there. Dad's fingers were slimmer than mine, but it still needed the additional use of a spoon to help lever the victim gently to safety and, even more gently, onto the closed lavatory seat for a rest, some breadcrumbs and a hastily wiped ashtray of water. I had identified our guest as a swift, a migratory species. The bird should have been on its way to Africa, flying non-stop and partying on a million tasty insects en route, rather than making do with mouldy breadcrumbs and a wet fag end on a loo lid.

While I kept a close watch on our quivering visitor, Dad cautiously dismantled its lethal window trap. For some minutes, not a breath, not a wing flap. Then, finally, we saw some signs of life, as the swift teetered awkwardly towards the edge of the loo, fluttered its wings – and plunged more or less head first onto the lino, bewildered but still in one piece.

Not nearly as bewildered as I was. 'It can't fly!' I whispered urgently. 'Is it broken wings, Dad?'

'Maybe, maybe not. Hmm, nothing else in your animal book?'

I shook my head.

'Well, I could be wrong but I seem to remember that the legs of some birds – like swifts, perhaps – are too weak to push themselves up into the air. Yes, come closer, take a look – there's hardly anything of them – can you see?'

He was right.

'I think what they probably have to do first is to drop down, from a cliff or a rooftop or, well, not from a lavatory seat, anyway.'

'Not high enough!' I agreed, nodding wisely.

'Exactly, drop down to a point where the air pressure against the wings is strong enough to stop them falling and start pushing them up instead for their journey.'

Brilliant! It would be a risky manoeuvre but what other choice did we have except throw the poor creature into the air and hope for the best? We ruled that out and decided to rely on nature and the bird itself to know best and take over. So Dad, ever so carefully, moved the bird close to the window sill's edge and then retreated to join me, fingers crossed as we prayed for a good outcome.

We didn't have long to wait. Without a second thought, it seemed, our fearless hero courted certain death by flinging itself off the sill. Then it recovered almost at once in a dramatic arc that carried it high, as Dad had predicted, and away as swiftly as a swift.

Wow! We watched until it disappeared into the blue, surely chirping a grateful thanks to the window sills of the world – and perhaps even to us. Although I had long been aware that my father knew practically everything there was to know in the world, it was still a surprise to discover he was an expert on birds as well. I couldn't help but congratulate him.

'Oh, thank you,' he said modestly. 'But I think I need to sit down. Give me a hand, will you?'

In all the excitement I had not noticed that our drama had exhausted him. He was unsteady and looked pale, with half-awake eyes, so I took his arm to help him up the rest of the stairs. He stopped me. 'No, no. Just let me stay here. A few minutes' rest on the vacated throne of a heroic little bird would be an honour.' He lowered himself onto the closed toilet seat. 'By the way,' he went on. 'I'm really not as clever as you think. You know a lot more about birds than I do. No, I believe the way we solved our tricky problem today had less to do with swifts and more to do with – dare I mention it – physics.'

I stared at him goggle-eyed. 'Physics?'

He nodded rather smugly. 'You've heard of the famous apple, haven't you? Isaac Newton? Gravity? Equilibrium, energy, laws of motion and all the rest of it?'

'But you once told me you hated physics!'

'Did I? No, I don't think so. I said physics is something of a mystery to me, too – I certainly said that. But what would we have done this afternoon without it, eh?' He drew closer. 'Wasn't it physics that helped us save a little life?'

That stopped me in my tracks.

'Now, make us cup of tea,' he went on, 'and I'll join you when I've got my breath back.'

I left him in peace. After I had the tea ready just as he liked it (no milk, no sugar for him, plenty of both for me) and he hadn't appeared, I went down and called through the door but there was no answer to my 'Dad, your tea's getting cold!'

I was about to try again when I heard a sound that everyone in the family had hoped never, ever to hear again. It was the sound of Father being sick.

My hand stayed in mid-air for a long time before it dropped to my side again. I stared bleakly at the door and did nothing except panic. He hadn't been sick for weeks and weeks. I'll go in to him. Where's Mum? No, he'll come out on his own. Is it locked? He's fine, must be. I'll wait in the kitchen. I'll stay here. Smash the door down! Rescue. Do nothing. No. People are often sick. Fetch him out. Why isn't Mum home?

I was leaning against the wall by now, sliding slowly to the floor, eyes shut, hugging my knees and feeling sorry for myself.

'What are you doing?' asked my father, as he came out from the toilet, holding on to the door for support.

'Er, waiting for you.'

'Ah yes, the tea.' He began to take a deep breath but gave up halfway.

I got to my feet. 'Are you all right?' I asked, succumbing to the world's most stupid question when someone clearly isn't. He nodded benignly and I followed him into the kitchen. Once there, he ignored the tea and opted for a rest instead. I helped settle him down in his armchair with a rug. 'I'll tell Mum when she gets back.'

'Tell her what?' he asked.

'Well – that you've been sick again.'

He sat up. 'I haven't been sick since I came out of hospital – you know that.'

An 'oh' was all I managed.

'Although you are not altogether wrong. I did overdo things this afternoon – my own fault, should have known better by now. But it's nothing sinister, you know, so let us not worry your mother about it. It would only upset her.'

It certainly would, I thought. 'I won't say anything,' I promised.

'Anyway, we have a much happier story to tell, haven't we?' He settled back again, his eyes beginning to close.

'Shall I turn the light off?' I asked.

He gave half a nod and I tiptoed out of the room, wondering why my father's explanation left me feeling uneasy.

Mum returned home soon afterwards and sensed the change in Dad; she needed no hints from me. She had no difficulty persuading him to have an early supper, an early night, a lie-in in the morning and a late Sunday breakfast with the family.

Her plan worked wonders. He was certainly livelier and more relaxed than the day before – perhaps than any day before – and a two-egg (!) omelette Barbara managed to rustle up from out of nowhere was an extra bonus for him. The highlight of the morning was Dad telling us about the swift. From the first word to the last, he gave a tender, beautifully worded, almost poetic account. We hardly breathed; we hardly moved. Even I kept quiet for once, but I glowed with pride when he credited me as the ideal partner in our two-man team.

Later that day, I took myself off to a quiet corner and squirmed in embarrassment as I recalled my earlier impulse to break down the lavatory door. What had I been thinking of? Was it really panic – or had I been planning to rescue my ailing father from imminent death and destruction in yet another 'showbiz' attempt to win personal glory as his saviour? I could hardly bear to be alone with myself.

The autumn weeks that followed were sunny ones in our home. There was less of the daily tension that had been dogging us for so long. One late evening at the very beginning of December, when Tom and I were already in bed, we heard Father tuning his cello in the living room. It was the first time in months that he had done more than merely look at the instrument, but with Christmas only a few weeks away he was clearly eager to practise. A wartime Christmas was necessarily a muted affair, with presents, plum pudding, decorations and other trimmings and treats often in short supply or missing altogether. We could bear all that, but the idea of a cello lying silent in a corner would have been unbearable.

Dad didn't let us down. He played our favourite carols, both English and German ones (all with a Jewish lilt, of course); we sang them; and Barbara – who had saved up enough money to buy her own cello – managed to cover both skills at the same time. The magic was there, as always, and the year ended on a much happier note than expected.

It was not until halfway through January that the cancer took its grip on our dad again. Dr Manasse came more than once to discuss the future with him, Mum and possibly Barbara as well. I was only told what I needed to know: that Dad would be staying home and only had to visit the hospital for one or two tests, if that.

As the days went on, Dad had to spend more and more time in bed. I could see him only when he felt strong enough. All our family's birthdays were spread over the first months of the year and Dad became visibly weaker as each one went by. Tom's was 28 January, three days before Dad's. By that time, Dad had lost more weight again. We were all at home on Mum's birthday at the end of February when he asked to see each one of us children separately in his bedroom. I had no idea why. Tom and I waited in the hallway as Barbara went in first.

A few minutes later, she came out in tears and ran straight to her room. Tom was next and came out also crying. After some persuasion from Mum, I went in, too. Dad was in bed with his head raised on a pillow. He explained as gently as he could that he had not much longer to live.

After that, I couldn't take in anything he was saying. I knew it was all very important, about Mother and the family and looking after one another, but all I managed was to nod a few times at what I hoped were the right moments, and do my best to cry like the others as I left his room. I couldn't manage even that.

A fortnight later, on 13 March, a message arrived to say Tom had been taken to hospital after an accident at his workbench. Four fingers of one hand had been sliced off. Mum and Barbara both rushed out to get to him. Our father died nine days later – aged fifty-nine.

CHAPTER 10

Surviving

The loss of a much-loved husband together with Mother's desperate concern for Tom, who had been moved to a hospital much further away from home, left her with little else but grief beyond measure. Barbara, too, was inconsolable yet never failed to love and care for Mother and Tom. These must have been the worst days of our mother's life. And Barbara's, too. And Tom's.

It was different for me. I was secretly ashamed to be the one least affected among us as I had barely understood the gravity of my father's condition while he was alive – something that had been so obvious to everyone else. And now it was too late. It took years before I could begin to revisit those long-gone days of 1944, and learn to mourn properly.

Meanwhile Tom's life had come to a standstill. He found it hard to bear the phantom pains in his lost fingers and just trying to tie a shoelace could reduce him to tears. He became depressed, resentful, angry and despairing. Luckily, he was sent to a hospital renowned for its treatment of war-wounded servicemen. It was Tom's good fortune to be a patient there, and he did well. When he returned home, he had to endure more treatment and rehabilitation for many months. Then one day he fell in love with a Welsh girl and married her.

Barbara had left home before Tom to work as an interpreter for the American occupation forces in Germany. While there, she met a German-American and they soon married. It was goodbye to England and hello to America. Meanwhile my mum and I stayed in London and continued to look after each other nicely, though she did seem curiously indifferent to my needs at a time when the merciless force of nature was pushing me through an adolescence I feared might last even longer than childhood.

A retired PE teacher in whom I had once confided strongly advised that an extended adolescence might be of interest to arty-farty nancy boys, but should be avoided by all red-blooded men intent on a proper career in sport – which I wasn't. I decided I was going to pursue a very different career, having concluded I was an exceptionally talented performer. I had ideas above my station and no evidence as yet to back my claims of talent.

When the war ended in 1945, more than a million people celebrated in the streets. Crowds massed in Trafalgar Square and around Buckingham Palace. King George VI and Queen Elizabeth, accompanied by Winston Churchill, waved from its balcony. Princess Elizabeth and her sister Princess Margaret were allowed to wander incognito among the crowds and take part in the celebrations.

We, the loyal members of the North London Emergency Secondary School, were soon rebranded as pukka students of the

William Ellis lot, the spineless cowards who had panicked away from the realities of blitz, bombs and blackouts to live the life of Riley in the green and pleasant Shangri-La of Leighton Buzzard.

Actually, some of the spineless Ellis cowards turned out to be reasonably human when I got to know them. There was one, though, who was known to be something of a bully. He was much bigger than me, spotty faced and lacking in charm, so he was understandably more interested in smaller fry like me on whom to perform his dastardly deeds. One day he approached me in the playground with some horrid words of abuse to test my reaction and build up the courage to hit me. He found the courage. I found the jitters.

Quick thinking saved my life, however melodramatic that might sound. In less than a nanosecond I changed my blubbering look of fear into a friendly smile that made me look like a first-class fan of his witty banter. This confused him, which gave me precious moments to consider my response. But he rallied sooner than expected by calling me a dirty little German Jewish pig.

So I hit him.

His mistake had been to push his ugly face close to my nice one, but instead of my little fist landing on his primeval chin, it shot up a couple of inches of its own accord and dislocated his glasses hard enough to bring tears to his eyes and alter the bridge of his nose. He retired from the fray with the proper humiliation of a loser, leaving me to console my porridged fist and trembling knees. Oh boy, was I glad to be alive.

At home that evening, I gloried in my conquest. Hitting a comparative stranger, particularly a big stupid one, was a first for me – and defeating him with one blow deserved a good gloat for a while – but later, while sipping my bedtime cocoa, I had second thoughts. As a sensitive, caring fellow with little prejudice against my inferiors, I felt that my response to some silly words from an ignorant clod who knew no better was unworthy. I had used my considerable power all right, but what is power without mercy? No, I would need to make amends.

I put pen to paper and composed a friendly apology. I identified myself as a humble but dedicated student of linguistics and, from the best of motives, offered to advise him on a more acceptable use of our beautiful English tongue, pointing out some of the words he had chosen to mis-choose.

I suggested that 'dirty', for example, was a misnomer in a situation where its antonym might have been nearer the truth. I was not trying to confuse the poor boy with a tricky seven-letter word like antonym – not really, anyway.

The second word, 'little', on the other hand – credit where credit was due – was excellently chosen, with its nice touch of gentle humour targeted at me. 'German' was also a faultless choice – no quarrels there. 'Jewish' – also good, though only half-right in my case, but bless him, how could he have known of my mongrel credentials?

And, of course, 'pig' was a lovely, lovely three-letter word, even though considered impolite when referring to actual people. When linked to 'Jewish', however, it would suggest an ignorance of kosher practices that could offend.

I fizzed up the message with a playful touch of satire way over his head, sealed the envelope and, next morning, got my best pal

David (braver than me) to locate his whereabouts at school and drop my document into his prehistoric hands.

By the end of that day I received a quite disgraceful – and anonymous, can you believe – written reply in ridiculously pretentious calligraphy which was no doubt meant to impress me, but didn't. David and I spent a long time trying to decipher the rotten stuff.

See if you can make sense of it (reply not required, thank you):

Hitting & Faux-Swiftian Satire are the only Repartee GOD Grants the Inarticulate.

The real surprise was that this evil creature turned out to be a top-ranking William Ellis sixth-form swotting shitty A-level know-all!

It took me hours to surface from the injustice and start hunting for one of those silver-lining things people talk about. And – you may not believe this – there it was! Not just one silver lining, but two of them, tucked in the heart of the previous day's nanosecond!

When I had changed my expression at the speed of light to throw the villain off his guard, it was not the first time I had done something of the sort. I had done the same when I saw my father in his hospital bed. I did not speak of the latter to my new friend, David, but I couldn't help gloating a bit about how I had stopped time, changed the look on my face and thumped the William Ellis gorilla.

It is time to say a bit more about David. We had met one day during dinner hour when he was at a nearby table with some other pupils, who were listening spellbound to what he had to say and ignoring their food. I had turned to my immediate munching neighbour. 'D'you know who that is over there, talking to those blokes?' I asked.

He looked up momentarily. 'Yeah.' He burped and carried on munching.

'What's he telling them?'

He looked up again. 'Dunno. He does films.'

'Films? You mean he's a film star? Whew! What's his name?'

'Who cares?' he said and left the table.

I wasn't going to be satisfied with that. As soon as the film star's rapt audience started to disperse, I wandered casually over and introduced myself.

'Hello! My name's Sachs. I'm in 5C.' Then, more tentatively, 'I hear you're in films.'

He gave me a world-weary look. 'Listen,' he offered with the narrowed eyes and wrinkled brow of a Humphrey Bogart. 'If you want me to get you into movies, don't even ask, OK?' And he got up and left.

It wasn't the best of introductions but, as it turned out, an obsession with showbiz was not the only thing we shared. We were more or less the same age; lived not far from each other; each had a sister and a brother, and a good mother, and no smelly cats. Critically, we had each seen our father die. David's father had died not long before mine. That alone was enough to forge a growing friendship over the following weeks and, indeed, years.

David was, of course, no film star. His short career was limited to non-speaking crowd work, with occasional words to speak for a few extra shillings.

It was, on the whole, a disappointing CV but, as I got to know him, I couldn't help but appreciate his determination. His was the sort of character I could respect, so I gave him a thumbs-up.

'We've got something else in common then, haven't we, eh?' I said to him, one day.

'What?'

'Ideas above our station,' I said in my offhand witty way, hoping for an all-pals-together grin.

'I like to think of it as ambition,' he replied, po-faced.

It felt like a slap on the wrist for me. But I forgave him without necessarily saying so, and we tackled our final year of school captivity as good pals, doing not too much class work to carry us through to our exams, after which we could escape at last into the world proper.

David's ambitions were different from mine. An actor's life was not for him. He was fascinated by every aspect of cinema, from its humble beginnings of half a century before to its technical progress. Appearing in front of a camera was his way of finding a toehold into the world behind it. He knew I was far less focused on my future than he was on his, but he still offered to introduce me to Aida Foster. I was about to ask who she was, but he beat me to it.

'She runs a stage school in Golders Green. I'm on her books for film work only.'

Aida Foster had founded her school in 1929 almost as a hobby, but she became famous for supplying many of the pantomime 'babes' who took part in Christmas shows.

I was wondering what 'on her books' meant.

'We get on OK, so I might get you on her books as well, and Jean Simmons could even be around.'

'Who?'

'You don't know Jean Simmons? Oh dear, oh Lord. *Way to the Stars*? No? She still comes in for classes sometimes.' He broke into song: '"Let him go or let him tarry, let him sink or let him swim" – got a lovely voice on her – "he doesn't care for me and I don't care for him." She does that in *Way to the Stars* and she'll be off to Hollywood with a big contract any day now, you mark my words. And you've never heard of her!'

'Not really.'

'I wonder at your ignorance. Well, you can catch up when *Great Expectations* opens in the West End. You've heard of the West End?'

I nodded.

'Can't go wrong with David Lean, can you? Best director in the world. Genius! He knows a thing or two, I can tell you.'

I was pop-eyed by now. What was going on? *Way to the Stars*, genius, *Great Expectations*, Hollywood contracts! There was almost too much to take in.

Thanks to David, I did get on Aida Foster's books, a deal which required Mum's permission and me having to promise Miss Foster that every future engagement for the rest of my life would be booked through her. She must have had a lot of faith in my talent just by talking to me. Brilliant. I sensed that my journey to the top was going to be a pretty smooth one.

My first professional appearance actually followed not long after with *Hue & Cry*, the first of the smash-hit Ealing comedies made after the war. My role was to cover two days' filming outside Cannon Street station, much of which was a bomb site. Miss Foster said I would be a working-class schoolboy in a demanding role that required clear diction and extreme physical dexterity to cope with tons of rubble and mangled railway tracks while pursuing the villains – child's play for someone of my calibre. I was, of course, not alone in this critical action sequence. About 200 to 300 other boys of more or less the same age were supporting me. David was one of them.

I must have been favourably noticed by the Ealing casting department as, some months later, they wanted to use me again. This time the role was a working-class schoolboy of roughly my own age in *Nicholas Nickleby* – the classic Victorian novel destined for even greater fame as a cinematic masterpiece, again from Ealing Studios. Unlike the hundreds of boys featured in *Hue & Cry*, we lads at Dotheboys Hall were fewer than two dozen so I had a chance to stand out from the crowd.

When *Hue & Cry* reached our local Odeon in 1947, we were eager to review our efforts. David actually caught a glimpse of himself among the 300 others. I didn't manage to do the same, which was a pity as I thought I was good in the part.

Having made my mark, I had the brilliant idea of approaching the casting department for a modest speaking role I might offer to compose in the inimitable style of the hugely favoured author. Even a single one of his masterly sentences properly presented, preferably in close-up, might be a step up the ladder to success. I asked David what he thought.

'A hopeless pitch down the ladder to obscurity,' he said, and went back to the book he was reading. It hurt. It really hurt but, I had to admit, usefully so, once I had regained my composure. Later that day I plucked up the courage to ask him, 'Did you by any chance mean that, er, conceit is not ah, er, the same as confidence?'

He barely raised his eyes. 'Ten out of ah, er, ten,' he said and went back to another book he was reading.

Lesson learned. So, in the end, I didn't ask, and I didn't get. Life was tough, but hey, that's show business.

Well, not to worry. There was another silver lining coming up for me several months ahead, when we saw the finished film together. This time it was my turn to catch a glimpse of me! David hadn't been in *Nicholas Nickleby* at all, so I was one up on him. There I was, recognisable (as long as you already knew what I looked like) in the back row of the schoolroom, standing well out compared to the others. Best of all, I was right next to the first real film star I ever met – Derek Bond, who was playing the title role. He even chatted to me in between takes – and he even let me chat back! He was very nice.

I was not to know then that thirty years or so later the two of us would be in Hong Kong, of all places, to play leading roles in an all-British production of a popular West End farce. Our four-week season of dinner theatre performances at the highly prized – and priced – five-star Hilton Hotel with its famous Hilton Playhouse attracted a sell-out audience. We gratefully accepted the hotel's offer of luxurious suites and all other facilities they could provide including, of course, the regular Sunday lunchtime cruises on the hotel's private yacht.

Yes, life was tough, but hey, that's show business, too.

CHAPTER 11

Exam Fever

Back in the real world, our summer holidays were eagerly awaited by all except those at the end of their fifth year, whose enthusiasm was dampened by the challenge of imminent exams. I write of the – may I suggest treacherous? – School Certificate Examinations that required pass marks in at least five subjects of our choice from the curriculum, plus a further three compulsory ones: mathematics, English and a foreign language – French, in my case.

David and I had little reason to panic over the coming tests. We considered ourselves to be of well-above average intelligence. He had the precious skill of picking up facts and analysing them with a lightning speed I couldn't match, whereas I think I had the edge on him with a more sensitive and mature understanding of the world about us.

It was around this time the aforementioned treachery first came to my notice. It seems I hadn't been listening weeks earlier, when details of the three compulsory subjects were explained to us. David enlightened me. Failure to achieve a pass mark in even one of those three would be enough to deny us our school certificate. Full stop. End of story.

Ten minutes earlier and I would not have thought of myself as a potential loser, but now I went into slow meltdown and only just managed to hold back my *cris de coeur* from childhood days of 'Why me?' and 'It's not fair!'

Would failure put an end to my promising career? I wondered. No school cert. – no Oscar? No hey-diddly-de-dee, an actor's life for me? Just the nightmare of a labour exchange, a dole queue, and even – God forbid – a 'proper job'. Then there was my mother to consider.

David read my mind. 'We'll do all right,' he said.

'How d'you know?'

'We did better than all right at the mock exams.'

I shook my head, unconvinced. 'You might have done. I don't know.'

'I do,' he said and went back to the book he was reading.

I saw his point soon enough. I was now noticing other fifth formers with smaller brains whispering of injustice and strike action, and in corners of the playground even calling for bloody revolution. I thought it best to do a little extra revision but I needn't have bothered, and perhaps I didn't. There was no bloodshed in the end, anyway.

While waiting for the exams, David and I were busy plotting our careers; both of us had decided to leave school promptly at the end of term. David was keen to follow up useful contacts he had already made, while my plan was similar, but more subtle.

From our earliest days in Berlin, our parents had taken for

granted that their children would go to university. Fate dictated otherwise for Tom and Barbara so I was left as the only candidate to support our mother's hopes. She came from a culture where any respectable child from a respectable family got at least one degree. She was not exactly against my choice of career but would certainly have preferred something more worthwhile than life as a play actor, a mysterious profession of which she – and I – knew virtually nothing. But she loved me and was considering the idea of a drama school for me if I could not be persuaded otherwise. Whatever my ambitions, she was determined they would have to be planned in a thoroughly responsible way.

My selection of 'Exactly my view Mum, goes without saying, would never let you down, don't worry' and so on formed the gist of my responses. But I dreaded the possibility of a further period of hard labour in a sixth form, followed by more years in some stupid university. That would be enough to kill off all my fame and fortune dreams, half-witted as they were.

When, weeks later, at last our exam results arrived, I found them to be something of a mixed success. David had passed – and I had not.

UGH!

When I came home in the early evening, Mum told me the shocking news. To minimise her almost tears of despair, I comforted her with a near enough honest account of the results I had achieved in each of my six chosen subjects, never mind minimum of five, plus two out of the three unselected ones, namely English language and French. Fate had been against me. Despite extra revision prior to the exams (really?), I and others had been the victims of rogue questions on algebra, trigonometry and logarithms, unjustly passed off as mathematics! I was far from the only victim. It was a disgrace that those three gate-crashing interlopers should be allowed to bring failure to an entire exam. And everybody agreed with me in that! Oh yes.

It was at about this point I sensed things were not going as I had hoped. Instead of cheering my mother up, the very opposite was happening. She had by now stopped listening to me and my increasingly convoluted excuses. A few moments later, she gave a sigh.

'It is in the past,' she said, carefully avoiding my eyes. 'I will go to my room. Do not disturb. We will speak again tomorrow.'

She left me to myself. I was alone, lonely and guilty. I was upset that I had lied to her – not for the first time – and I was at a loss.

I didn't know what to do.

Her plan for me, I feared, was to do what was normal in our family. I should follow in the footsteps of my ancestors, go to university and get a few degrees and settle down to a normal life with a normal income.

But I had become obsessed with being an actor. Bizarrely – and you must remember that at that stage I knew far less about the realities of acting than I did about the okapi, Charles Darwin or Bulldog Drummond – I thought this would be much easier than becoming a zoologist, as I had once intended, or having any other 'normal' profession.

The next morning my mother was composed and had decided

how she was going to deal with me. She insisted that I did not leave school and would have to sit the school cert. again.

'What would Father have said?' she asked.

I had no reply to that. So it was back to school for another term. I was quite unable to focus on such delights as geometry and suspected I had done no better than previously when I sat the school certificate again.

I knew that I had failed and, one evening, I finally forced myself to accept what would be the inevitable disappointment. With real humility I said: 'I've let you down, Mother, and I'm so sorry and so ashamed.'

With those few simple words, I was leaving a hefty chunk of my childhood behind me, thank God. She sat in silence for some moments, before allowing herself a second cup of tea while I smiled affectionately and took a modest sip from my first one.

Then something extraordinary happened, which convinces me how much I wanted what I wanted. I was frightened I couldn't tell her, that the words I hoped to recruit for my cause would stay well out of reach, and that I would have to abandon all hopes of bright lights, when, to my astonishment, the words I hadn't found, found me instead.

I began hesitantly but I grew into the speech. With more and more conviction I voiced an unshakeable decision to master the many skills of my chosen career; to embrace enthusiastically the disciplines and commitments I would face; and to strive for perfection in everything I did on stage, on screen and on the wireless.

I bowed my head, glowing with pride and humility. And suspicion and awe. And surprise and gratitude.

I don't know where I got the inspiration. Perhaps I really did want to be an actor for better reasons than my slick, glib and unthinking conviction that it would be easy. I had summed up my hopes and dreams. An eternity of doom began to fill my being as her chin started to tremble.

'Yes,' she said at last, 'that is a wonderful target for you to study, Anderle.'

'Thank you,' I nodded.

She turned away and devoted her attention to clearing the table.

'Let me help you, Mother,' I eventually managed to croak. She seemed too engrossed to reply.

'Please,' I begged.

She shook her head gently, picked up the tray and made for the kitchen, leaving the last two biscuits behind for me.

I would be lying if I said I had profound motives for wanting to act. I was not interested in acting in order to explore the depths of my soul because I was far from sure I had one. I just had ideas above my station but I was stubborn and so my mother agreed in the end. My mother, however, was still the very practical woman who had cajoled exit visas out of the Nazis and, being practical, she decided that if I was going to be an actor I had better see the best. She took me to St Martin's Lane to see *Richard III* with Laurence Olivier.

I was knocked out by his performance. He was powerful and evil, but funny. I didn't know what *Richard III* was about, but when I got back home I started learning it. Seeing Olivier had made me even more determined to act.

Mum then insisted I get some basic training. So, before I left school, I attended some Sunday classes run by a director. He let anyone who wanted to become a professional come as long as, of course, they paid the fees. He was heavily into what we would now call improvisation. He would give us a subject, like 'Imagine you are on a train and a girl is sitting there and her nose suddenly starts bleeding' and expect us to turn this into a scene. I loved that because I could make it all up. You didn't have to learn anything. You thought about the subject and let your imagination take flight, whether it was a funny scene, a tragic one or just a slice of so-called normal life.

I went to those classes for quite a long time. One of the other would-bes was Maggie Smith. Neither of us would have guessed that we would both act in Dustin Hoffman's *Quartet* sixty-five years later.

After a while, I started to consider more formal training over and above that I was receiving at Aida Foster's. I can't remember whether it was my mother or me who discovered that the best drama school in England was the Royal Academy of Dramatic Art and that it had a kind of preparatory school. I soon found myself turning up for an audition.

I'd never done anything on an actual stage, not even in the school theatre, so I wasn't ready for what they threw at me. They said, 'Yes, it's good, very interesting, but you're very young and you're still at school.'

So far, so obvious.

'So, what you should do, perhaps,' they went on to suggest, 'is consider our other school up in Highgate. We suggest you do a term there and come back at the end of term and see what you've learned and have another audition here.'

I had no choice but to take their advice so I went to ParRADA, as we called it. It cost eighteen guineas for the term, which was very expensive as we had little money. They taught silly things I really didn't want to learn like diction and voice production. I just wanted to play Hamlet. To do that, I didn't have to know about the history of the theatre and whether Restoration comedy influenced Molière or the other way round.

But there was a silver lining again. Early in 1947 I played the Inquisitor in George Bernard Shaw's *Saint Joan*, a daunting part for a teenager. I had become friendly with an actor called O. B. Clarence. He had played the Inquisitor, I discovered later, in the first production of *Saint Joan*, which was organised by Shaw and starred Dame Sybil Thorndike. As he got older, O. B. Clarence settled for more benevolent, doddering roles in films – the most celebrated of his 1940s film roles was his brief turn as the Aged Parent in David Lean's *Great Expectations*.

Clarence offered me some good advice on how the Inquisitor had to seem kindly and friendly when he questioned those on trial but be ruthless. 'Get all the value out of Shaw's words,' he added, 'and you can't go far wrong.' Despite this well-meant advice, I was insufferably arrogant and left out part of his final speech because I, of the good memory, had not bothered to learn all the lines.

When I went back to RADA, they said, 'Oh, that is so much

better but you are maybe still young. Have another term in Highgate.'

So I did that. When that second term ended I went back to RADA to have yet another audition. They sounded like a stuck record: 'Yes, very good, but we think a third term would benefit you.'

By this time I was really fed up and, using my extensive knowledge of swear words, I thought 'Piss off'.

Then my acting ambitions were put on hold. My country needed me.

CHAPTER 12

National Service

The dreaded National Service. I didn't think I'd have to do it because I had only just become British. But then the official letter arrived announcing I must join up.

I resented it and thought I'd say I didn't want to do it. I had to have a medical and – I'm not proud of it in retrospect – I tried to cheat my way out. When I was interviewed, to the question, 'Do you have any problems?' I replied, 'Yes, I've got cancer.'

The army was having none of it.

My first experience of military life was taking a train with other raw recruits up to Catterick in Yorkshire, where we were put through eight weeks of basic training. We were trained to drill and, in theory, kill. When I'd qualified as a private class it was soon time for the army to decide what to do with me.

A gruff voice sounded, 'Yeah, o'right, come wiv me,' and I was marched into a room to face the sergeant major. He boomed, 'There's a board up there with all the jobs going. Now, what you wanna do, what you feel like doing? You can be a...' He rattled off my options.

What I didn't want to do, but I didn't dare say, was to carry rifles and drill up in Yorkshire.

'Do you wanna be a driver?' the sergeant barked.

I couldn't drive a car so I was a bit surprised when he added, 'A tank driver?'

'Er, no.'

'A signalman?'

'No, actually I'm an artist, an actor and I wonder if I might get into the dramatic part of the army.' I obviously dreamed I might be assigned to the Royal Light Thespians, which was hardly Drummond's old regiment.

Sergeant Sensitive snapped, 'Fuck off. I'll make you an orderly room clerk in the regiment.'

So for two years I was a rather orderly orderly whom Herr Plischert would have approved of. Everything was in *ordnung* as they said in Germany, which meant it was in perfect order. Form A was filed as Form A. Form B in triplicate was not filed as Form X in Serbo-Croat.

I ended up in a tank regiment in Dorset at Bovington Camp, but I'm proud to say I never drove a tank. I have found a photograph which shows me standing by a tank, but that is as impressive as it got. I should add one more military detail. We were not issued with rifles, which would be dangerous in a tank, but only with pistols.

I became a kind of secretary and looked after people's documents, pushing Form A in the direction of Department B, where no doubt it disappeared into Filing Cabinet C. Sometimes, I had to be on duty all night, ready to alert my superiors to any emergency. Living away from home for the first time was certainly an experience but, though I did miss Mother, if I'm honest I took it all in my stride.

I had one troublesome experience with a Trooper Mills, who had the bed next to me in the barracks. I lent him half a crown once but that was before I knew his full story. I had to check his documents and found that he had a history of disciplinary issues, one of which was under section 40 of the Army Act. He had been guilty of conduct prejudicial to good order and military discipline in that, on 24 July 1945, he had allowed himself to become infested with lice and was confined to barracks for twenty-eight days. I don't think he was much cleaner after that. And he still owes me the half crown. As I come from a banking family, with interest I calculate that would be £10,000 now.

But my acting ambitions were not put on hold. The army had surprising resources, which meant I got the chance to do some extraordinary things. One day my sergeant said, 'The colonel wants to see you because he has to be made up as a woman.' I had not joined a regiment Colonel Drummond would have disapproved of – the Royal Cross Dressers, or somesuch. It was just that Colonel Butch Manly (not his real name) was going to take part in a show.

I also helped to run a radio service in the regiment, which gave me the chance to act. Once we did a Noël Coward half-hour for Bovington's radio station. Three of us were in charge. I cast an Auxiliary Territorial Service girl, but she backed out so I had to step in and take over. After the Inquisitor in *Saint Joan*, I was now playing a grandmother – it was a bit of a change.

In the army I learned to obey orders, and I kept out of trouble. I even became a corporal but I had no natural authority. One guy in my platoon took the mickey out of me and bullied me. He sensed it wasn't me to set myself up as an authority figure. I just avoid trouble. I don't like giving orders – that's not for me.

National Service was supposed to last eighteen months but, just before I was due to leave, the Labour government – which had won a landslide victory after the war – extended National Service by six months. It was a horrible surprise and, when I finally left the army on 10 May 1951, I asked myself if it had done me any good. My feelings were mixed. In some ways it was good, but I hadn't needed the extra six months, as by then I was very clear that I wanted to act.

I had by now left Aida Foster's books and had some sense of what you had to do to get a job in my chosen vocation – and that meant visiting agents and hoping they would take you on. With the aim of building up my list of contacts, I made the round of the pot-pourri of agents. In my narcissistic soul, I imagined I'd soon be back on a movie set but this time I'd be playing a lead.

In the Woody Allen film, *Broadway Danny Rose*, the young – and not so young – hopefuls go up the stairs of office buildings, only for agents to slam the door in their faces with 'No thank you, we have nothing for you.' In *Some Like It Hot*, Jack Lemmon and Tony Curtis trudge from office to office and are given the bum's rush by one sleazy agent after another. Eventually, they have to pretend they are girls in order to get work. I have never had to go that far but I spent days walking up and down rickety stairs in the West End not getting anywhere. Then I had a piece of luck. A man I knew, who had an office just off Charing Cross Road, welcomed me not with the usual refrain that he had nothing for me but instead said, 'Maybe I can help. Now the war's over, we're starting *The Reunion Players* in Bexhill-on-Sea.' The cast of *The Reunion Players* was made up mainly of ex-servicemen. I qualified as I'd been in a tank regiment though, as I explained, I'd actually never graced a tank with my presence.

'You might be useful doing ASM work and playing a school boy or something occasionally,' the man said. The duties of an ASM, or assistant stage manager, he explained, included sweeping the stage, making tea, helping to get the properties and doing anything else the stage manager wanted. I was happy – I can't tell you how much.

As I begin to tell of my career as an actor, the tone of this book has to change. My life had started amid the horrors of Nazi Germany. Despite all my *knatsch*-ing, I had enjoyed a happy childhood until my father became ill. But now I was entering a totally different world.

The cast so far – Herr Plischert, Frau Fellenberg, Miss Taylor, David, Coop, Coop's weird parents, the goldfish fanatic and my own family – were, if I may use the phrase, ordinary people. I was about to enter a very different world, where I would meet the stars, would-be stars and some who were not quite the stars they fancied themselves to be. Some were extraordinarily talented – Alec Guinness, Dame Edith Evans, Rex Harrison, Noël Coward, Brian Rix, Eric Sykes, Peter Sellers, Richard

Burton and John Cleese – and a number of others were not. Some were quite human but some were such big stars, they soared into their own stratosphere.

Bexhill-on-Sea is not in any stratosphere. It is a Sussex resort and, blatantly, on the sea. Its theatre wasn't really a proper theatre. It was called the De La Warr Pavilion and had been designed by a German architect. It is seen quite often on television, especially in *Poirot*.

The repertory world was unique and very much of its time. In the 1940s, every seaside resort had its rep: Margate, Frinton, Bridlington, Minehead, Ayr, Ilkley, Worthing, Portsmouth and many others.

I had finally made it, or so I thought, by going to Bexhill. That's when I really began to learn what the theatre was all about. Artistic glory included making the tea, sweeping the stage, making sure the sound effects were on cue and often working all night. Best of all, I got occasional parts. My first appearance on the professional stage was as a really ancient pot man cleaning up the beer cellars. He was about sixty years older than I was. But my real artistic task was to play youngsters who were too old for the main actors to attempt. We staged an extraordinary mix of plays which ranged from the brilliant to the unspeakable. We even did *Macbeth* in a week and I played young Malcolm – probably with a bad Scottish accent, but it got me my first ever fan letter from a girl who had seen me in the play, liked what she saw and wanted my autograph.

I thought I was doing well. In fact, nine months after Malcolm, I made my debut in the new medium of television.

Norman Wisdom starred in *The Co Ed College with the Curious Curriculum* which hit the airwaves in May 1948 and I had a bit part. Norman, later Sir Norman, would crop up at various points in my career.

Despite my television appearance, at the end of the second season Bexhill didn't have me back. I assumed it must be because I wasn't very good or they thought I was lazy, even though I was still behaving like a good German boy who never argued with the authorities. But I recovered from my disappointment, which I soon came to realise is an essential skill if one is to survive in show business, and trudged around the agents again. At least now I could boast of a little experience. I managed to get other jobs, at first always as an ASM who, from time to time, got lucky and was allowed to play a small part.

One of my first jobs was on an Arts Council tour of Wales. For thirteen weeks we were in a different place almost every day, travelling from Cardiff to Bangor via many places with long and difficult Welsh names. The great fun for me, to my inner zoologist's delight, was that I got to perform the first animal part of my career in *Noah* – a monkey.

From 1950 to 1954, I went from one rep to another, sometimes just for one season or one project, but slowly it got better. The parts I played were a weird and wonderful mix and provided invaluable experience. We performed some established hits like Emlyn Williams's *Night Must Fall*, *September Tide* by Daphne du Maurier and *The Blue Lamp* by Ted Willis. We even did classics like Sheridan's *School for Scandal*.

The rep world had its hierarchies and when I moved up to the

Connaught at Worthing it was a definite step up from Bexhill. Proof: my pay doubled from £4 a week to £8 a week.

It still makes me smile looking at the programmes from that time – and especially the ads, which include gems singing the praises of dog parlours. Marion Ross, for example, would buff your poodle to the highest standards of canine beauty. For some reason in one programme it said that she had trained me!

I learned to take direction and, also, to be a little devious. One of my first parts was that of a young man. I got it because there was no proper actor in the cast spare and of the right age. I tried to make it interesting by giving my character an accent at the dress rehearsal. The actor I had my main scene with complained to our director, 'You know, he's not doing this right. Instead of doing it the way we rehearsed, he's playing a sort of character and putting on an accent.' So the director said, 'Well I will have a word with him.' And he did, asking, 'Andrew, what happened there?'

'I learned the lines right,' I said, 'but there was nothing interesting in the character; he was just saying words and I thought I'd put an accent in or character of some kind, so I did.'

'You put out your partner there and it is not a good idea.'

Obedient as ever, I said, 'Oh dearie me, I see, well, should I just do it the way you told me to?'

He smiled. 'No, just keep in what you did. It's quite good and I'll tell him.' So I got away with it.

While I was at the Connaught, Willard Stoker, a brilliantly funny man who was well known then in Liverpool, came to direct one play. I must have impressed him because he asked me to come back to the Mersey with him to perform in a well-established three-weekly rep company. And, to top it off, I was promoted to stage manager!

Actors being poor until – and if – they get pretty rich, I was delighted to get £9 a week, one pound a week more than at the Connaught. But I was a bit disappointed, having come from weekly rep where we had to learn everything fast. In three-weekly rep, it seemed to my know-all self, they wasted so much time dilly-dallying around. With ideas well above my station, I reckoned we were as good as the stars in the West End and woefully overlooked. I played Inspector Deep (the name still makes me laugh) in *Loyalties* by John Galsworthy. And I played my second Shakespeare part – not Hamlet but Snug the joiner in *A Midsummer Night's Dream*.

I was then offered a job which meant moving from the north-west to the north-east, to Durham, which in terms of pressure was the opposite of Liverpool. It was the last twice-weekly rep, which meant we had to do two performances every day – at 6 p.m. and 8.30 p.m. – apart from Sundays.

It was the first time I was promoted to being an actor, and nothing but an actor. For the first time, I didn't have to stage manage. It was a real breakthrough but it was too good to last. Just before the first night in a new show the director called me. The stage manager had disappeared. 'We haven't got all the props yet and I don't know where he is. I know you've done a lot of stage management, could you come in?'

'Oh Christ,' I said.

But you had to be a trouper.

The ASM was a girl, and we set about doing everything the stage manager should have done. We scoured local antique shops for props, but it was a panic trying to get everything done. We hadn't really finished by the time of the first performance. Halfway through it (I had a small part as a detective, coming on in the second act), the ASM said to me, 'You know, it's time you got your clothes on.'

'Oh hell,' I said.

I rushed onto the stage and forgot all my lines. I couldn't remember one word. The leading lady was baffled and didn't understand. 'What brings you here at this time of the evening?' she asked, desperately trying to prompt me into action. The ASM started shouting the words to me from the edge of the stage. Then, the director got in on the act and whispered my words in such a loud stage whisper I hardly needed to say anything, because the audience could see and hear him perfectly well. Fortunately I wasn't heavily reprimanded, rather to my surprise, because everyone knew I had done my best to stand in for the stage manager.

It turned out the stage manager had been last seen on a bridge over the River Weir, tearing ten-shilling notes to pieces. Reps were full of people with ambitions and frustrated ambitions; some had breakdowns. I heard later he had left the business and became so successful he was able to buy an island. He was lucky. Most settled for what they could achieve, which meant occasional work and often perpetual poverty. But nearly everyone had faith that one day they would be discovered and become a star.

Being in rep did give me the confidence to write to the BBC. I had better explain my method. I would find out the names of relevant producers, write individual letters to them and deliver them in person to the reception at Broadcasting House. I had been told the BBC was obliged to answer all letters. It worked well enough and I was duly summoned to Broadcasting House, which was then a temple of culture.

I clearly remember the first time I walked into the temple with the accuracy Herr Plischert would have expected of me, because the BBC provided you with what looked suspiciously like a school report card. Mine said that after my audition, I was not going to be called for a second one.

It felt like a terrible rejection. And when one is rejected, one hopes for something to make you feel positive. It was around this time I started to keep reviews. It's natural, when you are so dependent on how people react to you. I have never belonged to the splendidly detached who say they never bother to read reviews and don't care whether they are good or bad. I was joyed over (I haven't lost my grammatical wits but am twisting the language to make a point) when I got good reviews so – vanity, vanity – here is what one said about my performance in *The Release*: 'Andrew Sachs was so right for the part it is a pity he is not seen more often.'

Being old enough to be realistic, I doubt Noël Coward read the review but my next job took me to Wonderland. Or, to be more accurate, Shaftesbury Avenue in the fabled West End.

CHAPTER 13

Noël Coward and the BBC

In 1952, when I was just twenty-two, I went back to Liverpool for Sir Noël Coward. He had written a new musical called *After the Ball*, based on Oscar Wilde's *Lady Windermere's Fan*, which starts with the Duchess of Berwick telling Lady Windermere her husband is betraying her with Mrs Erlynne, and giving Mrs Erlynne large sums of money. It turns out that Mrs Erlynne is Lady Windermere's mother and Lord Windermere reveals that he is protecting her true identity to save his wife from humiliation.

I understudied the hugely significant part of Lady Windermere's footman. I dreaded doing it.

The already famous choreographer Robert Helpmann was directing. He was very camp and funny and, since it was a musical, he made the characters prance all over the stage when they were singing. I'm not sure what Wilde would have made of it, but when Noël Coward came to see the rehearsals he went wild. He took one look at what Helpmann was doing and was furious.

'No, no!' Coward said. 'We stand still when we do the songs. I want them to hear my words.' He could be fierce. I remember at one of the rehearsals a cleaner was up in the gallery just doing her job. But His Sublimity – I mean Coward – got annoyed and shouted to her to 'SHUT UP.'

On one occasion, so I heard, Coward had reason to criticise one of his cast. Being particularly unkind, he told the actor that he was not very good. The actor was experienced and dared to reply, 'Mr Coward, I have to say I don't like being talked to like this. I have had thirty-two years of experience,' to which Coward replied, 'No, you haven't. You have had one experience thirty-two times.' It was a brutally elegant put-down.

Few dared pipe up against Coward, of course.

Coward made us work hard to get the play right as he saw it. We were all very excited the first night the show opened in the West End, which had always been the plan after opening in Liverpool. I looked through the hole in the curtain to see who was in the audience and saw Coward come in at the back of the stalls, receiving a round of applause. He had with him a beautiful young woman in a magnificent white dress. Everyone turned – and it was not only for him. After the curtain came down, he brought her backstage. It turned out that Coward's escort was Marlene Dietrich, who had chucked me under the chin when I was five weeks old. I had no memory of this (which is why it did not feature prominently in earlier chapters, modesty being my middle name) but my mother told me it had happened. Coward introduced her to me and, smiling, she shook my hand. That was it. I did not have the presence of mind or the chutzpah to remind Marlene of how intimately we were connected. Or perhaps it was just that by then I had become so English and, of course, one doesn't boast, old chap.

My part as the footman might have been small but I had made it to the West End my friend David had teased me about at school. Despite Coward re-directing the play, sadly it didn't do well. The fact that a musical written by Noël Coward, based on a play by Oscar Wilde, only ran for five months demonstrates that you never know what is going to happen in show business, that business which is eternally insecure.

To survive as an actor you need a certain temperament. You have no idea where your next part – and your next payday – is coming from. You need the hide of a rhinoceros as you have to get used to being turned down, have to get used to being poor and, though you are acting, you have to be nice to people you sometimes would rather drown in a barrel of Malmsey wine, as Richard III allegedly did. It occurs to me that no Shakespeare scholar has looked at the many murders in the Bard's plays in the light of the troubles he had getting cast and getting his plays performed. I suggest Sachs's theory of Shakespeare: Shakespeare had so many of his characters murdered because he subconsciously wanted to kill all the people who early in his career had turned him down with the Elizabethan equivalent of 'Don't thee call us, we shall calleth ye.' Well, it's as good a theory as the one Tom and I developed about the length of Dickens's sentences.

Emboldened from my brief stint in the West End, I tried again to get into the BBC. This time I fared better and the report of the BBC Drama audition read: 'Very much like this voice, remarkable range as accents, direction, good voice control, very versatile, nice to see such range, vitality, would be useful to have but his real resting place is with variety and features.' As I look at it, I'm pleasantly surprised. I didn't think it was as good as that; in fact, I remembered my audition as awful. But that was not the opinion of the man who auditioned me and I was finally accepted into the hallowed BBC. It felt quite wonderful. I have always loved radio; it is my favourite medium. If I'm being smart, I say it's because I don't have to learn the lines as you read the script while you go (carefully, quietly), but there's more to it than that.

The BBC Drama Repertory Company consisted of about forty actors and actresses. Being in the BBC Rep was very different from the anarchies of seaside rep. You had to turn up virtually every day. You had to get on with your colleagues, and we very much saw ourselves as a team. We were there to perform the plays the BBC had decided to do. There might only be three in the cast or forty; regardless, we had a routine. First, we would have a read-through and then we would launch into the rehearsals until finally all the rather primitive sound effects (that were the state of the art at the time) were recorded. The variety of plays we did was astonishing and a tribute to those who followed Lord Reith, the first director general of the BBC. I acted in *Mrs Dale's Diary*, which, having started before *The Archers*, was Britain's first soap; in comedies like *The Caves of the Vatican* by Howard Marian Crawford; and in rather intellectual plays like Elizabeth Bowers's *The Death of the Heart*. I was in a number of Chekhov plays too, like *Uncle Vanya* and *The Cherry Orchard*.

If you had a proper part you were listed by name in the *Radio Times*; small parts became subsumed into a credit that said 'Members of the BBC Repertory Company played the other parts.' If you had a truly major role, you made it in bold type just below the title. I achieved this landmark in *The Takeover* where I played Alex Marks. Then it was time to play an animal again – the dormouse in *Alice in Wonderland*.

As you get older you don't remember every single part you got, so it's lucky I have kept a scrapbook which pretty much records every part I ever played and, later, every script I ever wrote. I suspect now that what made me keep such a detailed record was anxiety, something actors are rather prone to because of the insecurities of our profession. When I look back, I'm amazed at all the plays I took part in at the BBC – one month I acted in seventeen different radio productions.

I was beginning to get the hang of accents, a very useful tool when working on the radio. In one programme I played an Australian announcer, a Lancashire cockle worker and a cockney bus driver. I was learning my trade partly because I worked with amazing actors like Timothy West, Frederick Treves and Prunella Scales, and another three who were legends – and some said even monsters: Dame Edith Evans, Donald Wolfit and Richard Burton. Many actors who commanded huge fees were willing to work at the rather modest rates BBC Radio offered because it seemed the decent thing to do and, on the whole, they still are.

Dame Edith Evans was wonderful in the film of *Tom Jones*, but she is probably best remembered for her shocked, piercing tones in *The Importance of Being Earnest* where she played Lady

Bracknell, Oscar Wilde's domineering Victorian aristocrat. The first time Dame Edith came to the BBC she had never acted on radio before. She marched into the studio and said, 'And which is the microphone?' As the microphone dominated the table, it was really impossible to miss. So we had a good laugh. The next time she came in, she did precisely the same thing.

BBC Radio was dedicated to bringing foreign drama to listeners and it managed a real coup in 1954 when the Third Programme, as Radio 3 was then called, produced *The City* by Ingmar Bergman, who was famous for films like *The Seventh Seal*. Whether on radio or on film, Bergman was Scandinavian gloom personified, except for his marvellous comedy *Smiles of a Summer's Night*, which Stephen Sondheim turned into a musical. One of the other highlights was Beckett's *Waiting for Godot*, with Kenneth Griffiths as Estragon and Nigel Stock as Vladimir. I played Lucky, who is kept on a lead and has one very long speech which starts – and continues – in a splendid verbal jumble. I will only quote the beginning of what is a remarkable speech that parodies academic and religious texts.

Given the existence as uttered forth in the public works of Puncher and Wattmann of a personal God quaquaquaqua with white beard quaquaquaqua outside time without extension who from the heights of divine apathia divine athambia divine aphasia loves us dearly with some exceptions for reasons unknown.

The BBC even did a play in Middle English called *The Lincoln Passion*. It was clearly committed to the experimental in the hope that the British public would learn to be worthy of its great broadcaster. And it did not pull its punches. I've kept a piece from the *Radio Times* by Donald McGuinney who produced *Private Dream and Public Nightmare*. Introducing the programme he wrote, 'You may detest this programme but I hope you will not dismiss it. Certainly nothing like it has ever come out of your loudspeaker if you are familiar with the idea of music.' Dumbing down? There was none.

The fact that I had been born in Germany got me one part: the role of Prince Albert of Saxe Coburg (I have shortened his title, which is nearly as long as the sentences Dickens wrote) who married Queen Victoria. I was not particularly experienced and played him as a rather nice man. The director gave me a lot of useful notes, suggesting I shouldn't be too soft. Prince Albert, he said, 'wasn't such a nice man; he was German, passionate and you want to show authority. He was power.' I've said on a number of occasions that I didn't have natural authority but I had to act Albert with gusto. I listened to the director and I seemed to have done it right. At any rate, they were pleased with me. An actor obviously relies on directors. Working with certain people was good – not just because they appreciated what I was doing, though, of course, that boosted my self-confidence, but because they guided and explained. One of the best directors became a friend: Glyn Dearman, who was himself a close friend of John Tydeman, who became head of BBC Radio drama.

By the late 1950s, I had played dogs, cats, aristocrats, servants and in Shakespeare, who knew all about versatility. Radio was not all paradise, however. Most studios were underground, and the atmosphere and air soon became stuffy. After half an hour spent in the airless Studio 6A, I would want to go to sleep. We also faced the problem of rumbling tube trains underneath us and were often forced to pause our recordings because of the noise.

One day, I had a phone call from the BBC to say that a Mr Tennyson (yes, descendant of the great poet) wanted to come and see me at home. 'We've got a bit of a problem with *Mrs Dale's Diary*,' he confessed. The radio serial followed Mary Dale, who was the wife of a doctor called Jim. Her diary was very middle-class and urban, quite different from *The Archers*. Today a soap about a doctor would be packed with messages – don't eat too much sugar, run around the block every day and remember your doctor is busy and stressed so don't contact the surgery unless you're dying and quite sure you're dying. Mrs Dale wrote a journal at an easier time.

'The director we wanted is not available,' announced Tennyson, 'and we're looking for a director for the show for a period. You've done a lot of radio. Would you like to do it?'

I was tickled pink, though couldn't help but wonder why anybody should want me to direct, as I'd never done it before.

Still, I was there for about six months, supposedly direct-ing the artists. I say 'supposedly' because Jessie Matthews, who played Mrs Dale, would not have allowed God to direct her. I had no chance. I was scared of her, and with good reason. She was formidable. She was born in the middle of Soho in Berwick Street, where her father had a fruit and vegetable stall in the market (it's still there). Jessie first went on stage when she was twelve, quickly became a star and was the first person to perform Cole Porter's 'Let's Do It, Let's Fall in Love'. In the 1920s and 1930s she was a huge star, but her fame wilted after the war. Fading stars are not always realistic. Jessie thought she was doing the BBC a favour by playing Mrs Dale. And Sachs was, of course, the little-guy director. It's a pity I never told this story to Woody Allen: he could have played me trembling neurotically as the diva went her own merry way with the script. I've never, of course, met Woody Allen so this will just remain a fantasy. Working with one of the great stars of the time, though, was good experience. Showbiz stars come in different varieties, just like those in the starry heavens. You get the bright suns, you get the sad, burned-out ones that have used up all their hydrogen or helium, and you get the Supernova or Superdiva type. I leave it to readers to work out which one Jessie was. Being a polite German boy, I'll just say I wouldn't want to do it again.

I loved being at the BBC, it was such a lively place to work. You played different parts and it was always challenging, though there wasn't a lot of stress (except for Jessie). I was also delighted to be working and to know where the next job was coming from. Ask any young actor who struggles – and most of them do. Having a job means you know where your next meal's coming from; you can even take a taxi when you need to, buy your own drinks and not have to borrow money. And often at the BBC you worked with the best of the best. On 8 June 1964 I was in John Osborne's *The Entertainer* playing Frank Rice. The monster, or legend, Donald Wolfit was playing Archie Rice, the part Olivier had played in the original production at the Royal

Court. There is a famous anecdote about Wolfit I cannot resist sharing. He was once asked if an actress who was playing opposite him was his mistress. 'No,' he apparently replied, 'but she will be soon.' He was a veritable wolf, it seems.

Another highlight was *The Three Sisters* with Paul Schofield, Jill Bennett, George Cole, Lynn Redgrave and Ian McKellen. It was some cast: the future Thomas More, the future Arthur Daley and the future Gandalf in the same play.

Somewhere in the BBC archives – and one should remember that George Orwell used the BBC as his model for the Ministry of Truth in *1984* so the archives run deep – there is a record of what Sachs, A was employed and paid to do. But there is something missing: in the late 1950s I started writing scripts on a freelance basis.

Many actors have the itch to write, but all too often it just stays an itch. Some great dramatists have also been actors: Shakespeare played the ghost in *Hamlet*; the French playwright Molière played the lead in all his plays. Coward acted in many of his plays and, in our own day, the American Sam Shepherd has turned in a number of fine performances. But writing was in my blood, thanks to my Tyrolean grandfather.

My first opportunity came not long after my work on *Mrs Dale's Diary* finished, when I became involved with another soap. *Dear Girls* was about a group who came to London to find their fortune but had to share a house in Belsize Park. I was learning a new trade and wrote seven of the scripts. My main storyline was about a bird, a very rare bird that made its home in the roof top of the flat, and the girls were upset by its smell.

I remember touring in Hampshire with John Slater, a fine comic actor who also wrote short stories. One review in my ever useful scrapbooks describes him as a kind of a cockney Fernandel. (Fernandel was a great French comic actor with a battered face who played the feisty Catholic priest Don Camillo in a series of films. John was Jewish, but why should that stop him playing a good priest?) We were going from one gig to another, playing leads in a farce, and we were having a chat in the back of the car. I asked him about his writing.

'You know, that's what I've always wanted to do and I think I could do it properly because I could think of a good title and the first line.' I suppose I did not consider *Dear Girls* to be real writing.

'Do you really want to write?' John replied.

'Yes, absolutely.'

'Well, I'll tell you what we'll do,' he said. 'We'll have a little game, you and I. Let's both write a play. Let it be a half-hour radio play, that's the easiest way to get it done. The first one who finishes the script will get half a crown from the other one.'

That would be like a tenner today. We were big gamblers!

'Do you want to do it?' he asked.

Yes I did. So we shook on it.

At once John found some paper and began writing in the car. I will always be grateful to him for setting me off on the writing path.

The proof of any writing is the way the audience reacts to it. I was, of course, nervous about my work so, as soon as possible, I wanted to see how people reacted to it. When I had written about three-quarters of that first script, I showed it to some of the actors we were touring with. I didn't get the reaction I hoped for. Their verdict was that every character sounded the same. 'We can't tell which is which, who's the hero.' I learned from their reaction and managed the first essential – I finished the play.

I went to see John, who paid up the half a crown. He then said, 'I'm not stopping there. Let's go on and let's have another half-crown bet for the first one who gets their script bought by the BBC.'

The fact that I was in the BBC Rep helped, of course. Eventually I got one of the directors to read my first effort. He agreed, which was pretty much all that had to happen for it to go ahead in those days. There weren't commissioning committees. I was on my way and I started writing quite a lot.

My first play to be broadcast was *Flat to Let*, in 1964. Many first plays are autobiographical but mine was not remotely so. As I struggled as a young actor, I was still living in the flat that my mother had rented and we were still getting along famously. My play, however, described a young couple, with a baby, who rent a flat without knowing that the place has a macabre history. Tenants always want to leave because of the strange things that happen there, but this particular couple take it. It turns out to be rather tragic for them. There is a moment when the atmosphere really affects the wife. Her husband is at work; the baby is crying. She knows there's something badly wrong. Then the baby's cry changes into a voice – a male voice, a horrible voice that makes her run out into the street. I was in the studio for the recording and the director said to me, 'Andrew, I don't know how we are going to do that voice. I've got it recorded as a wolf or something.'

I said, 'Oh no, it's got to develop from an ordinary baby's voice to start with and then into something very scary. Let me do it.' He agreed, and I made the baby's cry – something like 'eeeooow, eeeeeoow' – change gradually into the name of the mother, Mary. I think it went like this: 'Eeeooow, eeeeeoow, eeeooowlake, eeelake, lake, lake, lary, MARY, MAARY.' It was that sort of thing and they kept it in.

Today the media commission meticulous market research to work out who listened or viewed what, and what the audience thought of it. The BBC was a pioneer in this field. When I started to write, the head of audience research was Robert Silvey, and his team found that the audience reaction to *Flat to Let* was quite positive. 'Andrew Sachs made a good job of his first radio play,' *The Times* said.

After that, I continued to work as an actor, of course, but I wrote whenever I had the time, and I got another commission for a half-hour play from the BBC. *Fearful Adversaries* followed an evening in the life of Arthur Redant, a busker who found the world was against him. A rival busker pushes him off his patch; the police get involved; his sister refuses to let him stay in her flat because he is drunk. Arthur is a natural victim. Again, *The Times* was kind: 'In the short time at his disposal, Mr Sachs contrived to get a little bit beneath the tawdry surface and suggests the fault might not after all lie in the stars.'

It was estimated that the audience for *Fearful Adversaries* was 0.3 per cent of the potential listening public, which sounds minuscule until you remember the total potential audience was millions. The listeners interviewed by the audience research team were unflattering, however. They thought it 'a sordid story which didn't lead anywhere' and obviously had no sympathy for Arthur's sufferings.

But I was hooked on writing. I blessed my fate that I wasn't like my granddad, stuck in the Tyrol writing in an obscure German dialect and becoming so bizarre that I would do the kind of thing he did – and consume sandwiches filled with soap without noticing.

And during all of this, my comfortable life was transformed – and in a good way.

Around 1958, I had a girlfriend called Sue Marriott. We went to a dance at a Christmas ball, but I couldn't dance for the life of me and she wasn't too delighted. Some months later, I was invited to go to another ball and I asked Sue if she would like to come. She said carefully, 'I will if you get some dancing lessons.'

So I did.

And that's how I met the love of my life. And when you meet the love of your life, old girlfriends either fade away or become friends, as Sue did.

Melody, tall, slim, a dish since the moment I set eyes on her, had come to London from Newcastle, where she had just finished six months in rep, and was now running a dance studio in Oxford Street. I tried my luck with a course of lessons, but I wasn't very good. I went there about eight times and, at the end, I had to go to Melody to be assessed. She watched me dancing with my teacher, enduring a jive, a waltz and foxtrot. 'Well,' she said at the end of it, 'I don't think there's any point in wasting your money, Mr Sachs. I think this is as good as it's going to get.'

Melody has her own take on the story and I should let her speak for herself, so here goes:

After I had taken Andy through his dancing exam, he asked if I would like to come and see him on Saturday night at the Whitehall Theatre where he was playing in *Simple Spymen*. He said he would leave a complimentary ticket at the box office but, being in the theatre myself, I knew there was no way he would get a comp on a Saturday night. I thought he was charming.

After the show, Melody came backstage and found me in the dressing room I was sharing with my cast mate, Ray Cooney. He had arranged for his girlfriend to join us for supper and I was hoping Melody would come too. We all went back to my flat together. I made supper, and I have to confess that it was just eggs on toast. Melody remembers this critical moment, critically:

The egg was very hard and Andy had covered it with a wet lettuce leaf. It was cold and soggy and I couldn't actually eat it. Afterwards, when it was time to go home, Raymond and his girlfriend offered me a lift. I said, 'Yes, sure,' but Andrew was having none of it. 'No, no, darling, stay behind,' he said. I really didn't know if that was a good idea, but I did stay behind. We sat on the sofa together and he took my hand but, at that moment, the door opened and an elderly lady in a white nightie appeared. It was Andrew's mother. I thought, 'Oh my God, I'm getting out of here,' but his mother was sweet. She said, 'Oh no, dear, don't let me disturb you, I'm going back to bed.'

Andrew took a bottle from a shelf in the living room and held it up to the light. It had little sparkling things in it. I said, 'What's that, then?' 'It's gold *wasser*,' he replied. So he gives me this glass of gold *wasser*, which I sipped, and then, without warning, he put his arm around me, held me tight and kissed me. And I have to say, it was special.

From then on, we were inseparable. Shortly afterwards, I played a season in rep at Folkestone, but I always came up for the weekend. Andrew would meet me at the station in his bubble car and we would drive back to his place. 'One thing you can be sure of about me,' he would say, 'is that I'm not a jealous man at all.' I thought, 'Good job.' Anyway, we're driving up Regent Street one night in the bubble car – the bubble car is left-hand drive, so I'm on the inside – and as we pull up at the lights a sports car drives up beside us with two guys in it. 'Hi!' one of them said, so I said 'Hi!' back. Before I knew it, Andy had accelerated away as fast as his bubble car would take him – and that wasn't very far. 'How dare you talk to other men when you're with me!' he said. I thought, 'Right, well, I'll keep quiet now, he's a complete loony. Not to mention rather more jealous than he had said. I'll wait till I get out of the car and then I'll go home.'

But I'm glad to say she didn't. We never left each other again, though we had to fit our love in with work. And there were obstacles – as ever there are in the paths of love. Melody had married when she was eighteen years old, to a chap called

Stanley, and together they had two sons, John and Billy. Stanley had obviously seen too many B movies, however, since his ambition in life was to be a gangster. Mr Big Time he was not. He and his gang had decided to break into a post office and steal all the Parker pens.

One night, at Stanley's mother's hotel in Hastings, where the family was living, there was a knock at the door from the local constabulary. When she let them in, they asked one of the more unusual questions in the annals of British crime: 'Have you got any pens?'

So a bemused Melody fetched them a pen. That was the proof they needed to put Stanley away. Stanley was sentenced to years in the pen for nicking the pens, and Stanley's mother threw Melody and her two sons out.

But my Melody is tough and she moved to London, began work in the theatres and, lucky for me, started running dancing classes.

We were poor but happy. When Melody became pregnant, I moved her and her sons in with me and my mother. Our daughter Kate was born in 1961 but where was I? At work. And where was I the next day? Rehearsing. I wasn't introduced to my daughter until she was two days old. But she was worth the wait.

It became obvious we needed a place of our own and we soon found a flat in Belsize Square to rent. It had no furniture and we had to furnish the place with second-hand stuff from an auction. I was performing in a matinee at the Whitehall Theatre so Melody went to the sale alone and bid for what we could afford. She bought two single beds which had previously seen life on a ship – even the blankets had the ship's name on them. These beds were put in the small box room for Melody's two sons, John and Billy. Kate had a little cot.

What you get cheap is often junk and some of the stuff Melody had bought was so awful we threw it away immediately! I could make us sound like total down-and-outs and say we burned it all to keep warm but that would be a fib. But we never got anything on credit. We always saved up and then splashed out. We only broke that rule once – to buy a sofa.

Melody had bought a cardboard suitcase at the sale but we couldn't get it open. Intrigued as to what was in it, we eventually forced it open and found an array of cutlery: knives, forks, spoons, fish knives, corkscrews. It was an amazing collection and, in its way, as bizarre as my father's books that had somehow survived from Berlin and I was now moving to Belsize. We had so little and yet we had so much.

Melody has been trying to teach me to dance ever since we met. Once, I nearly mastered the tango – well, at least three steps. You'd imagine that a man who dances like an injured rhino would lack the skills to play in farce, which depends on timing, rhythm and physical dexterity. Fortunately, that does not seem to have been true of me, as we'll see in the next chapter.

CHAPTER 14

Drop Your Trousers All the Time

Hubris returns to haunt you. I had been the arrogant teenager who had been so critical at ParRADA and thought what do I care about the history of the theatre they tried to teach us? Nada, zero, zilch. I could be a good actor without being able to tell my Marlowe from my Pinero. That is why I have to rely here on help from research done by Brian, now Lord Rix, one of the best producers of British comedy in the 1950s and no mean actor.

Brian wrote an entertaining account of the history of farce, which he subtitled: 'Tragedy When Your Trousers Fall Off'. He argued that the oldest theatrical productions were of Greek tragedies, to which crowds flocked in awe in the fourth century BC. The second oldest were Greek comedies, to which crowds flocked to guff-awe in the fourth century BC. Greek comedy inspired modern hits like *Up Pompeii!*, which allowed Frankie Howerd to rampage with his innuendoes, and *A Funny Thing*

Happened on the Way to the Forum, the film of which starred the great silent comic, Buster Keaton.

To make it plain I'm not a *Dummkopf*, I also need to bring to your attention the works of Terence and Plautus, Roman writers who developed the genre. There was one difference from the farces I was to play in under Rix's management. In farces 2,000 years ago, the actors did not lose their trousers. Why? Because they didn't have trousers in the first or any place. They wore togas.

Farce managed to make audiences laugh for over 2,000 years without authors or actors feeling they had to drop their pants. In France in 1671, the great actor and theatre manager Molière wrote *Les Fourberies de Scapin*. Scapin is a rascally servant who is constantly up to no good and in trouble, but he does not ever lose his trousers, or remove anyone else's trousers to reveal, *mon Dieu*, his French knickers.

One key difference between French and English comedy is that the English are easily embarrassed about sex. We tend to attribute British embarrassment about sex to Queen Victoria. In fact, the never amused Queen was far from being sexless as she had nine children and was, as Monty Python would put it, 'a bit of a goer' till her beloved husband Albert died. *Monty Python*, being written mainly by English public school boys, avoided sex.

As you will have gathered by now from my equation with regard to literature, I believe maths should be applied to the arts. So I claim that it was in Britain that the famous equation $E = mc^2$ was proved:

E = exposure (of nether parts)

m = much

c = chuckling

chuckling squared = helpless laughter.

In his history, Rix noted that there had been a great tradition of British farce in the period 1900–1930, which produced long lasting successes such as *Charley's Aunt* and *Rookery Nook*. After the war, people wanted to laugh, perhaps because laughter made austerity more bearable.

Rix had a huge advantage when it came to being an actor and impresario. His family was rich, having made a fortune landing fish in Hull. In 1947, when he was only twenty-six, Rix formed his own theatre company. He ran seaside rep companies at Ilkley, Bridlington and Margate and did well. He then took the Whitehall Theatre, just off Trafalgar Square, and turned it into a mecca of farce. (I use the word 'mecca' advisedly, as one of his first hits was *Stand by Your Bedouin*.)

One of Rix's other hits was *Reluctant Heroes*, which ran for four years. It was timely, soon after the war, being the story of a platoon of utterly useless soldiers, a theme echoed oddly in *Carry on Sergeant*, one of the first *Carry on* films. Another hit was *Let Sleeping Wives Lie*, in which I played a harassed hotel manager. It made fun of American business where executives know success depends on having the kind of wife the company wants. When an American boss comes to meet his two English employees, they know their promotion depends on displaying a stable and happy marriage. Fat chance. One man pretends an Irish chambermaid is his wife, while another wife persuades an old boyfriend to replace her real husband, who is away playing golf. The full Monty follows: irregular sleeping arrangements, changing bedrooms and people in the wrong pyjamas which are always on the point of falling down. As the hotel manager, I cried as I watched my respectable hotel frack (the word seems apt in 2014) into manic chaos. Manuel and Basil Fawlty would have fitted in perfectly – and made it worse.

Rix encouraged a number of farce writers, including Ray Cooney, who became a close friend of mine. Describing the art of farce, Ray wrote:

> The importance of creating believable characters and relationships and how vital it is to start off as totally normal and only gradually (and feasibly) develop into the complications of the Middle Act and then the absolute chaos of the third act; ordinary people in situations outside their control.

I loved being part of the chaos, though many of the farces were not subtle when I think about them now. Rix argues that *Simple Spymen*, in which a couple of radio salesmen get mistaken for Soviet spies, and *No Sex Please, We're British* ranked alongside the best of Feydeau, the great French comic writer. Masterpieces or not, they delivered bellyfuls of laughs and long runs.

I did an audition for Brian around 1954. He hired me and told me to play a part on a tour of *Dry Rot*. He always came to see how his plays were doing. He was pleased and, from then on, I worked for him for years. He started me off on £40 a week, which was not a bad wage then.

The Whitehall Theatre was good training after the BBC Rep because farce requires verbal and physical precision. I learned timing, how to get the biggest laugh and to think about what had gone wrong when the audience didn't titter enough.

In 1957, after *Dry Rot*, I was at Richmond in *Lock, Stock and Barrel* where Ray Cooney and I played 'wide boys'. *The Stage* said: 'It is a farce that most British would agree is tried and trusted; they seem to like it, to be entertained.' Not all the reviews we received were good. Reviewing *Dry Rot*, *Evening Standard*'s Milton Shulman, then one of the most important theatre critics, sniped, 'Oh dear, now the rot really has set in.' Perhaps not the pun of the century. The lordly Shulman was not lacking in hubris himself; he called his own memoirs *Marilyn, Hitler and Me*. But he certainly wasn't impressed by the fact that audiences came from all over Britain and laughed themselves stupid at our farces.

The names of some characters show how crude some of the farces were; in one play there was a Colonel Gray Balding, who was balding. Colonel Gray Balding was cartoon-like compared to the colonels in Peter Ustinov's *The Love of Four Colonels* where a British, French, American and Russian colonel each try to wake Sleeping Beauty. As with so much Ustinov, the play draws on stereotypes: the stiff-upper-lip Brit who loves his dogs; the bureaucratic Soviet who is scared of his wife; and the American who is obsessed with therapy and would have done anything to meet Freud. Even better was *Semi-Detached* by David Turner, in which Olivier played a man who was determined to be seen as middle class, while his daughter did the unmentionable without knickers and became pregnant before she was married.

The success of the Whitehall farces was noticed by BBC Radio and it tried to explore how to do farce on radio – and apparently doing it in semi-secret. I've found this cutting in my scrapbook:

> Meanwhile the liveliest thing I heard from the BBC this week wasn't a laugh (allowed) for public hearing but deserves to be. It was a playback of Feydeau, recorded by the Welsh Well Group, a band of unpaid enthusiasts mentioned here recently to whom the BBC lends studios for out of hours recording. The group took on Feydeau partly for fun but chiefly to demonstrate that the farce can still be funny without visual aids. The point was unquestionably made, it was very funny.

It even praised one actor who played the Prince of Palestria as a talent 'of which the public should positively not be deprived'. His identity remains a closely guarded secret.

Brian then got his farce-workers into the movies. Probably the best remembered are *The Night We Dropped a Clanger* (1959), *The Night We Got the Bird* (1961) and *Don't Just Lie There, Say Something!* (1973). *The Night We Dropped a Clang*er starred Hattie Jacques and Cecil Parker. It starts with a VI bomb dropping, unexploded, on a chicken run in the south of England and followed the wacky adventures of those who found it.

I would not like readers to think that one of the happiest events of my life, which happened around this time, in 1962, had the slightest tinge of farce. Melody and I decided to get married. With Melody still married to Stanley, and the Parker pen bandit behind bars in a prison unknown to us, she hadn't been able to sue for divorce – no divorce, no marriage. Fortunately, he was finally released and we tracked him down; on the day the divorce was finalised, incidentally also Melody's birthday, we got married.

Being a pitifully paid actor, I was, of course, working on the day, which meant, of course, that I was in danger of missing my own wedding. Our wedding day became a military operation.

Early morning chez Sachs, and feeding the children was the first task of the day. With all the little ones fed, Melody faced the daunting mission of securing an all-important babysitter for Kate. Our flat was on the middle floor of a big house with one flat upstairs and one downstairs. Upstairs lived a rather grumpy woman (though her grumpiness was sometimes outweighed by the charm of her husband) who, with their front door on our landing, would always burst into our flat and make rather critical comments to Melody. Melody found her a bit much. Downstairs lived another fussy woman who wouldn't let us store our pram in the garden. Melody found her difficult, too!

But Grumpy Upstairs was a great babysitter, so Melody went a-knocking and asked her if she might mind Kate while she and I rush to the registry office.

Grumpy Upstairs looked aghast. It did not take a mind-reader to read her mind. It had never occurred to her that Downstairs with Three Children didn't have the necessary banns, rings and papers. My own mother and father lived in so-called sin before they married, which was pretty advanced in the 1930s, so perhaps we were merely continuing a family tradition. Thirty years on, our neighbour had failed to realise she was living in the swinging sixties in swinging London and so wafted a certain 'I'm shocked'. Still, she agreed to look after Kate (phew) and Melody took the two boys to the pictures for the Saturday matinees.

Children taken care of, at around 9.30 a.m. Melody and I rushed off in our red Mini and signed the till death do us part at the registry office on Haverstock Hill. It was an intimate affair, just us, my mother and my lifelong friend, David, from William Ellis School.

After the registrar had done his part, David took my mother home and I hared off to the BBC to work. Melody collected the boys, rushed home, rescued Kate from Grumpy Upstairs and set about preparing a buffet for the thirty guests who were coming that night. Later, after putting Kate into her cot, she dressed the boys in their best suits and hurried to change herself. She had just finished putting on her new blue dress from C&A – economic circumstances prevented her getting the outfit from Harrods – but had not quite finished putting the final touches to her make-up when the doorbell rang and the first guests arrived. I managed not to be late for my own wedding reception and we partied into the early morning.

It was a fabulous party with so many friends there to celebrate our day. The next day our flat looked like a tip, with champagne bottles, crisps and fag ends everywhere. It was all a great rehearsal for *Fawlty Towers*!

With her new husband back at work, Melody had begun the clear-up of a lifetime when the doorbell rang. It was two gents who had agreed to buy our red Mini which we had decided to sell because, frankly, we needed the money.

'Usually,' Melody said defensively, 'our place isn't such a mess.'

The Mini buyers didn't have the slightest interest in our domestic hygiene as long as the car worked. Being an ace negotiator, Melody took £303 off them – which was £3 more than I told her to sell the car for – and smiled them out. She was happy with her lot.

But the buyers of our red Mini were not, as the fongle in the engine didn't work. Don't ask me what a fongle is. How can I be expected to remember mere mechanical details fifty years on? They turned up again and we behaved impeccably – and refunded them a fiver.

I must now return to true farce. After his lease ran out at the Whitehall in 1966, Brian Rix moved his company to the Garrick, where he staged *Stand by Your Bedouin*. I played Hamid – and put on yet another accent. The programme for the show still amuses me. Usually theatre programmes are like political manifestoes – all glitz and not much truth – but there were two items which had a peppersniff of truth. The first concerned how *Stand by Your Bedouin* got its title. A conference was called and Brian Rix, Elspeth Gray, Gilbert Harrison, Wallis Douglas, Ray Cooney, Tony Hilton and my good self met at 10 p.m. Brian said, 'Well, now all we need is a title.' The first suggestion was *Fez to Fez* and *Yemen and Women*, do you mind … *Oranges and Yemen*, *What a Shower*, *Sordid Arabia*, *I Mecca Last Night*. At three in the morning, we gave up. The second day dawned with a rapid interchange of phone calls. One of the new ideas was *Dromedary Gets the Hump*, to which the consensus was 'You must be joking'. The next suggestions were *Gin and Bitter Yemen*, *Haifa a Moment*, *The Former Imam Shall Steal Them* and *I've Grown Accustomed to her Fez*. None cut the Arabian mustard.

Then, at 6 p.m., the phone rang and Tony Hilton suggested *Stand by Your Bedouin*. With a belated reaction to his service days, Brian was standing stiffly at attention. Relief all round. I was also confident enough to write an ironic CV for the programme which went:

Andy Sachs lost his trousers one chilly morning on Victoria Station. A passing talent scout from the Rix organisation, impressed by his own unique comic talent, handed him a contract. Several farces later he felt ready to tackle the great Shakespearian roles in his bathroom. Having reached the very pinnacle of obscurity he joined the BBC Radio sound department. After some more time as an actor and TV producing *The Dales* he was asked to go back to farces and here he is.

The irony was a mask for anxiety. Despite always working, I needed to make an economic crust. And we needed more than a crust as Melody and I had a growing family – and she had to deal with the less-than-perfect behaviour of her ex.

Melody had made it clear to Stanley that he was always welcome to see the boys but he had to make regular visits – he couldn't just turn up and expect to be greeted with love. Once, when Stanley made arrangements to see Billy, Billy got all dressed up in his dickie bow. He waited for two hours for his

Manuel and his infamous pet rat Basil, which caused chaos at Fawlty Towers, in a delightful cartoon by Nick Horridge.

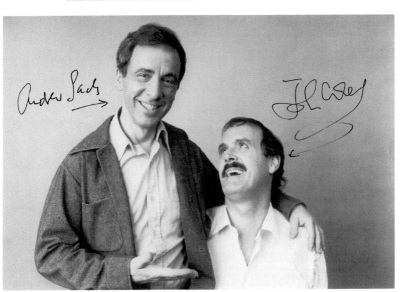

For once, John Cleese looks up at me.

Manuel fancies himself as an unbeatable matador.

Surprising Princess Anne at a Save the Children charity event.

Home sweet home. Melody makes up to me in our kitchen.

The picture above the mantelpiece is of my father when he was young.

Our dogs have always been an important part of our lives. On the left, skipping down the streets of Maida Vale with our blind dog Robbie, and on the right, Melody sits with Lizzie and Pepi.

ABOVE LEFT In Pinero's *Dandy Dick*, 1981.

ABOVE RIGHT This time I'm the hotel manager in *Are You Being Served? The Movie*, 1977.

LEFT With Nigel Hawthorne in a 1980 production of *The Tempest*.

BELOW With Glynn Edwards in a TV adaptation of H. G. Wells's *The History of Mr Polly*, 1980.

LEFT In *Glompus Van Der Hloed's Tales from the Crypt*, which aired on Capital Radio in 1981. I starred with Griff Rhys Jones and Mel Smith.

RIGHT As G. K. Chesterton's Father Brown.

BELOW Melody, me and our grandchildren. From left: Georgina, Kimberley, Charlotte and Billy.

A waxwork of Manuel tries to upset me on the roof of Madame Tussauds.

As Widow Twankey in my first pantomime, *Aladdin*, at the Cambridge Arts Theatre, 1991.

Recording the BBC Radio 5 production of *Tintin* in 1991. I played Snowy.

Joanna Lumley, Bob Hoskins, my daughter Kate and me. We voiced the characters of the animated series *The Forgotten Toys*.

On the cobbles of Weatherfield with *Coronation Street* stalwart Norris Cole. I played his brother Ramsay. © ITV Studios

Filming Dustin Hoffman's *Quartet* in the magnificent Hedsor House was sheer joy.

Billy Connolly and me in the lovely Hedsor House gardens.

Rehearsing for the annual concert. Billy Connolly, Tom Courtenay and Pauline Collins try to follow the score but with me as a debutante conductor it wasn't easy!

father before Melody decided to call time. Stanley telephoned and apologised and we gave him one more chance, but when he made another arrangement to take his son out and, again, failed to turn up, enough was enough and we did not allow him to make any more arrangements which he would only break.

I always thought of Melody's sons as my own and, indeed, I adopted them. I was absurdly pleased when they called me Dad. When I was home, I loved reading the children bedtime stories – tales of Tintin and Captain Haddock, they enjoyed them so much. I say 'when I was home' because, often, I was touring, bringing the delights of farce to all points of the compass. But absence does not just make the heart fonder. It can create tensions, and I am forever grateful to Melody for holding our family together. She always made everyone feel welcome and our home was a social one, a place for the children to bring all of their friends after school. Since we had yet to find our pot of gold, Melody would often cook a huge pot of stew for everyone to help themselves – which was even tastier. We were poor but happy!

One of my contributions to family life was to make sure Melody and the children had a lovely, slightly German Christmas, just as my parents had created for Barbara, Tom and me. My mother would enjoy all too few of these with us. When she was in her fifties, she had developed that very distressing disease, Parkinson's. She would often have the shakes so badly that she could never hold Kate when she was a baby. But my mother never grumbled. She always smiled.

I have said my mother was a heroine. She was also a heroine

to Melody, who loved her and sat with her for hours, talking away. Melody knew my mother would hate to have the children see her struggle to eat without dribbling – one of the many, many awful effects of Parkinson's – so she took care to feed her when they were alone.

Eventually, in 1966, my mother had to go into a home in Hampstead. Melody would try to visit every afternoon if I was in the theatre and couldn't get there myself. Kate liked to go too, because my mother had a little white-and-blue dish in which she kept Smarties. When Kate came to see her, she would open the lid and little Kate would dig in.

My mother had the knack of finding pleasure in small things. I remember once taking her for a drive in the countryside. We didn't say much but she smiled beautifully, never more so than when she just stared at a tree. Though she was always an immensely strong woman, I knew she always missed my Vati terribly, the man she had stood by through such turbulent times. They had been intensely happy together.

She lived until 1967 and when she died, I was heartbroken. She had looked after me with such love all of my life. After she was cremated, we spread her ashes among flowers, as she had asked us to do.

You grieve and you remember.

You grieve and you don't know how you will carry on.

You grieve and, somehow, you carry on.

You have no choice but to carry on.

I had a family to look after, and so I wrestled with my conscience when I was asked to go to South Africa with *Not Now Darling* in 1969. I was in two minds about it because of the Apartheid regime, but I had mouths to feed and a mortgage to pay. I hesitated: should I do it or should I not do it? Finally, I decided yes. We needed the money.

South Africa then was a brutal country if you were black and a wonderful one if you were white. I learned a great deal while I was out there and, if I focus on the trivial, it's because I don't feel qualified to give a précis of the political situation there. So my only story from the tour has to do with reptiles.

One day, the front-of-house manager at the theatre in Johannesburg told me a journalist wanted to interview me and to do it at an animal sanctuary because he knew I was interested in animals. The sanctuary had just saved a young deer from a forest fire, and they had had to house it temporarily among the snakes, alligators and crocs.

Having spotted snake handlers demonstrating how to extract venom from the reptiles, the journalist suggested I do something with the snakes which would make a good picture. I was mad and agreed. The man in charge, the snake maestro, told me to accompany him, and off he jumped over the wall that kept the snakes well away from the paying public. I followed him, thinking, I hope he knows what he's doing.

'We'll have this one,' he said as he picked up a particularly dangerous-looking specimen. He saw I was scared. 'Don't worry, it's not poisonous,' he soothed. 'Just put it round your neck.' I should have known better and yet I did what I was asked to do. I let them place Mr Fang around my neck.

Snake maestro then said, 'Try not to look behind you. Keep your eyes away from him because they can blind you.' The man was obviously Basil Fawlty's South African cousin.

When I got back to the theatre in Johannesburg, the front-of-house man asked me what species of snake it was. At this distance of time I've forgotten but back in 1969 I knew and told him.

'It's not poisonous,' he reassured me, 'but it's got rubbish in its mouth and if it gets too close to you, you have a bad time anyway because it vomits over you.' I had managed to avoid the snake throw up on me – something only snake experts know snakes are capable of.

A few weeks after my escape from reptile puke I returned to England, where I was fated to play a part that required me to look like Richard III with a basket of fruit on my head. I refer to my costume as Tapioca, one of the ugly sisters in Cinderella.

When I returned from South Africa, I also wrote *The Decline and Fall of the Empire* which was broadcast on Radio 4. The title gives the impression that it was about Britain's loss of empire, but this Empire was a cinema that was going to be pulled down. The play was a tribute to the cinema of my youth, when it cost only sixpence for a seat in the front stalls. A year later, I wrote a half-hour radio play about an eccentric married couple who had dozens of children. Timothy West and Prunella Scales played the couple. It went well and I harboured the ambition of turning it into a stage play – of which more later on.

But I still liked to do serious theatre and I had an exciting opportunity when I was offered a part in John Mortimer's *A Voyage Round My Father*. Mortimer was a barrister and a writer. His most famous 'real' brief was to defend the publishers of D. H. Lawrence's *Lady Chatterley's Lover* against charges of obscenity; his most famous 'unreal' brief was Rumpole, the feisty barrister who is able to confront judges fearlessly but is often intimidated by his wife.

A Voyage Round My Father is a personal and touching play, precisely the kind of play I never wrote. Mortimer wrote it about his father who had been a blind and cantankerous barrister, and who was played rather brilliantly by Alec Guinness. Jeremy Brett, famous later as Sherlock Holmes, played his son. Most of us had more than one part; I had three and, later, four.

I found Guinness very approachable and we got on well. One evening, he called me into his dressing room. His was on the ground floor and mine was five floors up. Alec knew I came from Germany and wanted some information about Berlin and what my childhood there had been like. I was only too happy to tell him everything I remembered. He had, he told me, agreed to play Hitler in a film based on his last days in the bunker.

A few days later, he invited me to his dressing room again. He said, 'I just wanted to introduce you to the production people on my film because I think I would very much like you to play Goebbels.'

Wow, I thought. What an irony. The mongrel plays the pure Aryan.

A few days later, Guinness said, 'Of course, I'm not casting this but I think you would be very good.' A few weeks later he apologised, 'I'm afraid they've got different casting for it.'

'It doesn't matter,' I replied. You can't be an actor if you can't stand rejection.

Having been rejected, I was very surprised to be summoned to a flat in Knightsbridge where I met the producer of the Hitler film. I had no idea why he wanted to meet me. We were chatting normally, when from behind a man said in an Italian accent, 'Yes, that is fine but not so much hair.' Instead of playing Goebbels, I discovered I had been cast as the person who married Hitler and Eva Braun just before the Allies took Berlin.

Since I began this book by describing the effect Hitler had on my life and that of my family, I want to say something about *The Last Days of Hitler* and Alec's performance. He had lived through the war but I was amazed how little he knew about Hitler. He had accepted the view Hitler was a madman and a diabolical fiend but he had never studied him. Alec prepared meticulously, reading a great deal. He discovered that, although Hitler was only fifty-six in 1945, he was pretty senile by then. The assassination attempt in 1944 left him partially paralysed. He couldn't lift his feet much off the ground. He hardly had the use of his left arm. His head shook. He was taking an enormous amount of pep pills to keep going and the pills were damaging him.

The Italian producers arranged for a certain Herr Boldt from Hamburg to brief Alec. Boldt had been with Hitler just before his death and showed Alec how Hitler behaved so that he could perfect his mannerisms and obsessions. I wondered what my old teacher Herr Plischert would have made of that; the Hitler he had revered had been seen as a heroic figure, not one verging on senility. Alec decided he would not adopt a German accent. As an actor, I understand the point Alec made in the *New York Times*:

> As an actor, I cannot possibly make Hitler a sympathetic figure.
> I can only make him human. I must see only Hitler's point of
> view. I'm afraid I'll be most hateful, and, as a precaution, I've
> asked the company to take out insurance against an attempt on
> my life. They think I'm being frivolous, but I'm not. It's for my
> wife's sake.

My father was an insurance man. I wonder how he would have assessed the risk of Guinness being murdered because he played Hitler as a reasonable man. At first, Alec thought Hitler was the finest performance he ever gave but, as the critics were not rapturous, he came to think that was exaggerated.

An odd thing happened during the run of *A Voyage* (I was still in the play, of course, but had slipped away for my day marrying Hitler). I got one of the most peculiar requests I ever had. It started innocuously: 'I hope you don't mind me writing this card, also could you please send me your autograph. I hope the show is going well and the best with it. I enclose a stamped addressed envelope so please can you send a pair of your socks.'

I was in theatre with Alec and told him, 'They want me to send my socks.' I passed this around the cast and one actress said, 'He's written to you, has he?' She added, 'I keep getting these letters from the sock man asking what do you do when you first come into the theatre dressing room, how do you get dressed or undressed and more – it's weird, isn't it?'

Our correspondent was a collector of memorable socks. I have consulted some authorities on the subject of the sock collector. They suggest that the author was a primitive foot fetishist. The top-class foot fetishist is proud that feet and feet alone provoke his erotic fantasies. The sock collector was an imperfect foot fetishist, however, as he also wanted descriptions of people dressing and undressing in the dressing and undressing rooms. I can only wonder what made him like that.

That brings me to the long-running farce, *No Sex Please, We're British*. The show opened in 1971 and the lead was first played by Michael Crawford, who made it something remarkable. His agility was astonishing and I admired him enormously. He climbed up things, down things and fell off things in a way that Milton Shulman, who complained there wasn't a real clown in *Dry Rot*, should have admired. The farce was well written but Crawford's brilliance raised it to a different level. I realised when I was asked to take the part that I couldn't match some of his physical brilliance. At best I sometimes got close. In my early teens, my frequent trips to the zoo often saw me spend time in the children's playground close by, which also had some gymnastic equipment, parallel bars, single bars and rings. I met two older guys who regularly practised there, who showed me a few things and how to swing on the bars. It turned out I could do such simple acrobatics quite nicely. It was very exhausting to do eight performances of *No Sex Please* a week, however, and I went through three shirts in a show.

The play was so demanding it was a miracle I had only one

accident. The set was a big room which had a real hatch leading to the kitchen. Twice in the play the hatch was open and I would jump through it to escape someone chasing me. At the end of the play, I had to do the same thing but this time the hatch would be locked; I would instead run around the settee. As I was running, I felt something go in my foot. Though it was just before the final curtain, I fell on the floor and – so much for my athletic prowess – I could not get up. It was awful. When the others took their bow at the end of the show I forced myself to stand – I have no idea how. Actors learn to take knocks. And the show must go on; it did and I did.

In 1972, I was offered a very different part: that of Albert Einstein in an American TV drama documentary. Melody still thinks it is one of the best things I've ever done, though much of what I did was just to read from his letters to his wives. When he wasn't rewriting the laws of the universe, Einstein had a vibrant love life. The make-up made a deep impression both on me and Melody. I really looked more like Einstein than myself. You can make up the face but not, alas, the brain. I had always struggled with physics, as the reader will know. Nevertheless, I managed to impersonate the greatest physicist of the twentieth century, but did it mean I understood the theory of relativity better? I leave that to your imagination squared.

CHAPTER 15

Fawlty Towers: Part One

The lessons I had learned in nearly twenty years of playing farce were about to serve me well in a classic that Plautus and Terence in their togas would have been proud to have written.

In March 1975, soon after I started in *No Sex Please*, John Howard Davies, a BBC producer, and John Cleese came to see it.

I'd worked for the latter John at Video Arts, his company in Oxford Street which made corporate videos – even *Monty Python* did not pay that well, so John had to sweat at the corporate coalface. The idea was that if one made learning about business amusing, executives would pay attention to essential management skills, such as how not to insult your clients and other aspects of running a profitable business.

Especially in his Basil Fawlty persona, John Cleese gives the impression of being manic and self-centred. That only shows what a good actor he is. In reality, John is kind, thoughtful and sensitive. He knew that our daughter Kate was a fan of *Monty Python* and arranged to take us out to lunch for her birthday. He had asked what she would like as a present. Kate said she would love a recording of one of his shows. He turned up with the whole set of *Monty Python*. She was knocked out. I use the phrase advisedly. Later, I too would be knocked out by John – but not in quite the same way.

After John had been to *No Sex Please*, I got the message that he and John Howard Davies would like to see me and would like to offer me the role of a Spanish waiter named Manuel in a new programme to be called *Fawlty Towers*. This, he explained, was a comedy he had written with his wife, Connie Booth, about a small hotel which was always on the verge of chaos. Meryl Streep, one of the greatest actresses of our times, has spoken about how hard she has fought for some parts in her career. I hardly fought for the part of Manuel but I was absolutely thrilled to be offered it – though I wasn't sure that I could do a Spanish accent. This was Jewish angst at its peak. I'd played a dormouse, a monkey, cockneys, a French foreign minister, a Hungarian carpet salesman, not to mention Prince Albert of Saxe Coburg, so I really should have had the confidence to do a Spanish accent.

Couldn't the waiter have a German accent instead? I asked.

The answer was a definite no. Manuel was a Spanish waiter who got everything wrong, not a German one who would get everything right. Or in *ordnung*.

So I threw myself into studying Spanish accents and exhausted the mounds of material stuffed into the BBC library. I listened to hours of tapes of Spanish people talking English. On set, the BBC provided a Spanish speaker whose mission was to check I pronounced properly the squeaks of Spanish that Manuel would utter when bashed, beaten or boiled by Basil. No viewer ever complained about Manuel's authenticity – or, if they did, I never got to hear about it. So I practised my Español, as we say in Barcelona. And my '¿*Que?*', which is Spanish for 'What?' or, indeed, 'What the Karl Dickens', or perhaps 'What the Cervantes'.

Doing the show required something of a juggling act as I was committed to *No Sex Please*, but the theatre and the BBC somehow worked out a way I could make all the rehearsals and recordings for *Fawlty Towers* without missing any performances in the theatre. It helped that we did the dress rehearsal and recording for *Fawlty Towers* on a Sunday, when there was no performance of *Sex*, as it were.

John had the idea for *Fawlty Towers* when he and Connie stayed in a small hotel whose owner was outrageously rude to them. They could not quite understand how such a place could survive but it did; the series it inspired has now gone down in television history. Basil Fawlty (played by John) runs the hotel with his sharp as steel wife Sybil (played by Prunella Scales). Sybil knows he creates chaos and is not to be trusted with drink, builders, guests or, in fact, anything.

The hotel has three permanent residents – two old ladies and a retired major. The staff are Polly the maid, played by Connie Booth, and Manuel, the Spanish waiter (me), who is all too often persecuted by Mr Fawlty.

The first rehearsals were a little tense but many of us were far from strangers. I'd worked with John and with Pru Scales, as I first met her, when I was a lowly assistant stage manager at Worthing rep theatre in the early 1950s. She was married to

Timothy West and we had become friends early in our careers. Then, we were all struggling through hard times to establish our reputations and raise families. These days we still talk about how we somehow got through it all.

John had been central to *Monty Python* but he wasn't the big star he became later and the BBC had serious doubts about the scripts. Internal reports complained they were not funny and far too long. They had a point about the length. When we got together to read, it became clear the scripts were going to over-run, so John and Connie had to slim them down.

As a result of this cutting and re-cutting, the script blossomed into something truly wonderful and innovative. We had no idea, however, that we were making historic TV and that the shows would still be screened, in countries as far-flung as Argentina and Zambia, nearly forty years after they were first made.

My performance as Manuel owes something not just to the physical comedy of *No Sex Please* but to something that happened when I was in *Mrs Dale's Diary*. A young foreign actor had joined the cast, but he didn't speak very good English. The sad truth was that he was not able to do the part properly. During rehearsals the director took him aside. 'This is no good,' he said. 'You do not speak English well enough.' The young man started to defend himself, 'But you know I can learn this, please let me do it.' It did not work and he was let go. I really felt empathy for this young actor. After all, in 1938 I had been taught the mantra 'I am a little German boy and I don't speak English' (despite PC Reginald's best efforts). I remembered that boy when I started to think about Manuel.

Manuel has a good opinion of himself but he is pretty humble and he loves Mr Fawlty and will do anything for him, no matter how much Fawlty abuses, insults and hits him. As it turned out, the hitting was not all play-acting. One abuse of Manuel took place when we recorded 'The Wedding Party'. Basil is the stereotypical uptight Brit, and one of the enduring mysteries of *Fawlty Towers* is whether Basil and Sybil ever had sex; the general consensus is no, which would explain why Basil is perpetually frustrated. Whether or not he had marital nookie, Basil certainly wasn't going to have carryings-on under his roof unless the carriers-on were married – and probably not even then. It could have been called *No Sex Please, We're Fawlty*.

In 'The Wedding Party', however, Basil is confronted by lust suppressed and rampant. The guests include a couple who have come to Torquay for a wedding and have the hots for each other, and a French antiques dealer, Mrs Peignoir, who flirts with both Basil and Major Gowan. Even the staff's hormones are going full tilt. The usually sensible Polly is being very seductive to her boyfriend on top of the front desk and ice queen Sybil is flirting at the bar. Not with Basil, of course, who compares his wife's giggling to 'machine-gunning a seal'. Basil is frustration personified in search of someone to take it out on.

And who is the take-it-out-on victim?

A poor Spanish waiter from Barcelona.

At one point in the episode, the frustrated Basil runs into the kitchen, grabs a frying pan and attacks Manuel – a neurotic Brit determined to protect the virtue of his hotel.

I have tried not to make this memoir too heavy but I must

now introduce an intellectual theme. In his great film *Rashomon*, the Japanese director Kurosawa tells the story of a murder from four points of view. Each version is sincere and each is utterly different. Memories of the frying-pan fiasco may never win the Grand Prix at the Venice Film Festival, as *Rashomon* did, but here is View One – mine.

We had rehearsed the frying-pan scene a great deal. The pan was one the BBC had specially padded so that it would not break my skull. It worked perfectly at the dress rehearsal. The pan bounced off my head in full harmony with BBC Health and Safety rules.

When we recorded the show live in front of the studio audience, it went wrong, and painfully so. Somehow there was a mix-up, and, unbeknown to John, the pan left for him to pick up was not a prop, as we had discussed, but a real metal frying pan in which you could cook a nice paella – and he brought it down *wooomph* on my poor head.

He hit me so hard I couldn't get up. Of course, he apologised, in his own way, offering me a Babycham and a big kiss.

John's recollection is rather different. He maintains that we would never have rehearsed such a scene, just discussed it; that it was always to have been a real frying pan, and it was only to be a glancing blow as I turned away – but that somehow I got the timing wrong, moving upwards and backwards at precisely the wrong moment. Ouch! Of course, he apologised at once.

Am I right? Is John right? Kurosawa suggested all the versions of *Rashomon* were true – but as it was John who wrote the 'Wedding Party' script, and he is a good deal younger than

I am, I'm certainly happy to bow to his superior memory. One thing's for sure, we're not going to fall out over a frying pan!

Comedy is a risky business, as another moment in 'The Wedding Party' makes clear. In another scene, Basil comes running to Manuel and says there are goings-on upstairs. Then he takes me – Manuel – outside the hotel to get a ladder, determined to catch the sex maniacs at it. 'Hold the ladder,' he tells Manuel while he climbs up. He finds the window shut so, pretending to check the windows, he peers in and sees the couple inside. Feigning great shock and outrage, he loses his balance and topples backwards – as he is supposed to. But when the ladder clattered down it missed my nose by a whisker.

In another episode, I was actually burned quite badly. I need to explain this carefully.

The subject of the episode: there was to be a fire alarm practice so all the staff and guests would know what to do if there were a fire. Accordingly, Basil tells the guests and staff that at eleven o'clock there will be a fire alarm practice.

The first mix-up: the guests don't quite understand what Basil is saying. He gets into quite a state and, as usual, things go wrong.

The catalyst: the fire alarm goes off, but before 11 a.m. Stubborn as ever, Basil insists that it is not the real fire alarm. It is meaningless.

But it is not meaningless. The truth is that in the kitchen, Manuel has actually managed to start a real fire accidentally. The people outside, in the immortal phrase, 'know nothing'. Manuel panics in English and Spanish. He runs out of the kitchen and into the lobby and screams, 'Oh, Mr Fawlty, there is a fire!' To which he gets the kind of reaction Basil often gave him. Manuel has got it all wrong. 'Oh no, go away, go away,' he dismisses his frantic waiter. Obsessed with one thing, the fire drill, Basil doesn't realise Manuel is talking about a real fire. True farcical confusion. There is a real fire. No one in the hotel apart from Manuel knows there is a real fire. They all think Manuel is pretending there is a fire because, as usual, he knows nothing. Confused? I'm not surprised!

From there, the chaos intensifies. Manuel screams 'Fire!' two or three times and manages to get pushed back into a burning kitchen.

And now I have to switch to me rather than Manuel. I was starting to smoulder and was really in pain. I had become the victim of overconfident stunts (so-called) experts. They had given me a waiter's uniform that had been treated with 100 per cent BBC-guaranteed fire retardant on it. The uniform, I was promised, would smoke and look dangerously hot but it would just feel warm.

'Yes,' I said. 'That's fine.'

Never trust stunts experts. This was one of the worst experiences of my career. When I was rushing in and out from the kitchen trying to warn Basil, the jacket actually got really hot and, at the end, I had to take it off. It wasn't a very good fire retardant. My arm was frazzled red skin. It was extremely painful.

John could have killed the whole of the BBC; he made a great fuss, quite rightly. I was sent to a doctor in Harley Street who told me I would have scars for the rest of my life. The sum total of the BBC's compensation for being scarred for the rest of one's life came to £700. The next day I had to return to *No Sex Please*.

In one scene, I had to catch a number of encyclopaedias – they were glued together just to make them heavier – which were thrown at my chest. The pain from the burns was such that I was unable to catch them properly and fell backwards. The reader will note that in *Fawlty Towers* a ladder nearly de-brained me. Now I was the victim of a literary mugging that could have been devised by the Marquis de Sade.

In fact, the Harley Street doctor was being alarmist so I never could complain about the BBC's compensation. The scars lasted a few years, though for a while I couldn't bear to have my arm uncovered in sunlight.

John gave the show his all. When we finished rehearsals and were about to record in front of the live audience, he visibly moved up a gear. His adrenalin went into overdrive. Nervous energy poured from his every pore. His performance was sheer genius. I caught a repeat of the episode 'Gourmet Night' from the first season recently. High comedy and farce sometimes need perfectly focused manic energy. John had that brilliantly and was wonderful to play against. It was always a real challenge.

For all this, the first series of *Fawlty Towers* was far from being an instant hit. The shows were on BBC 2 and the first reviews were hardly to die for. 'Long John is short on jokes,' said Tony Pratt in the *Daily Mirror*. Peter Buckman in *The Listener* complained that 'John Cleese was hardly a good character actor and then I am sorry to say stuck his unfunnies in my ribs.' He went on:

Most regrettably of all, a large part of the business revolves round that venerable stooge – a Spanish waiter with faulty English.

While not for a moment accusing Cleese and Booth of racism, jokes about dagos and wops horrified some Americans who were watching with me, and once this had been pointed out, I began to notice all sorts of racist jokes.

Then the tide turned. Clive James had been on holiday when the series started but when he caught up with it, he wrote that the show had him retching with laughter. Peter Fiddick, the veteran reviewer on *The Guardian*, said that as it blended so many different types of laugher it should fail, but that 'Cleese and his cronies continually pull it off'. As one of the cronies, I was delighted.

The audiences grew and the once-sniffy BBC saw it had a hit on its hands. In 1976, it repeated the series, BAFTA nominated John for Best Light Entertainment Performance and the show won the Best Situation Comedy award. I basked in the glory – and the pleasure of making millions laugh. I was gratified also to have received a nomination at the Royal Television Society for Best Light Entertainment Performance. Manuel wasn't such a dumb waiter, after all.

CHAPTER 16

Chichester and Sound Experiments

After the first series, John and Connie needed time to write a second one, so I went back to the actor's merry-go-round. First stop was the Chichester Festival Theatre which had developed a considerable reputation under an Australian, Keith Michell, who was both an actor – he played Henry VIII in the TV series – and a producer. He lured Michael Redgrave to play a memorable Uncle Vanya there and he persuaded Rex Harrison to act in *Monsieur Perrichon's Travels*, a comedy by the French playwright Eugene Labiche, who wrote or co-wrote a total of 176 plays.

Rex needed a good deal of rehearsal and constant attention. The cast actually complained about him to Keith Michell but all Keith said was that they should just 'get on with it'. Around opening night Rex made up for it. He invited the whole cast to the beautiful house he had rented nearby and was very gracious as the giver of the party. After the last performance, he gave another party. There was a piano at this house and the cast said that they wanted Rex to entertain them. At first he was reluctant, but we persuaded him and he performed 'I've Grown Accustomed to your Face' from *My Fair Lady* quite beautifully.

There's something magical about seeing a performance in private. Maybe the truth is that even after fifty years in show-biz, I am still starstruck. If I see a pianist playing Mozart at the Albert Hall, yes, I enjoy it. But I enjoy it 100 times more if they are playing at a little gathering. Then it's magic. I tend to cry joyfully and tears come down my face when there is somebody that really moves me. I do that more when I am close to the performer and it is private.

I was not just in Chichester to act. Keith Michell gave me a real opportunity. I had turned the half-hour play about the married couple, *Made in Heaven*, which Timothy West and Prunella Scales had performed on the radio, into a full-length play. I was rather proud of it and asked Keith to have a read. He loved it and agreed to stage the play, hiring Wendy Toye to direct.

Unfortunately, I was still in *No Sex Please* so I couldn't go to rehearsals and see how my play was being produced. The result was I couldn't contribute anything. Even when I saw it finally, I didn't have the courage and the confidence to tell them what I thought was wrong and how the production could be improved. One of the problems was that the sets were exaggerated, with huge settees which made no sense to me. It was meant to be just an ordinary room in an ordinary home.

Melody and our children came with me on the first night. Patricia Routledge, who played the role of the mother, was wonderful, and Tony Robinson was superb. He played the child from a toddler to when he was a teenager.

Made in Heaven was in a repertory with *Othello* and Henrik Ibsen's *An Enemy of the People* so the competition was terrifyingly strong. Ten out of twelve reviews panned it. After that, I thought, oh well, that's the end of me. However, two years later the play was translated into Swedish for the National Theatre there, and adjusted to suit local audiences. They asked me to go over for the first night. The theatre was packed and the audience liked it. It ran longer than anticipated and they kept it on for a whole year, so that did cheer me up.

During this period, BBC Radio continued to offer me good opportunities. I've explained that I've always been interested in wildlife so it's not surprising that one part that stands out is that of a Russian dog. I was cast because I could bark convincingly – not a skill they teach at RADA, I suspect. The play was based on a Russian novel where a scientist gets the idea that dogs can be trained to talk. This itself was based on the work of Ivan Pavlov, who won the Nobel Prize for his work on conditioning animals.

In the play, the scientist finds me and gets me to, well, sort of talk. Then it's like *Pygmalion* with me as Audrey Hepburn, but canine. The scientist invites people to see this wonderful spectacle of me talking. He was very pleased but there were problems. While I was quite good in human talk, I might cock a leg at the curtains of the big room for a pee – something Eliza Doolittle never did, even when she was furious with Professor Higgins.

Anyway, playing the dog got me a Performance of the Year award.

At its best, the atmosphere at the BBC allowed us to experiment. After Chichester, I had the idea of doing a play without any words. I loved radio but I had the idea that a radio play did not have to be just a litany of voices and words. There must be other ways, I thought, of getting something across on radio. I challenged myself to think of sounds – not words – that would be understandable immediately. The best I could think of at first was a refrigerator. To know exactly what is happening, you need only the sound of the opening of the door. No words, please, the sound is enough for people to know what is going on. Therefore, if one could put together a series of recognisable sounds and create a relationship with each other in sequence, one could do something interesting. So that is what I did. The only actual words in the play were 'the' and 'revenge', the play's title.

I played the central character, a man on the run who escapes from prison for one reason only: he wants to get the man who sent him to prison and kill him. I think the best way of conveying the nature of the play is to set out the script. The recording was done in such a way that the audience was, as the script insists, 'at all times very close to the main character doing the same work, in fact, as his ears. This applies particularly to his breathing of which we are always nearly always aware.' I added that I hoped that closeness would help give a clearer perspective to some of the scenes.

FADE IN

1. Birds, slight wind through trees.

2. MAN approaches through shrubbery until very close. He has been running and is puffed out.

3. Suddenly, in the distance, a prison siren or alarm.

4. MAN gives a sharp intake of breath. Stifled groan of fear.

5. Announcer: 'We present *The Revenge* – a radio play without words.'

6. We are with the MAN as he runs blindly through the undergrowth. He stops for a moment.

7. Dogs bark in the distance.

8. MAN runs on and approaches a slow-running river. He splashes into it and runs along the middle, breathing heavily.

9. Dogs get nearer.

10. MAN stumbles to behind rock, trying to get his breath back.

11. Police voices can now be heard indistinctly, as well as the dogs.

12. MAN takes a deep breath and submerges.

13. From underwater we hear a dog breaking through onto the bank, whining and sniffing for a moment, then going on again.

14. MAN surfaces and releases breath desperately.

15. Dogs go off in the distance.

16. MAN whimpers with exhaustion.

FADE OUT

FADE IN

17. Same river sound.

18. Owl.

19. MAN breathing regularly now but shivering. He wades out of

the water, dripping wet. His shoes squelch as he moves through shrubbery.

FADE OUT

FADE IN

20. Clock striking in the distance.

21. MAN approaches on gravel, shoes still squelching.

22. Singing can be heard from a pub about twenty yards away.

23. MAN stops close and tries car door handle. It is locked. He moves to another. It is open. He slides in on leather seat.

24. There is a shout from a slightly drunken customer at the door of the pub, who approaches running.

25. MAN gets out of car.

26. DRUNK arrives and stops. He gets less than one angry word out when MAN punches him twice.

27. DRUNK falls against car and slides to the ground with a moan.

28. MAN drags unconscious body away behind some bushes with effort.

29. He searches in pockets and finds money.

30. He takes off his own wet shoes and throws them into the bushes.

31. He takes off the DRUNK's shoes and puts them on.

32. He then starts to exchange clothes. We hear the DRUNK's tie taken off, shirt unbuttoned, trousers zip etc.

FADE OUT

FADE IN

33. Railway yard. Shunting at various distances.

34. Running footsteps dodging about until we hear the MAN's breathing. He continues walking and tries one or two of the

sliding doors on the goods wagons, until one of them proves unlocked.

35. MAN sighs with satisfaction, pauses a moment to look around, then slides door open.

36. We stay with him, as he climbs in and shuts the door again from the inside.

37. MAN walks to one end of the wagon and lies down on some sort of soft bundles.

38. The wagon, which is part of a train, starts to move. The MAN is startled for a moment, but then settles down for a sleep.

FADE OUT

FADE IN

39. Heavy West End traffic. Snatches of indistinguishable conversation: newspaper seller etc. MAN approaches. We stay with him as he walks down the tube station.

40. He goes into phone box and closes the door.

41. Dialling. The number rings for quite a long time. MAN hangs up, apparently satisfied. He leaves phone box.

42. He puts money into ticket machine. Clicks his tongue impatiently as nothing happens. He bangs machine. Ticket is produced with change. He takes it and walks to escalator.

FADE OUT

FADE IN

43. MAN climbing last few steps of another tube station. He reaches the top and walks out into street.

44. Sounds of very light traffic as he walks along. He turns corner into a quiet street.

45. He walks past children playing some kind of musical game.

46. Milk float. A small dog barks in the distance. Pigeons coo. There is a sunny, peaceful atmosphere in this street.

47. After some time, he turns in through garden gate along path to front door.

48. He knocks. Pause. Knocks again, loud and long. Longer pause in which children run by in the street. MAN shows his satisfaction with a grunt.

49. MAN walks along side of house, brushing against dustbins and tries to open a window. It is locked.

50. He breaks small window, fiddles efficiently with catch, opens window, climbs in quickly and shuts it from the inside.

51. Bending down, he picks up the pieces of glass which have fallen into the room and puts them in ashcan.

52. He opens a larder unhurriedly. Finds a tin which he opens and helps himself to a biscuit.

53. Moves over to fridge and opens it. He takes out a bottle and shuts fridge door.

54. Pulls drawer open, rummages through cutlery until he finds a bottle opener and opens it. Slight fizz. He drinks gratefully straight from the bottle.

55. He puts a plate on the table. Opens various jars, tins and a bread bin etc. Starts to cut bread.

56. There is a noise outside the kitchen door.

57. MAN catches his breath and is absolutely still.

58. Noise is repeated.

59. MAN, breathing quietly, goes along to door and suddenly pulls it open.

60. A cat meows.

61. MAN relaxes. The cat rubs itself against his legs and purrs.

62. MAN goes back to cutting board and makes friendly noises to the cat.

63. He puts something on the bread and starts eating.

64. Taking the bottle and still eating, he moves out of the kitchen, through the hall and into living room. The door creaks slightly as he opens it.

65. He goes to settee and sinks down into it, still eating and drinking.

66. After a moment, he gets up and switches radio on. He tunes into pop song with presumably – though not recognisably – English words.

67. Goes back to settee and relaxes on it with cat purring. Begins to breathe regularly.

FADE OUT

FADE IN

68. Slight snoring.

69. The radio is now playing quiet classical music.

70. Car approaches outside. Stops. Car door bangs.

71. MAN wakes with a start.

72. Footsteps outside approach front door.

73. MAN quickly switches radio off, treading on cat.

74. He shoves plate and bottle under settee.

75. Goes to curtains and hides behind them. Breathing very close into curtain.

76. Front door bangs, steps approach. Living room door opens with slight creak. We hear SECOND MAN come in humming to himself.

77. He moves about for a few moments, then goes out of the room and can be heard turning on bath taps, still singing.

78. Cat purrs close by and rubs against MAN's leg. He kicks it impatiently.

79. Presently MAN moves away from curtain and across room to door. He opens it slowly. It creaks slightly.

80. He goes upstairs, bathroom sounds get a little clearer. The taps are turned off and SECOND MAN, still humming, gets into bath.

81. MAN goes quietly towards bathroom door and stands immediately outside, breathing tensely.

82. He opens bathroom door cautiously. Humming and bath sounds much closer now.

83. MAN approaches until he is immediately behind SECOND MAN.

84. MAN's breathing very close but quiet.

85. Suddenly SECOND MAN stops singing and freezes. He turns around and gasps with alarm and fear.

86. MAN pounces on him and pushes him under the water.

87. SECOND MAN breaks surface and screams but is pushed under again immediately.

88. Gradually struggle ceases. Some bubbles. Then quiet except for MAN's very heavy breathing. He is trembling and in a high state of excitement.

89. He takes his hands out of the water and shakes them into the bath. He pulls out the plug.

90. He leaves bathroom and goes downstairs and into living room. The door creaks slightly.

91. He lights cigarette and inhales deeply. He calms down a little.

92. Lifts phone. Pause. Dials 999.

93. Cat purrs.

FADE OUT

END

The killer had done what he wanted and got revenge. The play received enormous attention and was performed twice in one evening on Radio 3. Many people wrote to me, including a blind man who was very interested in the world being represented just in sound. The play even made the prestigious *Hi Fi News*. A number of teachers wrote to me and I've kept the letters. One ran: 'I have just played a tape of your radio play *The Revenge* to my class, who share language and learning problems. If you can imagine a dozen children listening with rapt attention to every sound, it is a real delight.' He added he was glad to share the pleasure 'in the stimulus your play has provided for these children'.

He included some letters from the children. One read:

Dear Mr Andrew Sachs, I like the story of *The Revenge*. I like the bit where you killed the people … and I like the bit where you run away from the police and can you make another play please.

Amusingly, *The Revenge* received an award in Barcelona. Manuel would have been proud.

CHAPTER 17

Fawlty Towers: Part Two

There was a big gap between the first series of *Fawlty Towers* and the second one, I think partly because of difficulties between John and Connie. When we started the second series, we were all gathered in the same rehearsal room we had used in the first series. John came in and I wondered where Connie was.

I answered my own question at once. She's probably parking the car downstairs. But when a few minutes later Connie came in, she and John behaved so oddly I wondered whether they had actually come to rehearsal together. She went over to John and said, 'Hello, John. How are you?'

He said, 'Oh lovely, yes, thank you. Did you get here all right?'

I wondered again. What does that mean?

We soon discovered they had separated but they were always very professional in rehearsals. If it was difficult for them, they did not show it to the rest of us.

If Connie had not written that second series with John, it wouldn't have been the same. She had a powerful say, and sometimes she overruled him. Even then, she did so rather gently.

'I'm not doing this, John,' she would say, tut-tutting away, but her annoyance would quickly dissipate. They were both perfectionists and wanted everything to be the best.

Despite what we later learned about their fraying marriage, John and Connie would often make up and even have a cuddle. I can't write the word 'cuddle' in the context of *Fawlty Towers* without thinking of the passion that Manuel provoked in the Greek chef in one memorable episode. As usual, Basil has aspirations to rival a five-star hotel, so he organises a gourmet evening to show his establishment has gastronomic class. He hires a top-class Greek chef who is supposed to have a sublime touch with roasts, sauces and fish. But Chef is temperamental. And more than temperamental. He is the only person to see Manuel as a love object. Manuel does not reciprocate, however.

Basil, however, couldn't care less about what Manuel might want and tells him, 'Now you've got to be nice to him, he is a very good cook.'

There was one moment which had to be cut out because the BBC was a prudish auntie. At one point, the besotted cook, instead of doing his Michelin star stuff, collapses against the wall in the kitchen, totally drunk.

The cook says, 'Ah, Mr Fawlty, I love him, I love him.'

Manuel replies, 'I don't like it, I never loved him.'

As Basil makes him get up, the cook throws up – but the BBC wouldn't allow that. All the audience heard was spewing and a gagging noise.

The second series was a huge success, too. After three episodes, the audience was eleven million. John was described as the British Jacques Tati, the great French comedian who made many wonderful silent comedies. He won the BAFTA for Best Light Entertainment performance. And he deserved it. I've said that most actors are insecure so, at the risk of blowing my own cornet, let the record show I was also nominated for Best Light Entertainment performance.

One of the pleasures of a hit is the fan letters and I was now getting letters addressed to Manuel as well as many requests, one of which has to be placed in the context of subsequent scandals.

Jimmy Savile's show *Jim'll Fix It* was one of the big hits of the 1970s. We now know that Savile was a serial sex criminal who abused the trust placed in him by many institutions – not just the BBC but hospitals including Stoke Mandeville and Broadmoor. Very few people had any idea then of his true character, and I was shocked when the truth became known.

After the second series, Savile contacted my agent and said a little girl had written in offering to teach Manuel English. I said I would love to do it. Savile made it quite a production. We went on location and a hotel had been made up to look like Fawlty Towers. I was asked to sit on the floor in the bar, dressed up as Manuel. The little girl was told all she had to do was call 'Manuel, Manuel,' and I would pop up from behind the bar, speaking atrocious English. Then, she could start to teach me. It was simple but quite charming, and it went off well. In hindsight, I shudder to think about it, though there was no hint of any impropriety on that occasion, I am relieved to say.

The media world was waiting to see if there would be a third series. 'We'll forget about it for a year,' John told us, 'and then decide if there's any juice left in it or whether we ought to try something completely different.' I hoped we would not abandon the series but it was obviously not my decision.

So, on the eve of my fiftieth birthday, I was in the happy position of having created a character recognised the breadth of the land. It was Manuel who was the celebrity, not me, and I have John to thank for offering me the role – it certainly changed my life. Though I enjoyed the fame my alter ego enjoyed, it became clear the third series was not going to happen quickly, if at all, and I went into my old spiral of doubt, fretting I would never work again and that we would end up in the workhouse. It reminded me of my youth. I felt I was going to have to go round the agencies again, as I'd done when I was starting out. I was only a little more confident than twenty-five years earlier, so I thought if somebody else offers me something I've got to say yes. That was my reason for doing *Dead Ernest*, a comedy series in which I died in episode one and was vacuumed up to Heaven. But I wasn't on cloud nine. It wasn't well written and as soon as filming began, I knew I shouldn't have taken the role. But I didn't want to be unemployed. I compounded the error when I did another series whose title I can't even remember.

If you believe that, dear reader, you'll believe anything. It's in the scrapbook, which strikes me as an odd word. It should be a book of things that one can scrap, destroy, discard, but it means the book of things we treasure because they hold good and sometimes not so good memories. I didn't have the confidence of some other actors, who can bat away the offers they don't like and say, 'Oh, I'm not going to do that, I'm sorry, no, no, no.'

Huge hits do have an afterlife, however, and the particular afterlife of *Fawlty Towers* was interesting as it involved the Germans, telephones, Madame Tussauds, an international cruise and Peter Sellers. I'll start with the Germans, as the episode in which a party of Germans come to Fawlty Towers is a classic. 'Don't mention the war!'

After the series was sold to Germany, the production company in Munich got hold of me and, as they had discovered I was German-born, asked if I would do an episode of *Fawlty Towers* in the German language. (How ironic, I was now going to play Manuel as a German!) So I went over there and played Manuel. I learned that at this stage they were not going to include the episode when no one must mention the war.

Later versions of *Fawlty Towers* shown in Germany, however, included the classic 'Don't mention the war' episode, which allows me to assert that the Germans are now sufficiently mature psychologically after many years of therapy to realise they lost the war!

This is Your Life was also a very popular show in the 1970s. Eamonn Andrews, who presented it, was one of the biggest stars on TV. The format was simple. The show covered someone's life in thirty minutes with contributions from family, friends and colleagues. It was entertaining, potted biography. The gimmick was that the subject of each show was surprised, as he or she had no idea they were about to be the hero of an episode. Thames TV's team, who made it, were adept at persuading the family and friends of their subjects to keep quiet and skilful at ambushing their 'victims'.

I certainly didn't guess I was in Eamonn Andrews's firing line when I was doing a photo shoot in central London. The organisers just told me we were to go to the record shop HMV in Oxford Street to sign some photos.

I was, of course, dressed as Manuel. I went up the stairs to the top floor and found a crowd of people waiting for me with photos to sign. I started signing and then I looked to my right and saw a man I didn't realise was Eamonn Andrews. Then, he announced himself and uttered his trademark, 'Andrew Sachs, this is your life.'

I was flummoxed and just said, 'What?' Laughing, I soon realised I was to be the subject of the big red book.

I was whisked off to the studios where I found Melody with a suit ready for me, so I changed, went into make-up and we got on with it. Eamonn Andrews was sweating so much throughout the recording he was dripping onto the book of my life. It was rather worrying, and I had to calm him down, just as Manuel had tried to calm Mr Fawlty sometimes. The show was, like all such shows, highly staged. Melody, Billy, John and Kate all took part, as did Leslie Phillips, who called me an 'enchanting fellow' and gave me a quick kiss; June Whitfield; and the diva Jessie Matthews herself, who appeared in a billowing blue gown. John Cleese recorded a hilarious tribute. My sister Barbara was in Kenya but recorded a message. My auntie Barbara was flown in from Munich and spoke remarkably good English. My brother Tom flew in from Toronto. I enjoyed it, even though sometimes it made it seem as if my whole career had been a prelude to playing Manuel.

After the end of the second series of *Fawlty Towers* and the excitement of *Jim'll Fix It* and *This is Your Life*, I wanted to rest, but I didn't get the chance. One day Melody told me my agent, Lynda Ronan, had rung at the crack of dawn and was coming round to discuss a new project.

'Lynda!' I smiled. 'That was nice of her!' That was the wrong thing to say. Melody complained Lynda had rung her ridiculously early and interrupted her beauty sleep.

I had, in much earlier days, dubbed my wife the 'Drama Queen of the Century', a questionable compliment perhaps, but one she soon came to appreciate by giggling modestly when I said it of her.

When she came over, Lynda told us I had been offered the chance to lecture on drama to the passengers on a luxury cruise sailing from Florida. I could be Professor of Drama.

'But be prepared,' Lynda warned. 'They'll want plenty of stuff on *Fawlty Towers*, of course, though what that has to do with drama is anybody's guess.'

'Oh, I don't know. "A Tragedy with Laughs!" wouldn't be far off.'

'I'll set up a meeting, yes?'

I groaned.

She wasn't going to let me get away with that. 'Never mind groaning. Try "Free Holiday". Try "Inspiring". It's not going to make you rich but they treat their lecturers like royalty.'

I was reluctant because of niggling doubts I've always had about the very thing they were asking me to do: feeding the public's urge to peel away the ins and outs of our profession in the hope of getting the low-down on backstage gossip I'd rather keep to myself.

'God, you're pompous!' my Drama Queen of the Century sometimes said. But my qualms stem from my first visit to a theatre when I was no more than five years old, an age when you're ready to believe anything. In particular, I remember being taken to see a Christmas play about a violin-playing beetle. The insect has his one leg hacked off by a horrible woodcutter, who is banished to the moon for his crime. The beetle enlists the help of two children and teaches them to fly. After thrilling adventures involving the Great Bear, the Milky Way and the Man in the Moon himself, they rescue the leg and glue it back on to the beetle using their spit, before returning home where they all live happily ever after. From the moment the curtain went up, I was spellbound.

I had come across creepy-crawlies before but never one twice as big as me, who walked on two legs like me, who talked like me, and could even dance and play tunes, not like me… What I was witnessing was wonderful. It wasn't a bedtime story. It wasn't pretend. This was real life! I knew that because it was happening right in front of me and I was part of it – almost in the front row!

I left that theatre deeply touched by the beetle, and desperate to meet him again someday. Unfortunately, my friend from next door then told me the beetle was not a beetle at all except on the outside, and inside it was empty and a man climbed into it every day. It was the man, an actor, who did the speaking. That was not the end of my disillusion. My friend added the beetle couldn't really fly and somebody else was playing the violin anyway. I felt betrayed.

What really persuaded me to sign on the dotted line was the contract Lynda had negotiated. If I would forgo my fee, management was prepared to invite the charming Mrs Sachs to enjoy the cruise with her husband in a first-class cabin, with a balcony and other benefits. We were happy at the prospect.

The cruise drama team was a good one; it included a choreographer who coaxed audience members on-stage to learn a routine; a theatre impresario who told us nail-biting tales of flops, hits, trials and tantrums; and a specially written radio play with the leading role to be played by a volunteer from the audience.

I was a familiar waiter without being a familiar face as far as the general public was concerned. But I signed up and agreed to include a tale or two about *Fawlty Towers*. I was torn. As the actor behind Manuel's moustache and mangled English, I had been able to hold on to a measure of anonymity that allowed me to play a wide range of roles with a good chance of not being recognised offstage.

The passengers loved the entertainment but their praise was often accompanied by discreet and sometimes less discreet curiosity about our work and personal lives. We were invited to judge competitions, attend quiz nights or have a go at karaoke, and at almost any time and almost any place on the ship, there could be requests for autographs, photos and general chats. A chirpy Londoner about half my age approached me one afternoon as I was on deck writing postcards.

'Hello, mate,' he said. 'Saw you last night doin' your stuff.'

I smiled modestly. 'Ah.'

'Bit of a surprise you wasn't Spanish, I tell ya.' He gave a short laugh.

'You're not the first,' I smiled back.

'Don't suppose I am,' he went on. 'I'm Sidney. Call me Sid.'

We shook hands. 'I'm Andrew. Call me Andy.'

There was a pause. I felt that a little ice might need breaking. 'Are you enjoying your cruise?'

'Top class,' he nodded.

Sid was a good talker: intelligent, self-confident, good-humoured and with a lively mind all nicely spiced up in a rich cockney sauce. A beguiling recipe. He came from generations of East End stock, about a dozen of whom were on the cruise, he told me.

'Wow!'

'Party booking! Costs peanuts that way.'

Sid had left school at fourteen hardly able to read and write but had got a skilled job he enjoyed. His wife and children were the love of his life. His two bright boys were destined to have a far better education than either of their parents, he said.

I gave up hoping he might reveal his reaction to our show, which shows how eager I remained for reviews, I suppose. Then, as he was leaving, he added, 'That talk of yours last night, Andy. I have to tell ya, that was a bit of an eye-opener for me. I never knew nothing about all that stuff, you know, like you was talkin' about, 'cos I never bin in a theatre before.'

'Would you go now?'

He thought about it for a moment, then shook his head. 'Nah – don't think so. Never been brought up to it, really.'

'And what about *Fawlty Towers*?' I offered with a hopeful smile.

'Nah, not really. I seen one or two of 'em with the kids. They love it. It's a good laugh. That's why I come last night, 'cos the missus was off with a girlfriend, and it didn't cost nothing and there was this photo of Emanuel as you go in. Don't look much like you though, does it? That's a joke in itself, eh?' He laughed heartily. 'No offence, mate.'

'None taken.'

'But that's what pulled me up, you know – that photo and then you goin' on about what you had to say. That was dead interestin'. You got one busy life, ain't ya. *I* never been round the world like you, mate. Doing plays! And all that telly, and Shakespeare and gawd knows what else.'

'But you're right in that I certainly love what I do.'

''Course you do. Like me. I love my work. But what beats me about you is where you find time for all that extra stuff when your job is nowhere near nine to five like mine. I mean, I don't get it.' He looked at me, puzzled. 'I mean, what I want to know is, have you *always* been a waiter?'

My brain skidded to a stop. Had I heard right? Did he really say what he said? Did he really think I was a real waiter?

I couldn't think what to say.

Sid didn't notice my blank stare and carried on with a bright-eyed smile. 'Yeah. That's what I can't get me head around. Well, another time, eh? Gotta go. See ya.'

And with a little wave, he went on his way.

The sun set; the seagulls soared; the spume spumed. I stayed on deck trying to pull myself together. A humid mist was beginning to settle on my soul. I should never have agreed to this cruise. It was all my fault.

Two days later, by the pool, Sid approached me once more. 'Hello, mate.'

I looked at him a little warily. 'How are you?'

'Great. I was tellin' the wife about you.'

'Oh yes?'

'And me mates. They made me look a right dickhead.'

'Oh?'

'They couldn't get over it, could they? 'Cos you never was a waiter, was ya? Not in real life.'

'Well...' I shrugged.

'Crafty little bugger. You never let on though, did ya? I felt a right banana. Oh dear, d'you know what they said?'

I started mumbling. 'Er, Sid, I'm ever so—'

'They said the look on my face was funnier than Forty Towels! Ha! We all had a good old laugh at that one, I tell ya.'

'You mean you weren't upset?'

'Upset? Wot's the matter wiv ya? No! I come to me senses, din' I? About time too.' Another laugh. 'No thanks to you, mind. Oh dear, oh dear – d'you fancy a pint then? You can't say no, mate. I owe ya!'

He made for the bar and, confused, I tagged along beside him. I rarely drink beer but I did this time and even managed a second half.

That Sid realised I was not a waiter was hugely significant for me, but he regarded it as more of a joke than anything else. I couldn't be so casual about it. I had to ask myself, had I changed at all? Well, yes, the cruise had certainly put a dent in my principle of honouring the magic of my profession.

Sid had never asked me to serve him but once I was taken for a real waiter, at the Grosvenor Hotel Park Lane no less. Melody had gone from supervising a dance school to designing dresses. Boy George was one of her clients. She had designed a wedding gown for a wealthy Arab family and I was invited to accompany her to the reception. As it started at 2.30 p.m. and my curtain for the show I was in at the time did not rise until 8 p.m., I could join her for the sumptuous feast.

As the dress was formal and it was a summer's day, I decided to wear my white tuxedo. Big mistake!

The hotel was crowded with excited guests. One of these assumed that any creature in a white tuxedo had to be a waiter so he took me by the arm and demanded I bring him a drink.

After explaining that I was a guest, Melody and I made our way to the buffet, where I was approached by yet another guest. 'Please,' he said, forcing an envelope into the palm of my hand, 'could you give this to the pretty girl standing by the band stand?'

Melody is never short of a good repartee. She smiled at the man. 'He is a waiter,' she said, 'but I'm afraid he is off duty this afternoon.'

Another incident in the afterlife of *Fawlty Towers* was being in a film with Peter Sellers. He began by behaving in a rather offhand way. I was given the small part of Hercule Poirot in *The Revenge of the Pink Panther* (1978), the last of the three films in which Peter Sellers played Inspector Clouseau. He wasn't exactly welcoming. I was there just for one day. I came early and had to wait because the director and he were at lunch. Peter Sellers finally arrived with the director, who I'd never met before, Blake Edwards. He said hello to me, which was one word of two syllables more than Sellers bestowed on me.

Then, during a break in filming, Sellers's wife, Lynne Frederick, turned up. Clearly she was a fan of *Fawlty Towers* as she came over to meet me and seemed pleased I was there. That changed Sellers's attitude and he suddenly became very friendly towards me.

More afterlife: Manuel was employed in some Spanish TV advertisements. But instead, they turned me into an Italian and called me Mario. Not '¿*Que*?' as in Spanish but '*Perquè*?' as in Italian. Why?

I think that was a question some companies asked themselves when they hired Manuel to make personal appearances. He/I majored – my once hero Stalin would have approved – in disrupting capitalism. We specialised in business conferences. Manuel would interrupt a managing director's speech by crashing in and telling Mr Chief Plutocrat he was in the wrong place. Ever helpful Manuel would try to improve the situation by escorting the boss out of the room, causing the kind of chaos that only an innocent abroad could.

The routine was sometimes used by charities. At a Save the Children event I interrupted Princess Anne who, of course, hadn't been told I was going to come in. I had glittery shoes, a Union Jack and a carrier bag of goodies. I did the usual fiasco Español, told her she was in the wrong place and would have to leave. Then Manuel realised who she was and bowed and scraped, hoping not to be hauled to the Tower. She took it in good spirits, though I never found out if Her Royal Highness was a fan of *Fawlty Towers*.

Manuel's attempts to find musical fame were less successful. In 1979 a producer suggested I sing 'O Cheryl'. The words went something like, 'I met my love in Estapona, I asked to her, "Will you be mine?" She tell me over a glass of vino she come from Ashton-under-Lyme.' It was not the quartet from *Rigoletto* – to which we will come later.

The perils of playing a character who becomes well known are quite well known. He is no longer under your control. You get confused; the public gets confused, too. At a fundraising dinner for the Lord Mayor of London, for example, the guests were introduced at the head of the stairs by a fully costumed flunkey who tromboned, 'Ladies and gentleman, Mr and Mrs Andrew Sachs of Fawlty Towers.'

Actually Mr and Mrs Sachs were of real Kilburn not fictional Fawlty, but the audience preferred the gloss to the dross.

I must now pause for a bit of honest self-criticism. As I write this, Daniel Radcliffe, the star of *Harry Potter*, has written a very sensible piece that criticises celebrities who whinge about the price of fame. The young wizard is right and smart.

Being a successful actor has its problems, especially if you play a character who becomes well known. The puppet comes to control the puppeteer and the puppeteer minds. It's a question actors have to face sometimes. Am I what I play or do I play what I am? (In 1990 Manuel made it into Madame Tussauds, the famous London waxworks, and I came face to face with 'the puppet'!)

I ask myself if I learned anything from being in *Fawlty Towers*. In some ways it was quite easy and I was just very lucky to have such a role. I didn't have to struggle to find how to play the part and seek the internal motivation: I did it automatically. I only rarely examined the motivations of my characters and hardly ever probed into my innermost life to find parallels between what I had experienced and what a character I was playing had experienced. In real life, I am proud to say I have never lost my trousers. Not yet.

My method was simple. I thought about the role I was playing and I would rely on directors and expect them to be guides. Sometimes what they said was not true and I would recognise that, but not argue very much. In the end if somebody was firm and insisted, 'This is what you are going to do,' I, ever the good little German boy, obeyed.

You could say the culture of my childhood made me obedient. I had been taught not to question my father or mother or any grown up. BBC directors had status and authority, even those who were not as good as they believed themselves to be.

In 1980, I got another big break which allowed me to play a character from his late teens upwards. H. G. Wells, the author of *The Time Machine* and *The War of the Worlds*, started as a humble draper in Sandgate, Kent. Once he had become successful, Wells decided to write a book that was partly autobiographical. Alfred Polly, his alter ego, was timid and never a happy draper. Wells wrote of Mr Polly: 'He hated Foxbourne; he hated Foxbourne High Street; he hated his shop and his wife and his neighbours;

he hated himself.' Polly was no Pollyanna. At the age of twenty, with money he inherits from his father, Polly sets up an outfitter's shop in Fishbourne. The next chapters feature a spectacular suicide attempt which ironically saves him from bankruptcy and gives him the courage to leave his wife, his shop and his town.

In 1949, John Mills played Polly in a film. The musical was itself turned into a film. I was following in stellar footsteps. I found the part challenging, but the director strange. He insisted on very low lighting, so in the first half there was virtually none at all. The show did not become more conventionally lit until later, when Polly makes it into the world and the open air. At the end of the novel, Polly muses:

> One seems to start in life expecting something. And it doesn't happen. And it doesn't matter. One starts with ideas that things are good and things are bad – and it hasn't much relation to what is good and what is bad... There's something that doesn't mind us.

We are, indeed, in the hands of fate. My fate was fortunate – I had managed to leave Germany alive and with both my parents alive. My father died tragically young but he had nearly six years as a free man in Britain. My beloved mother enjoyed nearly thirty years in London and though she had the miseries of suffering from Parkinson's at the end of her life, she had seen her children thrive and grandchildren come into the world.

Before reading Daniel Radcliffe's article, I might have whined that when I played in Pinero's *Dandy Dick* at Cambridge in 1981, one critic said that it was Manuel disguised as one very reverend gentlemen. '¿*Que?*'

Now I just smile sagely and turn to the subject of radio, where one is so easily anonymous as an actor. There, as I'd done since the 1950s, I could be all manner of men; anonymity is inherent in the medium. Radio 4, in fact, promoted me to running hotels when I played Bluntschli in one of my favourite plays, Shaw's *Arms and the Man*. Bluntschli saves the daughter of a rich Bulgarian family from being discovered in a compromising situation. But the girl is disappointed in him. He doesn't seem to relish leading cavalry charges. He turns out to be, the daughter snipes, a chocolate cream soldier rather than a hero. True, he says. That is because he is the owner of a chain of hotels, so he commands thousands of spoons, blankets and sheets. His military success is based on the fact that he knows how to keep his men fed and get them from one location to another.

Around this time I also worked with Eric Sykes, who had made a number of silent comedies. *It's Your Move* was one, a slapstick piece about a couple moving into a new home, who have the misfortune of hiring an accident-prone firm of house removers whose boss is Eric. I played one of the crew. That amazing comedy magician Tommy Cooper was in it, too.

I must now introduce the Czech theme. In 1986, I played Kafka's friend and publisher, Max Brod, in Alan Bennett's *Kafka's Dick*, the reviewers managing to my great relief to make no comparison between a Spanish waiter and Kafka's supportive and intellectual friend. The play was by a brilliant writer and starred Jim Broadbent, who was well on his way to being a star. It is set in the 1980s in Yorkshire. Kafka and Brod come back from the past to visit a Kafka devotee and his wife.

Kafka left instructions for all his works to be burned, instructions which Brod ignored as he reckoned *The Trial* (made into a great film with Orson Welles), the enigmatic *Metamorphosis* and many others were so brilliant they had to survive. As the play develops, it becomes clear Kafka had serious issues with his father. If he had lived in Vienna, he would have ended up on Freud's couch but as he lived in Prague, he ended up confused.

We all thought *Kafka's Dick* was bound to transfer to the West End. After a few months, however, the producer, Michael Codron, came to see us and told us that was not going to happen. Our run would end at the Royal Court. Don't call us, we'll call you. Or more likely not. The theatre is a fickle god.

I sometimes wonder what it says about me that I could get as much pleasure from doing slapstick, like Eric's film, as I could from political work like *The Prague Trial*, which involved two serious writers, Christopher Hampton and John Mortimer. The play had nothing to do with Kafka but focused on the attempt of my long-abandoned Communist friends to convict the so-called revolutionaries who fought for Czech freedom. I was proud to be in it, just as I was proud some years later to be in *Jumpers*, written by the brilliant Czech-born playwright, Sir Tom Stoppard.

There was more politics to come when I revisited my childhood city for a four-part TV documentary *Berliners*.

I wrote earlier about our lovely neighbour when I was a child in Berlin, the lady who served me wonderful cake. Of course, I had never expected to see Frau Fellenberg again after I came to England. But I did.

Berliners involved going back to Berlin after the wall came down and finding people I had known before I left for England. My aunt and a number of cousins had all survived because they weren't Jewish. I'm afraid that on my father's side of the family the story was very different.

I took my producer to the flat where we had lived; the doorbells had not changed and one still had the name of Fellenberg. I could not believe she might still be alive. I rang the bell. A top-floor window opened and an old woman called down, '*Jawohl, bitte.*' I knew at once who it was and reintroduced myself to my old friend. Naturally, she was amazed to see me after all those years.

She asked us up so we did so and told her what we were doing. My producer explained, 'We're doing a recce with cameras and we wondered if we could interview you.'

'Oh, shush shush,' she said, and gave us champagne and goodies from her fridge. They all tasted wonderful. But she hesitated about doing an interview.

When we left we said, 'Well, we are going to be here anyway so maybe we give you a call and perhaps we'll have a cup of tea while we're filming nearby.'

So when the time came we tried her again. She was shy still, but was prepared at least to do a little bit of an interview with us. It was wonderful, a very moving plunge into my past, because everything in her apartment was unchanged but still smart and tidy. The little stool was still there and she had even kept my cup as if I would return some day. I loved that memento of my childhood.

I have said that I have been fascinated by animals since I was a young boy. I still sometimes look at Brehm's book on animals that was in my parents' library and is now in my study. I have been lucky in that some of my work in the last few years has been to narrate wildlife films. It is not as glamorous, of course, as going into the wild and being on a photo safari but I find it absolutely enthralling. As it happened, in the 1990s the chance to explore the country and its wildlife was one of the reasons I decided to go to Australia. The trip taught me as much about union rules and monks as about wildlife.

Leslie Phillips, a fine comedian who first became famous in *The Navy Lark* as the lieutenant who couldn't navigate a toy duck in a bath, and I brought *Not Now Darling* to the Regis Theatre, Subiaco. You probably have not heard of Subiaco, which is a district of Perth in Western Australia, founded in 1851 by Benedictine monks from Subiaco in Italy. In the early sixth century Benedict of Nursia retired to the Italian Subiaco to think and pray. As a result, he founded the great monastic order which established the rule that, among other things, monks should spend part of each day in prayer, part in manual labour and part in study. I don't follow it myself, but I can see it would make for a balanced life. One of those who sought inspiration at Subiaco was the mediaeval animal lover, Francis of Assisi, who went on a retreat there in 1223.

When they arrived, the monks did not, as far as I know, get up the noses of the local monks' union. But Leslie and I did.

Australian Equity said we could not invade down under as they had their own, more than capable actors. British Equity argued with them and finally the Australians relented, but only on the condition we didn't play Sydney or Melbourne. We accepted and this was how we found ourselves in small towns with exotic names such as Waggawagga and Subiaco.

I had hoped we would get to see more of the wild eastern coast of Australia, but we didn't get that far. I never got to dive the Barrier Reef. But I did manage to visit Sydney Zoo, where I saw every kind of marsupial. They were refurbishing some of the cages but I hadn't lost my skill at working my way into the confidence of zoo personnel and quickly wangled a private tour which reminded me of my adventures in Regent's Park in my youth.

After that, in 1995, I had the honour of playing at the National Theatre in Jeremy Sams's wittily knowing production of *Wild Oats*, the 1791 romp by John O'Keeffe. Its plot centres on a young Quaker woman who disapproves of the frivolity of the drama but becomes smitten by a roving player. Worse, she develops a belated crush on the works of Shakespeare, and some of the actors who play him. The comedy both celebrates theatre and affectionately takes the Thespis (so to speak) out of thespians. The names of the characters are memorable: Ephraim Smooth, Farmer Gammon, Sir George Thunder, Trap and Twitch.

Some actors, especially the giants of our profession, carry on acting in the theatre until they are very old. Gielgud, for example, made a comeback to the West End when he was eighty-four years old. Though I enjoyed *Wild Oats*, I felt that, at sixty-five, it was time to stop treading the boards I had first trod in Bexhill.

I continued acting on the radio and one of my regular gigs became reading poetry on the BBC's *Poetry Please*. Then, in 2000, friends suggested I read rather more than a brief poem. They told me about Tennyson's *Enoch Arden* which tells the tragic story of two boys and a girl. The opening lines give most of the plot:

> Annie there is a thing upon my mind
> And it has been upon my mind so long
> I know that it will out at last. O Annie
> It is beyond all hope, against chance,
> That he who left you ten long years ago
> Should still be living – well then let me speak
> I grieve to see you poor and wanting help;
> I cannot help as I wish to do
> Unless – they say that women are so quick
> Perhaps you know what I have you know
> I wish you for my wife. I fain would prove
> A father to your children

The girl marries Enoch who is ruined and decides to go to sea. His friend Philip, meanwhile, has become rich and helps Annie because he loves her. I fell for the poem because it was all about good people. And not an evil man in there.

I found the poem beautiful and decided to do a one-man show based on it. I arranged for a friend of mine, a brilliant pianist, Victor Sangiorgio, to accompany me. We toured all over England, Wales and Scotland for three or four months.

I learned the poem by heart but I did not just rely on my memory. I had a lectern with a script on it on stage in case I needed it. That only happened once or twice. I would pause a moment and Victor would fill in with a piano accompaniment, so we got through any small lacuna. Tennyson's poem, like many Victorian works including those of Karl Dickins, is rather long. We cut it a little bit and the recital lasted about an hour. It was quite a feat to remember it.

I had better add that, as usual, I had to mix in a few anecdotes about, you guessed it, *Fawlty Towers*. Twenty years after the series had wrapped, audiences still wanted to know how we made it. Though I sometimes minded that Andrew Sachs seemed to have become Manuel, I am pleased to have been part of television history.

CHAPTER 18

A Distressing Time

Now I must come to the unpleasant incident that hit the headlines in 2008. I was busy with work, narrating TV documentaries and recording audio books and one of Sherlock Holmes's adventures for BBC Radio, when I and my family made the news – and this time there was no Manuel in sight. It was a hugely distressing time for all of my family.

Enter Russell Brand, the flashy young comedian, and his misguided companion, Jonathan Ross.

Until this sad episode, I had had no previous contact with either of them. During the recording of Sherlock Holmes (I was playing Dr Watson), I received a call on my mobile while enjoying a quick lunch at a pleasant outdoor street café not far from the studio. I wasn't quite clear what the BBC radio producer was saying, as the traffic was very noisy, but apparently Brand and Ross wanted to interview me for their show on Radio 2. It would be broadcast on Saturday night but had to be recorded now. Could I drop everything and do it?

I explained that I was unfortunately unavailable. The young producer kept ringing back, even though I continued to say I could not oblige due to my work commitments. The traffic noise made it hard to understand him, so after several phone calls I was still uncertain what he wanted or what exactly he was referring to. I wasn't particularly interested and I didn't have the time anyway, so hectic was my schedule.

The very hurtful mayhem erupted from my refusal, which was perfectly polite.

I had no idea that Brand and Ross would be so affected by my reluctant refusal. After it became obvious I could not be on the show, Brand decided to announce during the recording that he wanted to discuss my granddaughter, Georgina, with me, whom he knew. He added that she'd told him her grandfather had been Manuel. And it just got worse.

That evening, Melody and I listened to our answerphone messages, determining that the incoherent ramblings from those at the radio show were not worth listening to, before retiring to bed.

Since their behaviour affected all our family, I will let Melody take up the story, because soon after it all happened she jotted down her version of the events. Strangely, as you will see, there was unintentional comedy in the middle of our pain and embarrassment, though it wasn't recognised or appreciated at the time:

There's seldom a dull moment in our house and those fateful October days in 2008 were no exception.

At 3 a.m. I awoke to a call of nature. Careful not to disturb our beloved Cavaliers, the King Charles spaniels, by switching on the bedside lamp, I tiptoed quietly into the bathroom. I was returning to bed when I slipped on a silk dressing gown that had fallen on the bathroom tiles. There was a crack as I hit the floor. The pain was excruciating and my scream so loud it might have been heard at the end of our road, or so I was later told.

All the lights came on and there was Andrew standing over me in a state of shock while the dogs happily licked my contorted face.

'Not to panic,' said Andrew. 'Let's get you back on the bed.'

'Don't be daft,' I replied, 'I can't move.'

He did his best but to no avail and instead managed to roll me gently on the floor over two warm duvets. We rang the ambulance. And then we waited and waited. Nothing happened.

Dawn broke. We were still waiting. Finally an ambulance arrived and took me to a Hampstead hospital, where the medics parked me before deciding they could not cope with me there. The pain was so severe it was impossible. I eventually learned I had a broken hip.

Andrew managed to get another ambulance, which took us to a hospital I had been at before: the Hospital of St John & St Elizabeth.

Things required when having a hip replacement: one, a good surgeon; two, a good hospital; three, good nursing; and four, a good husband.

I'm grateful I had all four.

After a strong painkiller, I was waving goodbye to Andrew and our daughter Kate as I left for the theatre. Unfortunately, this time it was not to watch my husband on stage but to be placed in the hands of a wonderful surgeon who gave a perfect performance.

I will come back to Melody's account a little later.

With Melody in safe hands, I returned home to give the dogs their breakfast, telephoning my director as I went, to let him know I'd be late at the studio. Between Melody's accident and my work commitments, I couldn't say whether I was coming or going, and the intrusion of the people at the radio show only made a difficult set of affairs worse still.

As soon as the recording of Sherlock Holmes was over for the day, I drove back to the hospital. Melody was in pain and still a little groggy from the anaesthetic but in a surprisingly good mood, chatting with our daughter. Worried still about the fallout from my telephone exchange with the radio producers, however, after a while I left Melody with Kate and returned home to listen to our answerphone messages properly.

Instead of leaving me a simple 'We're sorry you can't make the show' message, Brand and Ross had gone into four-letter overdrive. They cursed, they jeered. They hadn't left one message but a series of them. What mattered so much was that they dragged in my granddaughter for no sane reason – except to have some fun at our expense.

The message they left was in no way private, but was broadcast in all its appalling unpleasantness that Saturday on Radio 2, the former safe and cosy home of the Light Programme.

I have always been a rather private man, which is why I have resisted the temptation of revealing the inside story. Part of me still wants to ignore Ross and Brand's sordid rantings, but I cannot ignore the whole subject – sadly, it wouldn't go away even if I tried. Brand and Ross were like two teenagers on the rampage, laughing at their own jokes, which is not something the best comics usually do. Their lewd banter was deeply hurtful for me, for my wife, for our daughter Kate and our granddaughter Georgina. It not only caused pain but huge stress to the family.

I certainly never thought I'd give my name to a scandal: Sachsgate.

Readers need to judge how Ross and Brand egged each other on, which is why I reproduce here some of what they said. What is so surprising is that Ross, a middle-aged man, did nothing to restrain either himself or Brand's 'performance'.

RUSSELL BRAND: Right, Jonathan, well this is unconventional.

JONATHAN ROSS: Don't worry, I'll blurt something out.

BRAND: Don't blurt something out, not on the answerphone, Jonathan.

ANDREW SACHS' ANSWERPHONE: Sorry I can't answer at the moment, but please call again or leave a message. Speak after the tone, thank you.

ROSS: Hello, Andrew.

BRAND: That's Jonathan Ross speaking now. Anyway, we

understand ... anyway ... we can still do the interview to his answerphone.

The two presenters exchange banter and then come the vile barbs.

ROSS: He f***** your granddaughter! [laughter] I'm sorry, I apologise. Andrew, I apologise ... I got excited, what can I say, it just came out.

The initial thing to note is that it is not Brand but Ross who first launches into abusive material and swearing.

BRAND: Andrew Sachs, I did not do nothing with Georgina – oh no, I've revealed I know her name! Oh no, it's a disaster. Abort, abort. Please watch that show. I am out of *The Bill*, starring Andrew Sachs, I'm out of *The Bill*. Put the phone down, put the phone down, code red, code red. I'm sorry, Mr Fawlty, I'm sorry, they're a waste of space.

ROSS: How could I carry that round in my head like a big brain blister all day? I had to pop it and let the pressure out. Like, it's really bothered us, though, he's the poor man sitting at home sobbing over his answer machine. If he's like most people of a certain age, he's probably got a picture of his grandchildren when they're young right by the phone. So while he's listening to the messages he's looking at a picture of her about nine on a swing.

BRAND: She was on a swing when I met her. Oh no!

ROSS: And probably enjoyed her.

I have cut out some of the next exchanges. To resume:

BRAND: OK, look, the truth is, Andrew, I'm ringing you to ask if I can marry, that's right marry, your granddaughter, Georgina the granddaughter.

ROSS: And I'd like to be a page boy.

BRAND: He wants to be a page boy. We're going to have a *Fawlty Towers*-themed wedding.

Then Ross, in a splendid display of hypocrisy, added on air: 'Our intentions were pure.'

They then decided to ring again, though they claimed they had to stop upsetting 'Manuel' and my family. And they referred back to that classic episode of *Fawlty Towers*.

ROSS: What should we not mention, the war?

BRAND: Don't mention the war, don't mention his granddaughter. Don't say: 'You only ever played Manuel.' Don't mention *The Bill* in a negative way. Yes! We'll just sing to him. I'll make up something as I go along.

ROSS: If you learn one thing from history, it's 'Do not repeat your mistakes'.

BRAND: Don't repeat them.

ROSS: So let's do it right this time.

BRAND: Thank God, Jonathan.

Again I have left some of the material out because I find it upsetting.

ROSS: The wonder of technology is such that we can keep doing this for hours.

BRAND: And even after the show's finished, Jonathan, we can find out where Andrew Sachs lives, kick his front door in and scream apologies into his bottom. We can just keep on troubling Andrew Sachs. Let's do it, right, OK. You pretend you're Andrew Sachs's answerphone.

ROSS: Hello, Manuel is not in right now. Leave your message after the tone.

BRAND (as the phone rings again): All right, Andrew Sachs's answerphone, I'm ever so sorry for what I said about Andrew Sachs.

ROSS: Just say sorry.

BRAND (laughing): I'll kill you!

ROSS: Don't say you'll wear him as a hat, just say sorry.

BRAND: Sorry, right.

It was exceptionally nasty and the text makes it obvious Jonathan Ross could not bear to be uncool or seem middle-aged, though he was nearing fifty. He wanted to act as if he were a young lad when, of course, he was nothing of the sort.

Melody, who was holed up in hospital for over a week while she recovered from her operation, was, as ever, a pillar of strength. I'll let her continue her side of the story.

Next thing I knew, I was propped up, bleary-eyed, squinting at a TV screen at the bottom of my bed and looking at Andrew in his little woolly hat. He was standing outside our house trying to control the dogs as he pushed his way through a crowd of photographers. They were shouting, 'What have you got to say, Mr Sachs? Give us a break. We're just trying to do our job.' But when I turned my head and saw Andrew sitting at my bedside I drifted back to sleep, believing it had all been a nightmare, that I was still feeling the effects of the operation.

Next morning, my nightmare was staring at me again from the TV fixed to the wall at the foot of my bed. As I was watching, a nurse came in. 'Roll over, dear,' she said, 'while I give you something to help with the pain.'

After a welcome dose of morphine, she left just as the

breakfast tray arrived with the newspapers. 'Here's the TV control,' the second nurse said and she also made a nippy exit. Wondering why they had left in such a hurry, I saw footage of Andrew and the story flash across the screen. I opened the newspapers and the story was splashed all over them. I was very disturbed that Andrew had had to listen to such hurtful nonsense. And there I was in my hospital bed unable to help him.

Another nurse came in and switched off the TV. 'The last thing you need is that rubbish,' she said. 'You haven't touched your breakfast.' I forced a few mouthfuls of scrambled egg down my throat. 'It tastes like metal,' I said. The nurse said not to worry as the medication sometimes caused such a reaction. The problem stayed with me for the rest of my stay in hospital. However, the food was not wasted.

Andrew was busy with work, visiting me, and looking after Lizzie and Jemima, our little dogs, so he hardly had time to eat. So my aversion to food served a purpose as Andrew ate my breakfast in the morning and then came back at night to polish off my dinner. At least he didn't starve. But I was worried about how the whole affair was affecting him.

The publicity was never-ending. Andrew was constantly followed by the press and with so much public interest the story just would not go away. Even Gordon Brown, the Prime Minister, said the behaviour of Ross and Brand was unacceptable and inappropriate.

We were at the heart of a media storm. Andrew was under enormous pressure and I was very concerned about him while I was trying to recover from my broken hip. But I was so proud that he maintained a dignified silence throughout, although knowing him the way I do I could see the terrific strain he was under.

If only these pranksters had thought about what they were doing and who they were doing it to before releasing their hurtful 'wit' in public. What a pity they did not think about the fallout for our family. From the number of letters and phone calls we received it was clear they had picked the wrong target. It was a comfort to read in the press that my husband is looked on as a much-loved national treasure.

It was good to get home again. Although I depended on a walking frame, at least I could help Andrew by being there with the dogs. I had been eight stone when I went into hospital and was seven and a half stone when I came out.

I was glad when Melody and her new hip came home. What she calls a media storm led to the BBC getting in quite a muddle. We complained, but at first the BBC stated they were 'not aware of any complaint by Mr Sachs'. I suspect that almost all previous directors general of the BBC – and not just Lord Reith – would simply have banned Brand and Ross for ever from working for 'Auntie'. The BBC found it hard, however, even to admit a complaint had been received. Eventually, they did apologise. One reason was the sheer volume of complaints: the BBC admitted it had received over 18,000.

By then reporters were camped outside our house but I only said, 'Oh, nothing to say.' Time and time again I said I had nothing to say.

As I write this, Shakespeare, the ever wise, comes to mind:

> Who steals my purse steals trash; 'tis something, nothing;
>
> 'Twas mine, 'tis his, and has been slave to thousands;
>
> But he that filches from me my good name
>
> Robs me of that which not enriches him
>
> And makes me poor indeed.

Brand and Ross had taken the good name of my family. Melody says I was upset and run-down, which she found unusual. And so did I. Many children who come to a strange country learn there are times when you have to be careful what you reveal of yourself, in order to fit in. I had always tended not to wear my heart on my sleeve lightly.

Melody and I both blame Ross more than Brand. Ross is a father with two daughters of his own. Melody wonders how a mature man and a father of girls could have behaved in such a way. She thinks he speaks before he thinks but she has not had the chance to say that to him or to ask how he would feel if his daughters had been ridiculed in public – which is a pity.

One of the letters of support we received that meant so much came from David Walliams, who surprised us by his kindness. David was one of Ross's best friends and wrote us this wonderful letter saying how disgusting he thought it was. It meant a lot to us.

David and I first met many years ago when I played his father in a television series. Melody is fond of him, too, and thought him a considerate young man with impeccable manners. Frequently he would pick me up and we would drive to work together. I remember his banter was always stimulating, so it didn't surprise me as I watched his rise to fame over the years. No one deserves it more.

Melody, who now considers David to be practically perfect, often wondered whether it was all down to his mother. 'I would love to meet her,' she would often say to me. She got her wish shortly after at my eightieth birthday party at The Ivy. It was a convivial evening with most of our special showbiz friends attending: actors, singers, comedians, agents and, of course, Brian Rix, now Lord Rix, who was one of my first employers over fifty years ago. And Ray Cooney, my lifelong friend, with whom I shared a dressing room in Whitehall farces.

Su Pollard turned up sparkling like a Christmas tree in an outfit that would make Dame Edna look drab. Su was always a showstopper. Some of our friends had brought their instruments with them (try and stop them). Chas McDevitt, star of skiffle and composer of 'Freight Train', showed up with his friends armed with their banjos, ukuleles, guitars and the odd mouth organ.

It was good to be surrounded by real friendship after going through all that unnecessary ridicule and bad mouthing. It had been a good night to lay the ghosts of bad memories and my friends had been there to help us.

The Ivy did us proud and we certainly needed a good diversion. The food was top-class and the waiters, who were used to serving a more restrained clientele in the private room, were enjoying the party spirit.

After blowing the candles out on my cake without starting a fire it was time for the speeches. I cannot repeat what some of our friends said about the terrible two but I will share part of the witty poem by Roy Hudd OBE, who insists on adding, 'I didn't get it for services to poetry!'

But 'Manuel' was the name,

And what was it brought him fame?

Being smacked around the ear'ole by John Cleese.

Now you must forgive me this

But I have to take the p… mickey

Out of that couple who pull schoolboy strokes.

Russell Brand earns lots of dosh

But looks like he needs a wash

'Cos he smells like his pathetic phone call 'jokes'.

Then there's Mister Ross

To the Beeb he'll be no loss

Though for years he's been their chat show's favourite anchor.

He can't pronounce 'Ross', he always says it's 'Woss'

Yes, he surely is a real TV top 'ranker'

I'm afraid what follows might lead to us all being sued for defamation of the little character they have… Sorry, I didn't mean that. So I will fast-forward to Roy's sweet ending.

But now I must end today, so can I simply say

To Andrew, 'Keep your foot hard on the pedal!'

And to Melody Sachs, his bride,

After fifty years by his side,

'By God, love, you deserve a bloody medal!'

The entertainment continued to be first class. Su Pollard won the race to the mike and belted out a selection of Judy Garland songs, followed by Julie Walters singing 'The Wedding', one of her greatest hits. Just as the banjo struck up, David Walliams arrived with his mother. A waiter guided them to our table and Melody's face lit up when David's mother sat next to her. The music was loud and I hoped they could hear each other. I relaxed when I saw them smiling and nodding their heads in agreement as they talked twenty to the dozen. I didn't have to guess what they were talking about.

Later on we were invited to David Walliams's party after his wedding. Everybody was there, as they say, and who should enter but Ross's wife and her two daughters. Ross was not yet to be seen. Melody remembers:

I wanted to say to him, 'Mr Ross I would like to ask you one question, "How would you have felt if somebody had said those things about your daughters?"'

She never got the chance, as Ross did not appear, as far as we could see.

The BBC finally started an inquiry, so I was asked to meet the director general, Mark Thompson. I was with him for less than an hour. He asked me detailed questions – when, why, where, how – that I found hard to answer after the weeks that had passed. I did not expect a grovelling apology but I did expect proper recognition that the airwaves he controlled should not be used to abuse someone – perhaps especially someone who had given the BBC loyal service. I did not expect special treatment but courtesy. So I must say I was surprised that Mark Thompson did not really say sorry, as I remember. I soon realised that he considered his job was to investigate what had happened, not offer solace.

To make matters worse, we then read an article that Ross's wife had written. In it she claimed I was very lucky because this publicity had got me a part in *Coronation Street*. The truth is that I had met one of its producers at a reunion of music hall performers some time before. He asked if I'd ever thought of doing a part in *Corrie*. I nodded. 'Leave it to us,' he said. When the offer arrived a few weeks later, however, it wasn't exactly Hamlet. They offered me a part which wasn't right for me. Some time before the Ross and Brand events, however, they came back to me asking if I wanted to play Norris's long-lost brother from Australia, who had come back to try and patch up his relationship with his family.

This time, it was very interesting and I was happy to accept. All this happened a long while before the Radio 2 disaster.

Mrs Ross should get her facts right before following in her husband's wake.

Both Brand and Lesley Douglas, controller of Radio 2, resigned from the BBC. Ross was suspended without pay for twelve weeks on 30 October, and later described the experience as 'fun'. Maybe it was fun for him, but it was excruciating for us. The BBC was fined £150,000 by the regulator Ofcom because of the incident.

We received much sympathy and hundreds of letters from

friends and members of the public. John Cleese, for one, was magnificent. Not long after it happened, he invited me to a variety show in front of Prince Charles for his birthday at the Wimbledon Theatre in November 2008. His call came right at the last minute and I did it that same day. He made light of the whole scandal as MC and we did a sketch together which he'd written to poke fun at how old we'd become. He was in a wheelchair and I staggered on as a decrepit Manuel with a stick that John promptly steals. John was on great form. The audience cheering the arrival of Manuel was very heartening at that point. The audience knew what it meant – that despite Brand and Ross's attack on me and my family, John was steadfastly with us.

I was happy to be able to repay John's support as he went through his difficult divorce with his third wife, Alyce. To cheer him up, a number of his close friends, including Barry Cryer, Ronnie Corbett and my wife and I, took him for a jolly lunch at The Ivy. Humour is always the best pick-me-up and we all began telling near-the-knuckle stories about each other. It ended up being a very funny and cathartic evening.

John had to pay for his freedom, so he devised a one-man show, which was largely about himself. I saw the final performance in Guildford and thought it was terrific, absolutely terrific. I admired, as ever, his resourcefulness.

Melody and I are still rung up by the press whenever Brand or Ross cause offence, but we have always declined to comment. Even when, during Channel 4's 2013 Comedy Awards, the whole distasteful saga was brought up again in a cringe-making double act between comedian Lee Mack and Ross, four-letter words in abundance (and even a mock apology), we felt it best to leave them to condemn themselves by their own childish performance, especially since the general public were quick to express their disgust, for which we are extremely grateful.

And we felt the same way when, a month later, on New Year's Eve 2013, while watching *Greatest Stand-Up Comedians* on Channel 5 with our son Billy, we were unexpectedly treated to an extract from Russell Brand's stage show. This included mocking reference, in Brand's usual full-frontal manner, to the whole painful affair of five years before and to our granddaughter.

As Melody philosophically put it, as we switched channels, recharged our glasses and wished each other a happy new year, 'What goes around, comes around – and may it be soon.'

For our part, this whole saga has been a painful experience that has damaged our family, and one we would like to put behind us once and for all.

CHAPTER 19

Not the Final Curtain

I've no intention of ending this book on a downbeat note. The phrase is appropriate because I became a conductor, thanks to Dustin Hoffman, star of *The Graduate* and *Little Big Man*. The joy of an actor's life is the surprises. You think you're down and suddenly the phone rings. *Quartet* came out of the blue.

Lynda Ronan, my agent, called to tell me I was wanted for an audition at Ealing, so along I went to the studio where I'd done *Nicholas Nickleby* and *Hue & Cry* sixty years earlier, when I really knew nothing. Sixty years on, and I was still auditioning.

The casting director, Lucy Bevan, and I had a long chat. 'Is Dustin Hoffman here, am I going to meet him for the audition?' I asked.

'No, no, he never comes, because he would want to employ everybody that he sees,' Lucy said. I could understand that as an actor. Hoffman must have had to audition early in his career – even Chaplin and Garbo at one time had to – and perhaps he remembered how stressful it could be, so he did not want to turn anyone down. Lucy invited me instead to record some lines and said she would send the tape to Dustin.

Later that day, Melody said to me, 'You know, I've got a feeling you've got this part. You have got this part.' My wife isn't just an ordinary drama queen but, at times, a clairvoyant one.

The next day Lynda rang up. 'Are you free tomorrow at two o'clock? Dustin Hoffman wants to meet you at a club in Portobello Road.'

Of course I was free!

I got there before 2 p.m. The club staff knew he was coming and had been told to offer me a drink. Dustin turned up with his American secretary.

We shook hands, sat down and he started talking, though at first he said little about the film itself. Finally, he started explaining the film, and gave me a book. I think he had brought a copy for every member of the cast. It was a Radio 3 classical music thing – a lovely book, especially as I quite like classical music. He also gave us each a DVD about a home for retired Italian musicians in Milan.

The overtures over, Dustin explained that *Quartet* was about a group of ageing musicians and singers who live in a retirement home. 'I want you to play the conductor,' he said.

To which I replied, 'But I haven't done any conducting.'

'We'll work on it,' he said.

He was very friendly, which made it possible for me to say to him, 'An odd thing happened yesterday, Dustin. My wife and I were watching one of your films which we'd seen before, *All the President's Men*.'

'What did you think?' he asked me.

I said it was wonderful and added that when we finished watching it, Melody said to me, 'I knew we had to watch this film at this particular moment because I've got a feeling about it.'

'Really?' Dustin said.

'Yes,' I said.

'Aha!' he smiled. 'She's a witch, like my wife. What's her name? I want to talk to her.'

Dustin's competent American secretary took our number so she could get hold of Melody.

When Dustin phoned, Melody found him calm, delightful and helpful. Filming with him was certainly fun.

Dustin's location team found Hedsor House, a very grand country house in Buckinghamshire that had been redesigned in the eighteenth century for 'mad' King George III and Queen Charlotte. The once royal residence was now used for receptions and weddings, and had all the genuine style that poor Basil Fawlty always aspired to with no success. It had been Nicole Kidman's home in the film *The Golden Compass* based on Philip Pullman's *Northern Lights*.

Now it was to be Beecham House, the home for retired musicians. In theory, the place should have had no financial problems, since it was connected with Sir Thomas Beecham, who was not just a great conductor but also belonged to the family that made a fortune out of Beecham's pills. When Jean Horton, a dramatic diva played by Dame Maggie Smith, comes to live there, she quips she is now housed on a sea of laxatives.

Despite its pharmaceutical links, Beecham House needs funds, so every year it stages a gala to raise them. All the residents are meant to join in and perform, but there are all kinds of niggles and ego wars. The event is organised by Cedric, a resident played by Sir Michael Gambon, who was so brilliant as Dumbledore in the *Harry Potter* films. The other residents include a great tenor, Reginald Paget (played Sir Tom Courtenay), who has lost his appetite for performing and is now keeping his brain ticking by teaching youngsters about opera; Wilf Bond (played by Billy Connolly), a singer who has had a stroke which makes him less and less inhibited; and Cissy Robson (played by Pauline Collins), a mezzo soprano who is losing her mind and memory. As I write, Billy Connolly has announced very sadly that he is suffering the early stage of Parkinson's, so the film was oddly prescient.

Years earlier, Reginald, Wilf and Cissy had played in a legendary production of Verdi's *Rigoletto*. The fourth singer in that production was Jean Horton (Maggie Smith), still very much a diva, who had never received fewer than twelve curtain calls. She's now broke, stands on her dignity and will not sing, partly because she has lost her confidence.

The quartet of the film's title is the quartet in the last act of Verdi's *Rigoletto*. The Duke of Mantua, who has seduced Gilda, the daughter of Rigoletto, now lusts after a prostitute, Maddalena. Her brother Sparafucile has been hired by Rigoletto to kill the Duke. Maddalena persuades her brother to spare the Duke and kill Gilda instead. As they often do in opera. Jean Horton had played Gilda, but the last thing she wants to do is sing the quartet again. It is not just for artistic reasons. When she gets to Beecham House, Reginald Paget refuses to speak to her. She had broken his heart long ago when they were married and she had had an affair with an Italian.

The joker both in the film and in reality was Billy Connolly. Always in character, he flirted with the nurses, organised secret deliveries of whisky and railed against the frailties of ages. He often made us all crack up.

Before the filming started, Dustin made sure I was given a crash course in how to wield the baton by a professional conductor, though my character did not just have to conduct the orchestra. I was a messenger of sorts between the rival egos and had to make sure that Cissy Robson, who, if you remember, had lost her memory, remembered to pass on a message to Jean Horton.

Despite the fact that I'd never conducted any orchestra, I got into the spirit of the music. So much so that I took the liberty, if the singers were off-key, of trying to get them into shape without being nasty, as I had seen Noël Coward be decades earlier. My jokes worked. To my utter surprise, they laughed. It was funny, they explained. I was relieved. I love getting laughs, as long as they are in the right place for the right reason – nothing is worse than making people laugh for the wrong reason, or when they are laughing at you, rather than with you.

Dustin was a considerate director but very sure of what he wanted – and a perfectionist. Often I finished later than expected but he was courteous and would ring Melody to apologise for keeping me so long. Working with old actors is not easy because though they have experience, their memories sometimes aren't what they used to be. Dustin was especially kind to one actor who could not remember his lines, always stared at the autocue but still got his words wrong quite often. The film is very true about some problems of old age – and not just memory. Billy Connolly's character complains about having to pee all the time and once has to warn the ladies to avert their eyes as he does so against a tree.

The end of the film is magical – but I won't give it away here for those who haven't seen it.

Dustin closed the film with a credit sequence which juxtaposed pictures of the cast as they were now – i.e. old – with photos of ourselves when we were young. It was effective, a meditation on the passage of time. How we were then – how we are now. I was asked to rummage in my scrapbooks and found an old picture of myself from my days in the army – not driving a tank.

The film, Dustin's first as a director, was a stunning success. It proved that one is never too old to try something new.

At the party after we finished shooting, Hedsor House's owner said that if I ever wanted to visit, my wife and I would be most welcome. Melody and I will take him up on that some day.

As I come to the end of my tale, I am surprised as ever by the unexpected twists of an actor's life, though I have come full circle. I started off in Berlin, the son of a lapsed Catholic and a Jew. It seems fitting that as I neared the end of this book, I was asked to read part of a massive history of the Jews written by the historian Simon Schama. At the age of eighty-three, I was given the privilege of doing part of the audio book, which took me through the many perils of part of my inheritance. Schama is not an easy author as his text is full of Yiddish, Hebrew, Aramaic and Ladino, the mixture of Spanish and Hebrew that the Jews who lived in mediaeval Spain used. But I learned a great deal about the constant persecutions and that reminded me, of course, of the dangers my beloved father had faced in the 1930s, the dangers I was too young to understand in many ways. Reading the text was a challenge – and an education. And though the title of my book is *I Know Nothing!*, I still love learning. What else, apart from love, keeps you alive?

Index

"As unexpected and amusing as the man himself."
GYLES BRANDRETH

SEIZE THE DAY
MIKE READ
THE AUTOBIOGRAPHY

400PP HARDBACK, £20

A fascinating romp through the life of a broadcasting legend, Mike Read's autobiography offers an exciting insight into his three decades in showbiz. From ventures in radio, television and music, to tales of sport, romance and the royals, Mike writes with candour and humour in equal measure.

Recounting his stints as a Radio 1 DJ on the *Breakfast Show*, a prime-time television presenter on *Pop Quiz*, a co-founder of *The Guinness Book of British Hit Singles* and a jungle star on *I'm a Celebrity … Get Me Out of Here!*, this high-energy journey encapsulates all aspects of the celebrity's vast and varied career. Mike has seized every opportunity, whether in pop, poetry or politics.

A story packed with scintillating anecdotes, witty observations and nostalgic recollections, this is an autobiography that hits all the right notes..

— AVAILABLE FROM ALL GOOD BOOKSHOPS —

**THE NEWS
IS READ**

BY
**CHARLOTTE
GREEN**

304PP HARDBACK, £20

**For twenty-seven years Charlotte Green was one of the most
iconic newsreaders on Radio 4. Her rich, velvety voice was a staple
on the radio and a treat for millions of listeners.**

rlotte joined the BBC in 1978 and became one of the regular readers on the *Today* programme,
/here her voice proved to be a reassuring constant in the midst of momentous occasions and
rrible tragedies alike – her bulletins have covered everything from the fall of the Berlin Wall in
39 to the 7/7 London bombings in 2005. After leaving Radio 4 in 2013, Charlotte joined Classic
FM, where she now presents an arts and culture programme, *Charlotte Green's Culture Club*.

 this highly entertaining and touching autobiography, Charlotte tells the story of the woman
ehind the voice, with all the endearing qualities that have delighted her listeners for years and
ned her various prestigious accolades. *The News is Read* is a must-have for anyone wanting to
spend a few hours in the company of this warm, charming and wonderfully modest woman,
whose writing is as engaging as her voice.

— AVAILABLE FROM ALL GOOD BOOKSHOPS —